# Infiltrating culture

The infiltrator may be a foreigner, a spy, a child, a cleaner, a woman. Like Donna Haraway's cyborg or Michel Serres' parasite, the figure of the infiltrator offers a powerful new way of articulating cultural difference and cultural practices. Issues of gender, race and age are all addressed in a subtle and forceful close reading of a series of texts – from Claire Bretécher's sharp-edged cartoons to Colette's recipes, from the diary of a Martinican cleaning lady to James Bond thrillers.

Mireille Rosello's analysis explodes the notion of binary oppositions: the insider/outsider, black/white, straight/queer, rich/poor, solid/fluid. The infiltrator, she argues, is an ambivalent figure, one who penetrates a closed territory only to expose the fantasy upon which power relations are founded.

Rosello's lucid and passionate engagement with theories of multiculturalism and hybridity marks this as a major step forward in the field of cultural theory. As a critique of power, it is a seminal text and will be impossible to ignore.

Mireille Rosello teaches in the French department
at the University of Nottingham

# Infiltrating culture

## Power and identity in contemporary women's writing

Mireille Rosello

MANCHESTER UNIVERSITY PRESS
MANCHESTER and NEW YORK

distributed exclusively in the USA and Canada by ST. MARTIN'S PRESS, New York

Published by Manchester University Press
Oxford Road, Manchester M13 9NR, UK
and Room 400, 175 Fifth Avenue,
New York, NY 10010, USA

Distributed exclusively in the USA and Canada
by St. Martin's Press, Inc.,
175 Fifth Avenue, New York, NY 10010, USA

British Library Cataloguing-in-Publication Data
A catalogue record for this book is available from the British Library

Library of Congress Cataloging-in-Publication Data
Infiltrating culture / Mireille Rosello
    p.  cm.
   Includes bibliographical references.
   ISBN 0-7190-4875-3
    1. French literature—20th century—History and criticism.
 2. Identity (Psychology) in literature. 3. Feminism in literature.
 4. National characteristics, French, in literature. I. Title.
   PQ307.I54R67 1996
   840.9'353—dc20       95-33690

ISBN 0 7190 4875 3 hardback

First published in 1996
00 99 98 97 96   10 9 8 7 6 5 4 3 2 1

Typeset in Joanna
by Koinonia Limited, Manchester
Printed in Great Britain
by Bookcraft (Bath) Ltd

To Ross Chambers

# Contents

# Preface

In a few years, or in a few decades, theoreticians, philosophers and sociologists writing in French may remember the end of the twentieth century as a moment marked by an interdisciplinary obsession: the constantly reiterated attempt to address the vexed issue of a hypothetical French national and cultural identity, and the determination to find a specifically French solution to the international issue of multiculturalism. In retrospect, we will perhaps wonder why it seemed so natural, so relevant to display such an intense curiosity for foreigners, immigrants, *beurs* or *Arabes*, and ask so many painful questions about French nationality and French values.

While the slow construction of Europe forces many old nations to reconsider the imagined contract of good neighbourly conduct, as well as the terms of their sometimes century-old alliances or disagreements, economic or national theories can no longer be dissociated from a redefinition or at least a rethinking of religious beliefs and practices, of ethnic communities, of sexual identities, all categories which are usually considered to be very alien to a certain idea of Frenchness. Grudgingly, the *République une et indivisible* resigns itself to the inevitable: a re-examination of what it is to belong, and especially to belong to its enlightened self.

In English-speaking western countries, it has become a (facile) stereotype to note that 'the French' are allergic to difference, to multiculturalism for example. For better or for worse, the type of discourse on difference which proliferated in the 1970s among philosophers, political thinkers and historians appears to have had little impact on French mentalities. On the other hand, we cannot rule out the possibility that theories and works of fiction written in French in the twentieth century may provide us with a specific way of imagining communities, otherness, inclusion and exclusion.

If French identity is multicultural, it is almost in spite of itself and this internal tension, or at least the undeniable presence of a certain form of reluctance to multiculturalist thought in recent studies has encouraged me to tread more than gingerly on the ground already occupied by such widely-discussed key-words as otherness, minority, or marginality. 'Infiltration', however, is not meant as an alternative key-word. Indeed, it is not meant as a key-word at all. Even more important than the concept of infiltration here is the figure of the infiltrator itself, this presence which, as I will argue, we are not used to recognizing or identifying, precisely because the infiltrator's success depends on his or her invisibility. Infiltration is not meant as a coda to the list of successively authorized but rapidly displaced labels such as assimilation, insertion or integration. Renouncing the comfort of such recognized Arianne's threads is part of the plan. Infiltration does not belong to any recognizable political platform nor does it appear systematically in the news or in the discourse of social agents. Yet, the word is familiar, charged with physical and metaphorical connotations that I intend to combine rather than separate in the context of a discussion of the relationship between groups and individuals, marginals and dominant cultures.

This study of infiltration talks about spies who penetrate forbidden territories, but also about water and its avatars: this book is both about rising damp and about the (symbolic) purity of water distilled by mountains. Infiltration as defined here is a field of cultural and political practices which are closely yet transparently related to the way in which we imagine and cope with porosity and permeability in our everyday life. Before becoming obsessed with the role played by infiltrators in our societies, I was perfectly happy to imagine that soils fall, roughly, into one of two broad categories: they are either waterproof or permeable, dry or wet, hard or soft. On the one hand, we have coherent and tightly structured soils, made of homogeneous and inseparable particles through which water will not find its way, and on the other hand, we have porous and friable soils, capable of absorbing moisture, easily permeated by liquids. And this image also means that water is visualized as an external element seeping through or traversing a solid structure. Naturally, this construction remains unscientifically grounded, I know that the distinction I establish between different types of soil is probably closer to some kind of Bachelardian rêverie than to the knowledge accumulated in other disciplines (hydrology or geology for example). I would never want to argue that, in order to be a suitably well-informed French citizen, it is useful, if not indispensable, to gain a thorough knowledge of the phenomenon of infiltration as analysed by scientific disciplines, by soil specialists, by engineers or builders or architects for example. And yet, the assumption that it is urgent to study cultural practices of infiltration, the claim that it is politically relevant to work out a theory of social infiltration is tantamount to the following hypothesis: first, we take for granted the distinction between solids and fluids, between permeable and waterproof soils, it becomes a sort of self-evident truth or reality, and we then do not hesitate to apply what is a relatively unexamined cliché to other fields of cultural knowledge. Being aware that my simplistic distinction between waterproof and permeable soils would be deemed profoundly naive by geologists does not prevent my imagination from constructing further political and social analogies based on the original binary metaphor. Without really formulating it, I have always implicitly equated impervious soils with heavily policed borders, with drastic controls of identity, with xenophobic villages or nations. Symmetrically, permeable terrains have always evoked open(-minded) communities capable of welcoming otherness, the enriching experience of encounters with difference: people allowing themselves to be 'poreux à tous les souffles du monde' [porous to all the breaths of the world] as Césaire puts it in Notebook of a Return to my Native Land /Cahier d'un retour au pays natal (Césaire 114–15).

Theorizing infiltration as a literary, cultural and possibly political gesture is about (re)discovering that the distinction between solid and liquid, is not necessarily the most economical way of metaphorizing the relationship between water and soil. This book seeks to appropriate this vision, to speak about other areas of rediscoveries, and to speak about other problematic domains such as the ways in which I represent the infiltrated soils of gender or ethnic and minority studies as a reader of literary or non-literary cultural productions. Rethinking the implications of how I define a solid, a fluid and their interaction, asking myself whether I treat infiltration as a positive or a negative phenomenon implies that I also rethink the way in which I position myself with regard to identities, communities, borders, nationalisms, genders and power, especially when, as a reader, I encounter texts or cultural practices that represent complex negotiations between power and powerlessness, responsibility, and pleasure.

First of all, 'infiltration' can be imagined as an activity which falls under the category of 'tactics' as defined by Michel de Certeau in his *The Practice of Everyday Life*: the infiltrator is defined as an agent who does not have a territory and therefore cannot afford to resort to 'strategies', 'le calcul des rapports de force qui devient possible à partir du moment où un sujet de vouloir ou de pouvoir [un propriétaire, une entreprise, une cité, une institution scientifique] est isolable d'un «environnement»' (Certeau 1980, 21) [the calculus of force-relationships which becomes possible when a subject of will and power (a proprietor, an enterprise, a city, a scientific institution) can be isolated from an 'environment' (Certeau 1984, xix)]. A 'tactic', on the other hand, would be 'un calcul qui ne peut pas compter sur un propre, ni donc sur une frontière qui distingue l'autre comme une totalité visible' (21) [a calculus which cannot count on a 'proper' (a spatial or institutional localization), nor thus on a borderline distinguishing the other as a visible totality (xix)].

Infiltration would thus be one of the ways in which a member of a relatively powerless or underrepresented group manages to 'pass', to transgress official and invisible barriers, and to enjoy (at least temporarily) the privileges supposedly inherent in the condition of belonging to a hegemonic group. Like water going through a layer of sand, the infiltrator would never have his or her own land, nation, origin from which to speak. I was thinking about those individuals who may think that they do not need to help destroy walls because they constantly jump over fences and land on their feet. I was thinking about people for whom difference does not always make a difference because they have learned how to negotiate their way through borders and frontiers, how to become ironic dwellers of hegemonic spaces. In our times, they are (often represented as) 'good Indians or not-so-black blacks', 'non-hysterical women', 'non-effeminate gay men', and 'feminine lesbians'. For the dominant group, they are the other of otherness. To adopt a (first) spatial metaphor, the infiltrator would not really be a nomad, a traveller, an explorer, a 'flâneur', but rather a commuter, the unglamorous avatar of the Parisian petit bourgeois whose tedious train ride to and from work is the ironically degraded and unromantic counterpart of early twentieth-century anthropologists' great explorations (Clifford 1992).

At first, I thought that this book was going to be about gate-crashers: they seem like ideal infiltrator figures those adroit and nimble children who know how to sneak into a cinema or crawl under the circus tent because, or even though, they cannot afford the price of the ticket. For such *resquilleurs*, late nineteenth- or early twentieth-century novels often express tenderness, admiration or envy (Hugo, Dickens, Sabatier). But the *resquilleur* always steals my neighbour's apples whereas the brat who sneaks into my backyard and steals my cherries is undoubtedly a delinquent, a dangerous thief who will end up robbing a bank. Inner city dwellers or the inhabitants of their French equivalent, the suburbs may have replaced the figure of the *resquilleur* with the socially menacing picture of a potentially violent delinquent who will not be content with wrangling his or her way into a cinema or a subway train but is instead involved in drug dealing and car thefts.

Perhaps discourse has changed more than our reality however: the infiltrator, once identified (for the successful infiltrator should remain invisible to power), will always be described either (or both) as the hero of a David–Goliath confrontation or as the parasitical noise which interrupts the normal drone of social conversations. In the same way as Foucault imagines that the insane played an integral part in their society before what he calls 'le grand renfermement' (Foucault 1972), it may be that the 1930s, which invented the word *resquilleur*, was a time when infiltrators were accepted as part of the system even if they were always envisaged as marginal fringe figures. In the 1980s and 1990s the dominant discourse seems to reflect an increasing fear of infiltrators. I wonder if our cultural imagination will soon confuse them with the word 'loubard' which evokes gangs and teenage violence. The discourse of the media, of political analysts, of sociologists seems to fear, rather than admire, the delinquent. Robin Hood does not live in the suburbs.

I do not intend, however, to write the history of infiltrators: adopting Philip Fisher's description of recent theoretical research, I recognize that my interest lies not so much in 'myths' as in 'rhetorics', and this book will be about the way in which infiltration as a metaphor can be used to resist power, especially as I am already creating a certain form of power when I choose to use infiltrational tactics (Fisher 1992, 232). Even if one analyses the fear produced by infiltrators at different historical junctures, one may never be able to quantify the exact degree of disruption generated because infiltration itself will be different, influenced by specific variables: each form of infiltration may be recognized or ignored, laughed at or repressed, depending on how and when it manifests itself. Its relative immunity also depends on which system is infiltrated, and by 'system', I mean a self-imagined discursive unity, which could be a neighbourhood, a household, an individual, or a national, racial, or religious community.

Depending on who tells the story, when the infiltrator is identified, expelled, or eliminated, either order has been restored, or an innocent victim has been killed. Once recognized as such, infiltrators are usually placed within

two different and incompatible historical narratives. Which is why the
resquilleur as a literary character is only, after all, one heroic and failed version
of the infiltrator. Even when a sympathetic narrative sings the praises of the
resquilleur, somehow the game has already ended, and the old inside–outside
structure has taken over once again. Infiltrators are a paradox or a short-lived
phase of infiltration because once the lawful insider (the owner of the garden,
the theatre-goer, or the government's armed forces) or the complicitous
outsider (the oppositional, marginal collective who feels represented by gate-
crashers) have identified them, they disappear as infiltrators: one must decide
whether to cheer or to shoot them. The successful infiltrator, on the other
hand, is like a silence which no one can claim to hear, like a thing forgotten,
which nobody is aware of having forgotten. When a detective is spying on
you, something happens which you cannot describe unless you know that he
or she is a spy (in which case, he or she is a failed spy).

As readers, however, we may find it necessary to analyse infiltration after
it has been narrativized, even if the story deprives the infiltrator of some of
his/her power by identifying him or her. The black woman who passes for
white is an infiltrator who sabotages the racial mapping, just as the mole who
works with colleagues for ten years while leaking information to the enemy
may trangress national or professional barriers. A Jewish woman who marries
a Christian man could be considered an infiltrator. An immigrant, whether
or not he or she clings to his or her 'original' culture is an infiltrator, but
telling their story is strangely contradictory. Moreover, the list of potentially
infiltrable territories is endless if, as I suspect, the metaphor of 'territories of
belonging' is always already constructed as an invitation to stay with one's
own, to adopt the same laws. Perhaps there may be no such thing as
infiltrators, rather a process of infiltration, the existence of which is attested
by various figures and narrative techniques. Infiltration cannot be defined as
a stragegy and, rather than looking for its metaphorical territory of definition,
it may be more useful to describe the various contexts in which it seems to
thrive, to look for the conditions with which it tends to be associated.

Infiltration is a way out of and into identity and entities. It is goes well
with revolving doors, with security guards who fall asleep, with pirates and
computer viruses. Infiltration is about mistaken identities and glitches in the
controls, it is about metamorphoses. It is about relationships, and it is also
none of the above. If I try to define 'infiltration' as a specific form of resistance
or a particularly remarkable way of transgressing frontiers, I suspect that in
the end, the definition I will reach will not allow me to distinguish between
'infiltration' and a million other practices of 'togetherness' used everyday by
people and communities and nations.

But I would not be too disappointed to discover that we are all infiltrators
if it allows us to imagine the possibility of a new dialogue between differently
conceptualized communities (ethnic groups or nations) whose subjects may
be in need of similar tactics. Infiltration is likely to occur whenever a
relationship is established between the singular and the plural, whenever a

subject, a body, an individual, an entity which perceives itself or is perceived as 'single' is connected to a group, a nation, a gender, a culture, a race, any entity which can be described as a collectivity. But the fact that I cannot isolate the category of infiltrators does not mean that infiltration does not exist. In the following chapters, I would like to examine what happens when the infiltrator speaks or when he or she is represented in a textual or visual space.

## Introduction

## From community to *départenance*

A famous legend in Mexico, 'The Revenge of
Moctezuma', suggests that if Hispanics are
ever to regain control over their own destiny,
it shall happen by infiltrating the aggressor's
terrain. One of the last Aztec emperors,
Moctezuma, instead of fighting Cortés, re-
galed him with gifts because of an ancient
pre-Columbian belief that the bearded man
was divine. No doubt that this was a tactical
mistake by the Aztecs, but their revenge will
one day take place, so the legend goes, from
within the enemy line. Hard as it sounds,
Hispanics not only aren't learning English,
they are forcing the country to speak Spanish
– to turn bilingual ... They aren't here to be
assimilated, but to disseminate their culture
... Hispanics have infiltrated the enemy and
are ready to deconstruct its very essence ...
The revenge of Moctezuma. (Stavans 1992,
119–22)

Timeo Danaos et dona ferentes

### The rhetorics and politics of a metaphor

Using a metaphor such as infiltration presents a risk: it offers an
origin as the matrix of thought without justifying it. Why, after all,
base a literary and cultural reflection on the chance encounter with a
representation of porous soils in an encyclopedia? How does one
legitimize the privileging of one word, of one cluster of phenomena,
as the starting point of a system of explanation and interpretation? I
do not think that I can provide a convincing answer for myself or my
readers. Instead, I would like to remain aware of this original fallacy,
of the eminently fragile quality of the building-block in the hope that
the monument erected on such an unreliable pedestal will retain a

degree of self-destructive arbitrariness and provisionality. Proposing infiltration as the key-word and visible title is meant as a slightly parodic and irreverent gesture in the sense that it does not justify itself but imitates others, as self-consciously as possible. After all, the question 'why a metaphor?' could be reformulated as 'why this metaphor?', which returns us to the problem of how infiltration is different from other metaphors.

Another question could be: why 'infiltration' rather than 'passing' or 'spying'? Or, why 'infiltration' rather than other powerful metaphors that have been used in recent theoretical monuments? I had a large variety of possible models of metaphorically grounded discursive systems at my disposal. Recent theories of power and opposition often share the rhetorical tactic of the founding metaphor. Deleuze and Guattari's Mille Plateaux opens with the distinction between the root and the rhizome, two forms of 'natural' growths which are then used to distinguish between oneness and plurality, centrality and marginalization, the self and the other (Deleuze and Guattari 1980). The plurality of the rhizome is itself posited as a reason to reject the new binary opposition between the two figures (21) and the rigid law of the One-Two (25). The visualization of different types of roots would perhaps be less relevant or meaningful to us if it did not contain a philosophy of the State, of nomadologie, of capitalism. Michel Serres's recent Le Tiers instruit also discusses the idea of belonging to a given community, of travelling, of different forms of foreigness, and the book slowly expands out of the metaphor of the swimmer who crosses the river. The metamorphosis undergone by a subject who leaves 'here' to go 'there,' who abandons the relative safety of the homeland, gives rise to a theory of education as 'métissage' (Serres 1990).[1] Foucault's much discussed, reappropriated and criticized visions of power also rely on the meaningfulness of 'fissures' and 'friability'. L'Archéologie du savoir implicitly valorizes the self-awareness of forms of knowledge that recognize that solidity is both an illusion and a norm:

l'histoire des idées s'adresse à toute cette insidieuse pensée, à tout ce jeu de représentations qui courent anonymement entre les hommes; dans l'interstice des grands monuments discursifs, elle fait apparaître le sol friable sur lequel ils reposent. C'est la discipline des langages flottants, des oeuvres informes, des thèmes non liés. (Foucault 1969, 179)

the history of ideas is concerned with all that insidious thought, that whole interplay of representations that flow anonymously between men; in the interstices of the great discursive monuments, it reveals the crumbling soil on which they are based. It is the discipline of fluctuating languages (langages) of shapeless works, of unrelated themes. (Foucault 1969, 137)]

Finally, I suppose it might be argued that deconstruction as a whole plays with and exposes the supposedly transparent process by which metaphorical thought is legitimized although deconstruction itself is forced to resort to the unavoidable imaging of its own mental activity. In a collection of particularly enlightening quotations from Derrida's work, Deborah Esch shows that deconstruction's goals are sometimes better illustrated by images of buildings, monuments, destruction, although 'The double gesture of deconstructive intervention, then, is not restricted or determined by architectural metaphors or the conceptual and nonconceptual orders they may be taken to figure' (Esch 1992, 376).[2]

What I expect from infiltration, when used in conjunction with a reverie of the fissure, rhizome and friability is two-fold: I hope that the infiltrator can achieve the political and social goals which I imagine are the ultimate purpose (or original cause) of feminism, black studies, minority discourses or subaltern studies, without necessarily resorting to a politics of identity. I also hope that infiltration can be a way of using binary oppositions (including the opposition between the centre and the margin, power, and powerlessness) against themselves, without having to exhaust one's limited strategic moment of intervention in a careful demonstration of how they deconstruct themselves. In that sense, infiltration is sloppy, inelegant, theoretically unsound, and much too limited in terms of context to even be called a theory. It is, at best, a gimmick.

My assumption is that (despite the popularity of previously mentioned theories of resistance or opposition) power is still understood, or at least understandable as a solid centre, a core, and this, despite the popularity of discourses which tend to insist on its diffuseness, its omnipresence, its differential quality. Paradoxically, even if we accept that there is no 'hors-pouvoir' (Chambers 1991, xiv), whoever is perceived as outside is also perceived as powerless, and powerlessness is a very real form of suffering. The centre is opposed to the margins, the Same to the Other, or the multiple, 'le divers', 'la diversalité', 'créolisation' (Segalen 1904, Todorov 1989, Bernabé et al. 1989, Glissant 1990), the mainland ('la métropole') is contrasted to the borderland (the local, the ex-colony, the country of emigration) (Greenblatt 1992). When power imagines itself as a

territory always under attack by outsiders, an oppositional desire to
concentrate on the outsider, to listen to the voice of subalterns,
disenfranchised communities, minorities, women, etc. is caught in
the dominant metaphor of centre versus margin. Saying that power
contains resistance to power may thus be reformulated: it is exceed-
ingly difficult not to adopt the same metaphor of territory, borders
and borderlands when my voice seeks to interpret other muffled
voices.[3]

Practically and politically, adopting the point of view of the
diverse, the border, the marginalized can be very useful. It creates a
mirror territory, the ghost of a powerful presence which both
imitates and parodies the structure that oppresses it. Seeing oneself as
a marginal subject engaged in a creative process of legitimization is a
valuable enterprise. I would not want to deprive myself of the
concept of 'safe houses' (Pratt 1991) or even of the 'closet' even if I
am painfully aware of the potentially devastating effects of
ghettoization. The role of theoretical constructs may be to distinguish between the moments when it is tactically efficacious to seek
to reappropriate closets and ghettos, and the moments when it is
destructive and self-defeating.

For example, when one talks about racism in France in the 1990s,
how does one continue to demystify the illusory universalism of the
Enlightenment without empowering forms of reflection that have
turned the critique of white mythologies inside out, and are now
using it to promote racist agendas? What Maxim Silverman calls the
'Racialization of immigration' in France does not seem to have
resulted in the healthy discovery that France is not a homogeneously
populated nation, united by a unanimously accepted definition of
culture (Silverman 1990). Instead, or perhaps at the same time,
discourses are produced which use the celebration of difference as an
argument to keep cultures separate. What was most infamous about
the speeches accompanying governmental attempts to throw immigrant workers out of the country between 1974 and 1977 (the so-
called 'politique de l'aide au retour') or the 1986 expulsion of 101
Malians, was that such openly xenophobic decisions were couched in
the language of anti-racism and the celebration of difference.[4] Oliver
Mizla, author of Les Français devant l'immigration, quotes Alain de Benoist
who declared in Le Monde (19–20 June 1983, 16):

L'immigration est condamnable parce qu'elle porte atteinte à la culture
d'accueil aussi bien qu'à l'identité des immigrés. Le mot d'ordre n'est pas

'contre les immigrés', mais bien: avec les immigrés, contre les forces et les idéologies qui aboutissent à la destruction de leur personnalité, comme de la nôtre. (Mizla 1988, 166)

[Immigration is reprehensible because it threatens both the host culture and the immigrants' identity. Our slogan is not 'against the immigrants' but rather: with the immigrants against the forces and ideologies leading to the destruction of their personality as well as of our own.]

After all, here is a case of power infiltrating the rhetoric of the emergent discourse of liberalization and, I should make it clear, I do not intend to allow much space for such events in the following chapters. Although I realize that it is theoretically untenable to claim that I will focus on infiltration only when it helps the powerless (since the model of the infiltrator should help me modify the spectrum of forces, and also because the very definition of power-lessness and powerfulness will depend of what the infiltrator does), I intend to presuppose that my historical position as a reading subject allows me to make reasonably safe bets about what type of infiltration I find more or less desirable. As a powerful echo, I suddenly recall a sentence from Patricia Williams's *Alchemy of Race and Rights*: 'In sum, I see the problem at hand not as one of my giving racism too much power, but of how we may all give more power to the voices that racism suppresses' (Williams 1991, 168).

On the other hand, in an attempt to oppose Benoist's infiltrational differentialism, I am not sure that I would want to go as far as Olivier Roy who, in a controversial yet very seductive article, proposes to rehabilitate the ghetto:

Soyons francs et n'ayons pas peur des mots: dans l'ordre social, la communauté réalisée, c'est le ghetto. Car celui-ci se caractérise par l'intensité de sa vie communautaire et par son organisation interne. Au delà des stéréotypes qui produisent les connotations extrêmement négatives véhiculées par ce terme chez des gens aussi différents que Jean-Marie Le Pen et Harlem Désir, ce type de formation sociale présente nombre d'avantages pour les populations démunies car la véritable exclusion demeure la pauvreté sans horizon. (Roy 1991, 54)

[Let us be honest and not afraid of words: within the social order, the ghetto is a realized community. The ghetto is indeed characterized by the intensity of its community life and its internal organization. Beyond the stereotypes which cause people as different as Jean-Marie Le Pen and Harlem Désir to attach extremely negative connotations to the term, this type of social formation has a number of advantages for disenfranchised populations since the real exclusion remains hopeless poverty.]

It may be that Roy's reaction is motivated by what he perceives as the latest developments of a constantly evolving discourse about immigration. Many French intellectuals do not resist the temptation to systematically construct the so-called Anglo-Saxon model as a threatening other. Even if Roy had not used the word 'ghetto', his attempt at suggesting that there are *some* advantages to the principle of 'communities' was bound to be perceived as provocative. In the France of the 1990s, a transparent national credo continues to resist the very concept of community to the point that the ethnicisation of social relationships is consistently presented as a typically American threat to a supposedly more egalitarian and homogeneous society. The 'ghetto' then becomes a convenient synonym for any form of coalition based on principles that I insist on imagining as foreign to 'my' culture. The ghetto is a threat to the Republic, the ghetto is what comes to 'us' from America, it must be in bad taste.

In the end, the principle of community is naturalized as what comes from Anglo-Saxon cultures, as if the United States or Great Britain were other planets where naive inhabitants cannot criticize their own theories and practices. Conversely, Anglo-Saxons critics perceive France as a country corrupted by individualism and assimilationist tendencies where individuals are always the victim of centralized power. Both analyses are relatively accurate. I also find them completely fruitless as they deprive each 'camp' of a chance to see itself as already infiltrated by the other's construction. When thinkers like Bruno Etienne fulminate against the American ethnic model and warn us against the disappearance of what he calls 'the public space', he forgets that ethnicity is constantly problematized and criticized within Anglo-Saxon cultures. In 1992, when he delivered the presidential address at the MLA Convention, Houston Baker did not hesitate to test the limits of the 'conventional multicultural vision' (8), quoting the work of 'the influential French anthropologist Jean-Loup Amselle, who contends that the very notion of discrete ethnicities is an artifact of his discipline ... "the very definition of a given culture is in fact the result of intercultural relations of forces"' (Baker 1993, 8).[5]

When a model starts being perceived by a foreign thought as indigenous to another country, another nation, another culture, the time may be right to precisely analyse the resistance to what has already become a process of interaction. Infiltration is already happening when Houston Baker invokes Jean-Loup Amselle or when Pierre Bourdieu and Hans Haacke publish a book called *Libre-échange* which is a transnational, transatlantic, transdisciplinary conversation between a sociologist and an artist.[6] As the recent and monumental *La Misère du monde* powerfully demonstrates, Bourdieu and his team of researchers are neither willing to dismiss the concept of community, of immigrants, of *banlieues*, of *beurs* nor to naturalize them as new solid and waterproof territories or enclaves. As Loïc Wacquant, one of the authors of *La Misère du monde*, puts it in his 'De l'Amérique comme utopie à l'envers' (America as inverted utopia):

La décennie 80 aura été marquée non seulement par la montée des inégalités urbaines, de la xénophobie et des mouvements de protestation des jeunes des 'banlieues' populaires, mais aussi par la prolifération d'un discours d'un type nouveau autour du thème de la 'ghettoisation' qui suggère une convergence subite entre les quartiers déshérités des villes françaises et des villes américaines. La thématique du ghetto, nourrie de clichés importés d'Outre-Atlantique (Chicago, le Bronx, Harlem...), s'est imposée comme l'un des lieux communs du débat public sur la ville. (Bourdieu, 169)

[The eighties will have been marked not only by an increase of urban inequalities, of xenophobia and of protest demonstrations by the young inhabitants of so-called working-class suburbs, but also by the proliferation of a new discourse around the theme of 'ghettoisation'. What is suggested is that a sudden convergence is taking place between the disenfranchised neighbourhoods of French and American cities. The theme of the ghetto, fuelled by clichés made in America (Chicago, le Bronx, Harlem...), has become one of the commonplaces of the public debate about urban life.]

For a re-evaluation of the 'ghetto' does not move beyond the transparently French vision of community as dystopia and such reappropriation of a devalued term has a price: in order to even hope that some magic transmutation can take place and that the ghetto can be claimed as a successful alternative to what the French call 'intégration', it may be necessary to pretend that the word 'ghetto' had no history before the eighties reinvented it as a derogatory phantasm emptied of its resonances of extreme terror. To reclaim the 'ghetto' as a positive term, it may be necessary (and are we ready to be responsible for such a premise?) to forget even for a while that the word could mean death pure and simple if its inhabitants were Polish Jews in the 1940s. It may be that Roy considers that the rise of the far-right in contemporary France and Europe justifies such radical rhetorical and conceptual means, but I suggest that such forms of reappropriation belong to the category that Paul Gilroy calls a 'short-term corrective' in the Black Atlantic.[7]

Does the discourse of the minority always have to inhabit interstices, borderlands (Anzaldúa 1987), to redraw boundaries (Greenblatt 1992)? Or can we imagine what new metaphors, what new imagined universes would result from the 'theorisation of creolisation, métissage, mestizaje, and hybridity' (Gilroy 1993, 2). The infiltrator neither rehabilitates the ghetto nor claims the border-land as his or her reappropriated territory. He or she goes along with power's fantasy that it is a coherent structure, a territory, a self from which otherness has to be excluded. Then, power may lose or divert some of its energy trying to impose this image of itself, power will be satisfied that its rhetorical tactics are a success attested to by the fact that counter-histories and oppositional voices rely on the original metaphors: the infiltrator pretends to believe that minority discourses, emergent literatures, sub-cultures often construct them-selves as satellites of the core, margins, borders, in-betweens. The belief in this pretence may be power's blind spot and its weakness.

At the beginning of Serres's Le Tiers instruit a little myth accuses power of self-congratulatory near-sightedness: when Arlequin, 'empereur de la lune' comes back from his trip to the moon, he can only report that everything over there is the same as what we know here. Serres interprets this refusal/impossibility of (inventing/see-ing) difference as an effect of power (Arlequin being himself 'hermaphrodite, corps mêlé, mâle et femelle', 'chimère, corps composite et mélangé', 'sang-mêlé, marron ou marronne, coupé', 15):

Royal ou impérial, qui détient le pouvoir ne rencontre, en effet, dans l'espace, qu'obéissant à sa puissance, donc sa loi: le pouvoir ne se déplace pas. Lorsqu'il le fait, il avance sur un tapis rouge. Ainsi la raison ne découvre, sous ses pas, que sa règle. (Serres 1990, 11)

[Whoever yields power, be it regal or imperial, will not meet anyone in space who does not respect his domination and therefore his rule: power is immobile. When power moves, it treads on a red carpet. And reason discovers only its own rule under its feet.]

Instead of looking at the margins of dominant territories to expose the sham of coherence, I want to focus on what calls itself the very heart, the centre, supposedly the site of higher concentration, purity, coherence, gravity. Influenced by what I think I understand of chaos theory, I would like to show that some invariance d'échelle is at work, and by demonstrating that the centre is one of the best examples of borderland, I would like to show that infiltrators are neither marginals nor excluded outsiders, but, in Mary Louise Pratt's words, that they are never safe (Pratt 1991, 39). As an infiltrator, the closer I get to the centre, the more obvious it will be that it is structured like the opposition between outside and inside. I have a rather vague hope that infiltration could thus be used as a metaphor for global creolization or hybridity: perhaps looking at what happens on the 'borders' is all the more valid as I realize that what power lets me describe as an epiphenomenon that only occurs on its borders is in fact what happens as matrix of the whole construction. When Mary Louise Pratt talks about 'contact zones' for example, on the one hand, I welcome the challenging displacement, but on the other hand, I wonder how the 'contact zone' can be constructed as different from the zone, I wonder if the 'contact zone' is not always already pre-dicted (literally) by the zone. Infiltration would hope not to be an art of the contact zone but the art of imagining the zone *as* contact.

In the meantime, I have to recognize that infiltration already exists as a concept, that power recognizes its existence and that it comes complete with very negative connotations. Infiltration seems danger-ous when we think of water as an element and of a porous terrain as another. Once the image of two separate unequal entities is accepted as a premise, then infiltration can be described, not as a desirable form of empowerment, but as the degraded image of power in its invading, imperialistic tendencies. Infiltration suggests a slow proc-ess of taking over, and the slowness connotes insidiousness and dishonesty. The idea that the new entity is creeping into a closely-mapped scene signifies danger. This, of course, is, in itself, a by-product of an imaginary organization of space which privileges territories and severely guarded frontiers. In such spaces, infiltration may evoke liquidation, neutralization, dissolution, and it is probably no coincidence that the 'natural' effect of water on solid ground can be described by way of metaphors which have been reappropriated (sometimes as euphemisms) by military discourses.

Infiltration is never very far from disgust, it is the name of unspeakable things growing in the dark. The dominant imaginary of infiltration is not utopian. When water infiltrates a dry ground, the system has failed, drainage and techonology are required. Infiltration evokes mouldy basement, deteriotated human-made objects and decaying organic matter. Humid houses are haunted with the ghost of rotting bodies. Infiltration smells bad. Not as bad perhaps, as

detergent and bleach, yet much worse at the same time for it
connotes an unacceptable form of ageing, of giving in to time
without ritualizing the passage from new to old. From the most
grandiose to the most humble level of (imaginary) human activity,
infiltration is feared and avoided. Infiltration is about death and
decomposition, it informs and contests the distinction between dry
bones and decomposing cadavers. As Bataille's classic study on
L'Erotisme suggests, a decomposing body spells contamination, it
points to an intolerable lack of difference between life and death.
Once the bones are dried, drained, whitened, then order is restored
and memory can be preserved, engraved on solid waterproof stones.
The granite of tombstones is a statement not only against forgetfulness, but against the specific performance of forgetfulness which
comes with overgrown graves and the misshapen statues of angels
who have lost a limb or a wing, half of their faces, or whose features
have been eroded.

Le désordre qu'est, biologiquement, la pourriture à venir, qui, de même
que le cadavre frais, est l'image du destin, porte en lui-même une menace.
Nous ne croyons pas à la magie contagieuse, mais qui d'entre nous pourrait
dire qu'à la vue d'un cadavre rempli de vers, il ne blêmirait pas? Les peuples
archaïques voient dans le dessèchement des os la preuve que la menace de
la violence introduite à l'instant de la mort est apaisée. (Bataille 1957, 53)

[The corpse will rot; this biological disorder, like the newly dead body a
symbol of destiny, is threatening in itself. We no longer believe in
contagious magic, but which of us could be sure of not quailing at the sight
of a dead body crawling with maggots? Ancient peoples took the drying up
of the bones to be the proof that the threat of violence arising at the time of
death had passed over. (Erotism 47)]

But the most menial jobs and banal daily activities also look like a
ritual and an incessant war against or a denunciation of infiltration.
Sweeping a room is about infiltration, dusting the furniture is about
infiltration. Taking the trash out requires an act of faith: the
unexamined, immediate belief that there actually exists an 'away', an
outside.

What would happen if our faith was suddenly replaced by doubt?
What if we had a clear vision of there being no away, no outside.
What if I suddenly become aware that taking the trash out implies a
theory of inside and outside, the outside being what can be allowed
to be contaminated with filth, leftovers, dust, without losing its
identity. Infiltration may become distasteful whenever it highlights

the arbitrariness of boundaries. Removing dust is a satisfying activity only if we do not construct it as displacing dust from one place to another, only if we forget that it takes a cultural discourse to identify dust as an external, undesirable element, if we ignore the fact that objects, things are made of, rather than covered with, dust. Metaphorically, if there is no away, if boundaries dissolve, a catastrophe occurs, even language probably disappears. A mouldy basement describes a space which I can no longer define as a juxtaposition of separate elements: dryness and water. It is not so much that humidity is evil in itself, although its stereotypical association with the feminine as nature may indicate that it is a metaphorically devalued element, but water is all the more dangerous as it is only identified through its effect on the overall structure. The catastrophe occurs when the combination of dryness and water results in a new space which does not even constitute a new border but a network of interstices, or what Irigaray would call a 'fluid'.[8] A swamp or a mangrove is more frightening than the ocean because it is lived-in rather than traversed. It is teeming with forms of humid, shapeless, vaguely monstrous lives.

Humidity, probably the most commonplace form of infiltration as a 'natural' phenomenon, is culturally attached to a whole cluster of seemingly unrelated evils: death, disease, decay, the jungle, and why not the feminine. In 'Cyberculture', an article on the use of 'morphing' and 'cyborgs' in recent science-fiction movies, Mark Dery remarks that evil is often portrayed, not simply as the feminine, but as what is gooey about the feminine, or by the feminine redefined as gooey.[9] It could be argued – and celebrated, that stereotypical constructions of the woman as the enemy and evil side of man have more or less disappeared from recent films such as *Aliens* or *Terminator 2* where the heroine is a powerful ally in the men's war of liberation. But as Mark Dery points out, this is achieved by recasting evil as the not-yet-dried-out woman. Linda Hamilton, in *Terminator 2*, is acceptable as a 'man of steel' (Dery 1992, 504) in the same way as Sigourney Weaver, in *Aliens*, can only win by accentuating her own robotic side during the final duel against the oozing, sticky monster: 'The mensche's machine's pathological fear of the glutinous feminine goo that will gum its gears is manifest both in *Terminator 2* and *Aliens*, and is given ironic spin by the fact that the masculinist protagonist is in fact a woman' (Dery 1992, 505). The machine is glorified as order, dryness, meaningfulness, while the

parasitical force which interrupts its smooth and powerful motion is
an acceptable combination of sense and non-sense, life and shape-
lessness.[10]

Thus, cyborgs are infiltrators if the 'pleasure' and 'responsibility'
(Haraway 1991, 150) involved in conceptualizing them does not
bring me back to the reverie of the third, the in-between. Announc-
ing that her 'Cyborg Manifesto' is an 'argument for *pleasure* in the
confusion of boundaries and for *responsibility* in their construction',
Donna Haraway suggests:

In the tradition of 'Western' science and politics – the tradition of racist,
male-dominant capitalism; the tradition of progress; the tradition of
appropriation of nature as a resource for the production of culture; the
tradition of reproduction of the self from the reflection of the other – the
relation between organism and machine has been a border war. The stakes
in the *border war* have been the *territories* of production, reproduction, and
imagination. (Haraway 1991, 150, my emphasis)

The cyborg will function as infiltrator as long as I do not see him/
her/it as the third species, occupying the unstable yet recognizable
territory between humans and machines. In the same way as the
infiltrational potentials of subjects described as bisexuals (or trans-
sexuals, or cross-dressers for example or even sometimes women)
may depend on their refusal to be dialectically reinscribed as a third
gender.

The dilemma of infiltration when applied to politics is the
ambivalence of the instability of the inside–outside opposition: on
the one hand, infiltration is unavoidable, there is no pure system
because, precisely, there is no away. Draining a field is a self-
defeating enterprise if one does not visualize water as being driven
away from one's field rather than into another field. No system is
ever pure of strangeness, of foreignness. No communication is free
from parasite, but at the same time, I cannot conceptualize communication as parasite without losing the capability of communicating
(Serres 1980, Paulson 1988).

Even if there is no unproblematic *hors-texte*, *hors-pouvoir*, 'away',
at the same time, there is always an obvious, transparent, given
level of inside–outside, at every articulation of our thinking, be it
practical or theoretical. In fact, rereading Bataille's formulation, I
realize that he can only problematize our supposedly instinctive fear
of indifferentiation by reintroducing an unquestioned difference
between 'we' and 'they'. I am expected to naturally identify with the

'il' of 'il ne blêmirait', just as I am also expected to recognize the foreignness of the 'primitive people' who honour dried bones, even if these 'primitive' tribes are presented as a more immediate and real 'us', as a form of humanity that supposedly instinctively exemplifies what 'we' are bound to experience.

Politically, the infiltrator suffers from the same ambivalence. Power has a vested interest in eliminating infiltration from its own molecular structure, so to speak, by describing it as a specific form of dishonest invasion: a Trojan horse, the Greek mètis (Détienne and Vernant 1970), the 'strength of the weak' (Lyotard 1978). When identified, anticipated by a powerful text, when inscribed in a narrative which posits infiltration as a danger, it is construed as an external element, like the sting left in the flesh by a bee. It is perceived as what creates a site of disruption and pain, but not as what might change the overall structure. Power has a vested interest in describing the infiltrator not only as an unethical 'war machine' (Deleuze and Guattari 1980) but also as a self-contained (though small, inferior, microscopic) other. Infiltration is described as the betrayal of a non-evolving system, rather than being analysed (for example) as a metaphor of constant change, conflict, difference. Power strives to establish a difference between itself and the infiltrator by accusing him or her of unacceptable tactics. I argue that it is also a containing strategy to present the infiltrator as a limited circumscribable glitch. When Angie Chabram-Dernersesian describes the positioning of Chicanas within racial, cultural and political discourses, she points out that:

their gender is disfigured at the symbolic level under malinchismo, an ideological construct signifying betrayal which draws inspiration from the generic Malinche. (Chabram-Dernersesian 1992, 83)

It could be argued that 'malinchismo' is one of the names given to infiltration, each different name being an attempt at either dismissing its potential for change as unreal and utopian or at demonizing it as an agent of chaos. I wonder if recent horror or science-fiction movies do not reflect the second tendency. Ridley Scott's 1969 film *Aliens* defines horror as the possibility that the bee's sting may turn into a steel-piercing body secretion to which no border is immune. In this film, the infiltrator, brought back on board by a sense of solidarity to one's own (in spite of the strict rules of quarantine that should protect the system from infiltrators, Kane is reintroduced into the spaceship regardless of the fact that the limits of his body are no longer clear), brings with him/her/it the horrifying possibility of incomprehensible juxtaposition or symbiosis. Here is how Linda Zwinger tells the (infiltrated) story of infiltration:

A mysterious 'thing' has merged horribly with – and/or invaded and penetrated – crew member Kane's face – Kane's subsequent status is for a time uncanny and ambiguous: he is not quite alive and not quite dead; he is the creature's ... what? Victim? Lover? Spouse? Food? Mother? (Zwinger 1992, 75)

This is neither a celebration of infiltration nor a critique of the alien per se. The ludic, almost jubilatory tone recognizes that what is being attacked is not a border but the very molecular structure of the body, the molecular structure of the definition of strangeness, of the relationship to otherness. Infiltration resists being positioned as a third place. The 'truth' (or lie) which power would rather ignore and that infiltrators will take for granted is that every soil is porous. Infiltration as a tactic occurs when a subject no longer wants to convince the dominant group that its borders can always be redrawn, that its margins constitute sites of endless negotiations and conflicts. The infiltrator is convinced that foreignness is molecular (each particle of the dry soil is in fact susceptible to juxtaposition with humidity, water is never on the outside), but will not necessarily decide that it is worth imposing his or her vision of the structure as truth. In fact, the infiltrator may well decide that its status as foreign to him or herself and foreign to the self-declared centre is relevant to his or her gestures but should not be publicized as such.

Therefore, infiltration is not an image of 'métissage' because it does not imply that two supposedly distinct elements (two cultures, two discourses, two races) actually blend to produce a third term. I am not talking about the assimilation or integration of foreigners. Although métissage presents obvious oppositional possibilities, I choose here not to rely on a system that pretends to take for granted the possibility of hybridity as mixture, blend: I would rather not suppose that it is possible to identify separate essences that (sometimes violent) contact will finally cause to amalgamate. The picture of the infiltrated terrain is not about borders, is not about a third place, is not about mélange, it is about juxtaposition.

Talking about infiltration is a way of analysing relationships within a community and between elements as difference, a way of also paying attention to 'the differences between' and 'the differences within' (Johnson 1980, x). In other words, I treat identities like performed roles, knowing that the performance involved is not necessarily controlled by the subject of the enunciation. Rather than imagining that the foreigner, the Other, is the undesirable leftover of any subject's construction, rather than seeking to avoid otherness (because the risk of eliminating difference has proven insurmountable), I would like to play with Kristeva's notion of being foreign to ourselves (Kristeva 1988). It is illusory to pretend that communities, subjectivities do not function as powerful and self-contained sites of exclusion and inclusion. The 'we', in Kristeva's title may be a tell-tale and ironic signal that the concept of being 'étrangers à nous-même' is still a utopian construct since it cannot do away with the invention of a community based on exclusion from 'us'. Infiltration may be what lets me position myself 'Beyond Identity' while knowing that there can never be any 'beyond' unless I focus on a few micropolitical sites in order to ascertain what level of disorder, change and ambiguity is created within the always already infiltrated status of each core, centre, homogeneous subject or community.[11]

## Infiltration, identities and communities

When I imagine a historical context for this book, when I try to examine my theoretical assumptions, I realize that I wish I knew how to apply infiltration to my own discourse. I find it difficult to describe (create) the territory or territories which I could claim to infiltrate, even more difficult to formulate what relationship I would hope to establish with identifiable theoretical positions, and at the same time, I would feel somehow delinquent if I refused to clarify a few of my premises.

I assume that I am writing at a time when what has been called 'identity politics' is under attack from two distinct positions: on the one hand, a certain tradition fears the dissolving effect of what is loosely referred to as post-structuralism, deconstruction, post-modernism on so-called Western culture. Emergent discourses are being opposed as a dangerous threat to supposedly transparent literary and social values. I have to recognize that if emergent discourses continue to be the object of sometimes vicious attacks, it is because categories called 'women', 'minorities', or 'gays' can no longer be ignored nor declared irrelevant to the humanities. As Epstein and Straub remark in the introduction to *Body Guards*, African-American history and gay and lesbian history 'grew out of a modern move to claim identity and community as sources of psychological and political strength' (Epstein and Straub 1991, 8) and the same urge to build constituencies certainly appears in other minority groups.

On the other hand, the concept of identity is also criticized within these same oppositional formations, in much the same way as 'essentialism' was problematized in the 1980s (Fuss 1989). Partly under the influence of Foucault, recent criticism has preferred to emphasize a performative definition of identity. Judith Butler suggests, for example, that Foucault's work 'offers a counterwarning I think to those who might be tempted to treat femaleness or the feminine as an identity to be liberated' (Butler 1992, 348).[12] She goes on to state that

to take identity as a rallying point for liberation would be to subject oneself at the very moment that one calls for a release from subjection ... If identity imposes a fictive coherence and consistency on the body or, better, if identity is a regulatory principle that produces body in conformity with that principle then it is no more liberatory to embrace an unproblematized gay identity than it is to embrace the diagnostic category of homosexuality devised by juridico-medical regimes. (Butler 1992, 355)

At the same time, it does not take much cultural competence to be convinced that identity has been, is, and will continue to be 'a politically efficacious phantasm' (Butler 1991, 13). In everyday life, it does not take much competence to distinguish between a child and an adult, a black person and a white person, a man and a woman. Rather than focusing on what is unstable in these categories, rather than focusing on the border in the hope that liminality will destroy both the opposition between centre and margin and the principle of the opposition itself, my reading strategy consists of identifying figures who accept or pretend to accept an identity (including when they are marginalized and excluded) as a recuperation of the bad faith of the powerful.

In the end, talking about infiltration does not allow me to position my discourse within or beyond identities. I would like to ask, instead, what tactics one uses in order to act *as though* identity were as problematic in the street as in a theoretical article. How does one read when minorities or women are always imagined as oppositional dwellers of a borderland? I suggest that there is a gamble involved in the study about infiltration: I invest in the hope that it is possible to claim and question identity and community at the same time through a redefinition of the concept of belonging. The infiltrator is multiple and uncertain of his or her real affiliations. But rather than creating more ambiguities, instead of blurring frontiers, his or her game is to perform a lack of ambiguity. When the infiltrator 'passes' for a member of a group to which he or she knows that he or she does not belong naturally, transparently, the ambiguity of the performance of belonging, of being at one with the others, exposes the fact that each performance of identity is also similar to his or her game. If the infiltrator's insertion into a structure that imagines itself solid is relatively successful, then the identity of all the other members of the supposedly natural community is brought into question. Infiltration does not exploit the borders of identity to create ambiguities, rather, it uses ambiguities to invent provisional and discursive stagings of identity, or, to adapt Homi Bhabha's definition of hybridity, a 'metonymy of identity'.[13]

The infiltrator's repressed desire may thus be described as a phantasm of *départenance*. I understand *départenance* as a multiple movement away from the very concept of belonging (*appartenir* in French). *Départenir* would thus entail a gesture of departure, a deliberate renunciation of partnership, an always defeated attempt not to belong. I imagine *départenance* (both the process of 'departening' and the unattainable state of *départenance*) as the ultimate and unreachable goal of the infiltrator, the dynamic element in his or her choice of everyday tactics. As Serres puts it in a series of interviews with Bruno Latour:

Mais me pousse surtout une forte propension à «ne pas faire partie de…», car cela m'a toujours paru requérir d'exclure et de tuer ceux qui n'appartiennent pas à la secte. J'ai une horreur quasi physique de la libido d'appartenance. Vous noterez qu'elle est rarement analysée ainsi, puisqu'elle soutient toutes les ambitions cuisine la morale la plus répandue. (Serres 1992, 35)

[But I am especially driven by a strong desire 'not to belong to…', because I have always seen belonging as what demands that I exclude and kill those who do not belong to the sect. I have a quasi physical horror for the libido of belonging. Note that it is very rarely analysed as such because it founds all ambitions and simmers within the most currently accepted systems of ethics.]

Of course, this desire or oppositional libidinal construction is not only impossible to conceptualize and theorize, it is also ironic given that the infiltrator's tactics consist of imitating or mimicking (that is, creating by an effect of simulacrum) the identity of the group within which he or she seeks to 'pass', and given that the attempt to 'pass' can only be based on a simulacrum of identity even if the infiltrator does not believe in identity (his or her own included) other than as a performance. Infiltration is about inventing *départenance* as a goal while knowing that contemporary strategies have to rely on community, identity, on categories such as race, nationality, mother tongue, sexual preference, or second generation.

As a result, I do not think that infiltration can be idealized as a more successful form of oppositionality. It cannot even be imagined as an ethical position. Talking about the rhizome, Deleuze warns the reader that 'Il y a le meilleur et le pire dans le rhizome: la pomme de terre et le chiendent' (Deleuze and Guattari 1980, 13). Because even *départenance* could potentially be used as a way of excluding an 'other', infiltration is ironic as long as one understands irony as the archetypal self-reflexive trope: irony is aware of the irony of being one step ahead of one statement and one step behind the statement that is about to reappropriate it (Chambers 1990).[14]

## A word on the corpus

Before ending this series of provisional reflections on the theoretical, political, or literary implications of infiltration, I would like to comment on the juxtaposition of texts found in the following chapters. I wonder if readers, glancing at the table of contents, will be alienated by a sense of impossible synthesis, by a feeling of unfamiliarity. Another way of saying this is that I am perfectly aware that I would have difficulty identifying 'the' reader or 'the' audience to whom this book is addressed. Asking myself who is my public or even what public is implicitly invented as a community by the corpus I have chosen, will, I hope, prove rather unrewarding. I would rather ask myself what kind of reading technique is implicitly requested from a reader who has not necessarily heard of (let alone read or studied) the so-called primary texts.

I can and will emphasize many axes of coherence and many forms of resemblance between the books: all these texts were originally written in French (although not necessarily in metropolitan France: Michèle Maillet and Françoise Ega are from Martinique). They were all written during the twentieth century (although the difference between Vivien's and Ega's styles and assumptions will probably convince some readers that the label is at best useless if not downright confusing since the writers cannot be said to have shared the same historical or social experience). What is perhaps the least debatable category (all these texts were written by women) is also what creates disagreements and discordance between them (for example, Vivien refuses infiltration, Maillet's infiltrator figure can be said to be divided into two distinct female characters, Colette's form of infiltration of genre is not presented as gender-oriented). The literary genre of each text does not constitute a core of sameness either. In fact, trying to define the literary genre to which this corpus belongs will certainly prove self-defeating: although one might point out that every text is written in prose (but is a cartoon considered 'prose'?), it may be impossible to find a term for what kind of prose is represented here: I could not find a meaningful category to subsume a first-person narrator diary, a collection of short stories, an epistolary novel, journalism, recipes, etc.

Preserving the difference between books and acknowledging the distance between my readers' implicit canon and the corpus studied here can be offered as a modest and symbolic gesture towards an infiltrated conception of French studies: when one's discipline is infiltrated, one will find foreign elements at the very core of one's area of study. And these disparate elements cannot be rationalized as an emergent corpus either: Vivien, Ega, Maillet and Colette are not supposed to form a new community united by race, gender, class, or sexual orientation.[15] As far as my readers are concerned, I expect that specialists of Caribbean literature will be familiar with Françoise Ega and Michèle Maillet, but they may not know Vivien's work very well, especially not her prose. On the other hand, scholars interested in gay and lesbian studies will certainly have read and perhaps written about Vivien's short stories but Ega and Maillet will not be so recognizable. I anticipate that feminists or teachers or students of French who have spent some time in France will know about Bretécher's characters, but I see no reason to anticipate that such readers will have therefore been tempted to read Colette's or Sand's recipes even if these last two names are by far the most familiar items from the point of view of a traditional canon.

Even infiltration is not a unified category in these texts, although I have tried to group two main forms of infiltrational practices: Bretécher, Ega and Maillet exemplify what could be called the infiltrator as a figure. None of these authors openly focus on infiltration as a theme, but each story features one or several ambiguous characters whose relationship to the world of discursive power could be described in terms of infiltrational practices. Bretécher's children of a feminist mother, Ega's Martinican housecleaner and Maillet's victims of Nazi concentration camps illustrate, in very different ways, the complex negotiations and survival techniques of those who choose (or are forced to) pass, spy, interpret, learn, play. The second part of the book is devoted to the hypothesis that infiltration could be considered a genre or a counter-genre: Colette and Vivien may be described as infiltrators within a certain canon and I hope to show that their writings parallel their positioning or lack thereof by both adopting and subverting the conventional limits of recipes, short stories and by infiltrating the distinction between gender and genre.

I suggest that these texts do not necessarily have something to say to each other, I do not propose to force them to engage in a dialogue albeit heteroglossic. If they relate to each other, it is as infiltrators, which means that whatever disruption they create is practically unnoticeable, and also that my highlighting them as infiltrators constitutes a paradoxical and ambivalent gesture of 'outing'.

## Notes

1 See Lionnet's *Autobiographical Voices: Race, Gender, Self-Portraiture* for an analysis of the implications of the lack of satisfactory English translation for the French word *métissage*.

2 See especially a passage from *Mémoires* where Derrida writes about the 'allegorical bent of "deconstruction", a certain architectural rhetoric' (Esch 1992, 375), and a quotation from an interview on deconstruction and architecture (Esch 1992, 377). See also Esch's analysis of the case of the 'bugged' American embassy as revealed by a front-page story of the *Washington Post* (April 1987). She offers this 'story of superpower intrigue' as an 'allegory of events taking place elsewhere, in the ostensibly reified and circumscribed sphere of literary studies' (374). The interesting and original aspect of the bugging system was that 'the devices ... were embedded in the precast concrete block and reinforcing bars used in the construction of the embassy walls and floors' (374). Esch makes the point that even after the bugging system was identified (once the 'vulnerability of the structure itself to wholesale deconstruction' (375) had been exposed), 'neutralization' was still not the obvious option since it entailed 'deconstructing' part of the building (and the 'cost would equal what the United States had already spent to erect the chancery, with the total amounting to most of the sum appropriated for construction in the first place' (374).

3 Ross Chambers's *Room for Maneuver* is one successful metaphorical exception because it

evokes a cornered discourse eager to preserve its freedom of movement on the borders of but also within a more solid central structure.

4 For a subtle and disturbing analysis of the ways in which 'racist' and 'anti-racist' discourses mirror each other, see Pierre-André Taguieff's *La Force du préjugé: essai sur le racisme et ses doubles*.

5 Houston Baker was referring to Jean-Loup Amselle's *Logiques Métisses* published in Paris in 1990.

6 Although I am slightly worried by the title (as *libre-échange* places the book of interviews under the aegis of an enomomic euphemism that betrays the literal meaning of each of the elements of the compound word), I finally decided that I must place my hope in the ironic reappropriation of a limited 'freedom' attempted by the two authors throughout this original 'exchange'.

7 Paul Gilroy uses the expression to concede that there may be some value to what he otherwise perceives as the dangers of what he calls 'experience-centred knowledge' (53). See also pages 213 and 214 of his uncompromising *The Black Atlantic* for a moving attempt at opening a dialogue between Blacks and Jews that would not relativize the Holocaust: 'I want to resist the idea that the Holocaust is merely another instance of genocide. I accept arguments for its uniqueness. However, I do not want the recognition of that uniqueness to be an obstacle to better understanding of the complicity of rationality and ethnocidal terror to which this book is dedicated' (213).

8 See Irigaray's *Parler n'est jamais neutre* (281–93). I want to thank Annie Pritchard for pointing out that Irigaray's 'mechanics of the fluids' could be interpreted as a direct critique of Sartre's definition of his existentialist project as the elimination of the 'viscous'. Irigaray both takes into account the fact that the fluid and the solid are gendered and she reappropriates the distinction itself as a way of opposing binary thinking. Like Deleuze's 'rhizome,' the fluid is what escapes the very opposition between the solid and the fluid. On the relationship between femininity and the viscous, see Sartre's *L'Etre et le néant* (667–78).

9 'Morphing is the punningly named, computer-based image processing technique that gave *Terminator 2: Judgment Day* much of its technodazzle, enabling the T-1000 – a killer android possessed of protean powers – to dissolve seamlessly from a slight, feline policeman into the sinewy, taut-strung heroine, Sarah Connor, in the film's climactic moment' (Dery 1992, 501).

10 See also Mark Crispin Miller's *Boxed In: The Culture of TV* (306–7): 'Finally, Ripley manages to snuff the Alien only by turning herself into hyper-masculine/robotic: she encases herself in a mammoth robot-exoskeleton, which – powerful and dry – allows her to crush the shrieking mother-figure as if it were a giant, juicy bug' (quoted by Dery 1992, 505).

11 'Beyond Identities' is the title of the 55th issue of *Transition*, edited by Kwame Anthony Appiah and Henry Louis Gates, Jr. See also *Transition* 58 (1993), entitled 'Passing'.

12 See also Gayatri Spivak's key-note address 'Teaching for the Times' published in *MMLA* (25.1).

13 See Homi Bhabha's 'Signs Taken for Wonders' originally published in *'Race,' Writing and*

*Difference* and his 'DissemiNation: Time, Narrative and the Margins of the Modern Nation' in *Nation and Narration*. Both chapters are reprinted in *The Location of Culture* (102–22 and 139–70).

14 A shorter version of this text has appeared in a collection of articles in honour of Ross Chambers published by the *Canadian Review of Comparative Literature/Revue Canadienne de littérature comparée* (edited by Jonathan Hart 1995). Let this note be a necessarily inadequate way of reiterating to what incalculable extent this book is indebted to Ross Chambers's work as a whole and more specifically his reflexion on oppositional manoeuvres.

15 I am not insisting, for example, that the texts studied in this book have been unfairly neglected and should now be included into obligatory syllabi and reading lists. I would rather remember Gerald Graff's warning that 'conflict avoidance is built into the familiar 'add-on' principle of departmental and curricula change' (Graff 1992, 63) and that 'teaching the conflicts' is a more valuable strategy even if it goes 'against one of the sacred taboos of pedagogy, which is that students should be exposed to the results of their elders' conflicts, but not to the conflicts themselves' (Graff 1992, 81).

# Why do little boys play with washing machines and why do little girls lie about it?

> A functional change in a sign-system is a violent event. Even when it is perceived as 'gradual', or 'failed', or yet 'reversing itself', the change itself can be only operated by the force of a crisis.
>
> A celui à qui je dois tout.[1]

Children could be considered as the arch-infiltrators because it is assumed that they are incomplete adults, grown-ups to be. Children are encouraged to imitate parents, to do as they are told, because we know better. Our goal is to transmit our cultural patrimony, our social status (at least), our religious beliefs and culinary habits. Most of the time, I view childhood as a stage, a state of temporary ignorance and naivety which one overcomes as one grows up. The desirability of growing up does not preclude nostalgia for this pre-lapsarian and supposedly ideal moment of innocence. But nostalgic feelings cannot be separated from the a posteriori construction of childhood as a neutral space, a blank slate on which the efforts of educators will imprint knowledge and supposedly power. Like Bataille's 'primitive' people which would supposedly evolve to reach our level of civilized understanding, like women who need men's guidance, like immigrants who should strive towards assimilation or its new and improved counterpart, integration, children are seen as a draft version of the adults they will become. Allusions to the fact that children are not this void, emptiness and lack of future adulthood, will be perceived as exceptions to the rules or provocative statements. When the narrator of Colette's *La Maison de Claudine* looks for the best way of describing a wild cat which she considers the most 'natural' creature she has ever 'owned', she writes: 'je pourrais écrire qu'elle se comportait en enfant candide, s'il y avait des enfants

## UN COUPLE

Claire Bretécher, Les Frustrés III, Paris: Presses Pochet, 1978

candides' (Colette 1986, 1062) [I could write that she behaved like
a candid child if there were such a thing as candid child (my
translation)]. Such self-conscious statements are an apologetic form
of resistance to the unspoken myth of childish candor. The etymological whiteness in candor is the same whiteness that makes a blank
cartridge a harmless rehearsal, a powerless imitation of the real
thing. Adulthood, on the other hand, is a supposedly stable and solid
soil. It functions like presence and being in our western metaphysics,
it is imagined as a moment of plenitude, a climax to which every
child aspires and at which every old person may hope to have
remained poised. Short of having read Derrida before the time when
one is expected to know how to read, what can a child do but accept
his or her status as a more or less dangerous 'supplement' and
construct him or herself as a more or less successful infiltrator
(Derrida 1967, 203–34)?

When I started reading Claire Bretécher's 'Un Couple',[2] I remember being disappointed by what I thought was a particularly obvious
and unambiguous message. The story seems to represent patriarchal
society at its most caricatural: two children are enacting a most
unimaginative version of the family romance, adopting stereotypical
gender roles which seem obsolete or reactionary. Such essentialist
gender roles, I reflected, had long been criticized by feminists and I
doubted whether we absolutely needed yet another parody. I
thought that readers did not have to be particularly versed in feminist
theories to identify the children's roles as some of the most rigidly
conceived gender scripts possible. I remember thinking that
Bretécher was usually less predictable and boring.

Here we go again, I thought. The little girl does the dishes and the
little boy fixes the car and the washing machine. Although the little
boy does not speak much in the story, he confidently states that
women's talents are limited and the little girl does not object to his
generalization. In fact, both children agree that gender determines
what one might call disciplinary expertise: 'les bonnes femmes, ça ne
connait rien à la mécanique' [Girls don't know nothing about
mechanics]. Not only do they agree that men will naturally perform
better in certain areas but they also despise other (feminine) areas of
knowledge. What women do is devalued and described as lacking or
incompetent. 'C'est normal que les femmes connait rien à la
mécanique puisque c'est un travail d'homme' [Of course girls know
nothing about mechanics, that's a man's work]. The little girl

justifies the 'norm' by means of a tautology (it is not a woman's work because it is a man's work) in a rhetorical move which barely disguises the ideological premise as 'common sense' or good old 'popular' 'traditional' evidence. The little girl does not object to the little boy's narrow description of her abilities, rather, she steals back a little power by pointing out that her so called 'ignorance' can be seen as a successful adaptation to a situation which she does not question.

Her complete willingness to perform her role was however the first element which intrigued me and aroused my interest: even though I was tempted to accuse the little girl of complicity, self-oppression, I started thinking that it was too easy to colonize this text by imposing a rigid oppressor/victim grid upon its fictional characters. Paradoxically, this cartoon also represents a perfect system, a noiseless utopian space from which all friction is absent since the norm is reinforced by both protagonists, since neither expresses disagreement or pain. Some readers may indeed choose to point out that the story is 'fair' in its 'equal' stereotyping of women and men: the little girl complains that men 'sont tous des souillons' [they are all slobs] wallowing in grease. In a sense, 'Un Couple' represents a harmonious and idealized family romance, an ideological status quo which both characters seem perfectly happy to accept.

My own reading however is a friction-ridden activity: as a historically situated reader, I am aware that feminist activists, thinkers and writers have vehemently challenged such patriarchal structures, and I realize that this 'charming' picture is not supposed to be charming. Something, somewhere, is slightly wrong in this picture. Whether or not one is a self-declared feminist, such stereotyped portrayals of men and women may strike us as obnoxious because feminist thought has sufficiently infiltrated our society to function as knowledge and colour our interpretation of 'Un Couple': I would be surprised if, after the first few frames, we did not assume that an ironical and probably critical distance separates the female author from her young characters. In other albums, Bretécher relentlessly lampoons a certain post-sixty-eight urban, parisian, middle-class intellectual community. We may thus assume that the portrait is a virulent satire. The lack of minimum discrepancy between the children's discourse and the most recognizable stereotypes will lead us to suspect that only a strong dose of irony can lend comic relief to this sad perfect picture and justify its inclusion into the Frustrés as a whole.

If we agree that irony pervades the first part of the story, we may assume that the scene represents and denounces a society in which children's playful reenactments testify to the power of gendered expectations which deprive little girls and little boys from any latitude with regard to their socio-sexual inheritance. The characters are depicted as the innocent and powerless recipients of a discourse about gender difference which infiltrates their games. As children, they reproduce a model which they are not theoretically equipped to criticize, we assume that they are unthinkingly and 'naturally' imitating their parents. Perhaps a reader does not need more information to infer that this representation is meant as criticism and satire.

Bretécher's story, however, continues past the first nine frames and the author obviously takes advantage of the laws of linear reading to make her point. At the end of the story, the reader who thought that she had guessed the real meaning of 'Un Couple' is in for a surprise. The last frames problematize our first reading by adopting a more nuanced and interesting position: when the mother steps into the narrative frame, the little girl hastily interrupts the game and silences the little boy who was obviously on the verge of committing a serious political blunder. She stops him from telling the mother about their games and we, readers, become her accomplices, or at least, witnesses to her sudden change of tone. I argue that the abrupt switch in the story shows that the *status quo* is always already infiltrated, even if, as linear readers, we were at first led to believe that the children were buying into the stereotypical distinction between male and female roles.

If the child is capable of switching so convincingly to a totally new discourse at an instant's notice, we have to assume that she was not modelling herself on the mother who would disapprove of the game and who obviously did not pass on traditionally sexist stereotypes. The boy does not seem to know that the discursive and ideological foundation of his game is subversive, but the other child is aware of breaking a rule. By silencing her brother, she contains the discourse of a game within the limits of a children's fantasy world and does not encourage direct confrontation.

But the end of the story also seems to belittle the political desirability of infiltration: the last frames of 'Un Couple' constitute a discouraging conclusion. Apparently, the efforts of a whole generation of feminist thinkers and activists have been of no avail. Children are bad students. They have not learned what we wanted them to learn and history is not being rewritten. Prior to the mother's intervention, a feminist reader may be concerned by the sexist underpinnings of 'Un Couple', but she could reassure herself that such portraits were anachronistic or that Bretécher's fictional universe was not meant to represent a cultural norm: we might choose to hope that she was mocking an ultra-conservative fringe of the population that we will prefer to judge ignorant or backward.

Unfortunately, the character of the mother cannot be rationalized as a reactionary element: she symbolizes a form of radical, articulate, informed feminism and she has been acting as a feminist teacher for her children. Should we conclude that Bretécher's message is that the 1970s' generation of French feminists has been utterly powerless to modify women's roles and that infiltration is a form of change which does not make a difference? The story certainly reflects on the difficulty to infiltrate old gender structures and on patriarchy's remarkable tendency to perpetuate itself in spite of oppositional forces. But it also laughs at feminism's failure to formulate theories which children could absorb as a result of cultural immersion.

The mother's arrival is a narrative turning point which forces us to rethink the elements of the problem and robs us of the reassuring impression that we had understood the gist of the story, its humour and satirical thrust. This is an example of textual overbidding:[3] as if it were not sad enough to have to admit that nothing has changed, that feminism has had no influence over our culture, now the story suggests something even worse: that female children are perfectly willing to conform to an old-fashioned and traditional division of gender and work roles not in spite of but because of feminism. Feminist discourses have indeed infiltrated our culture but they have produced the adverse and unexpected effect of reinforcing patriarchal standards. 'Un Couple' thus raises serious questions about the history of feminism and about the way in which one transmits knowledge about gender roles to another generation.

## How does one inherit feminist knowledge?

In the last frames, the little girl repeats a (feminist) lesson indicating that the mother has been an efficient teacher. The little girl is obviously correct in assuming that for her mother, the desirable feminine role is to be 'driving to the office in the Volkswagen' while the husband 'does the dishes'. Why then is the lesson repeated and not assimilated?

In a sense, the mother's education has achieved some measure of success since the little girl has acquired a familiarity with feminism but her knowledge is used as a self-contained performance. It does not become a lifestyle. Of course, the pattern is not specific to the acquisition of 'feminist knowledge': in fact, whoever teaches 'feminism', 'history', or 'culture' is probably better off keeping in mind that many different discourses, unequally recognized within the discipline, will function as rivals and incompatible 'lessons'. The difference however is that when one learns history, the desirable result is that one will eventually 'know' something about history whereas when I teach 'feminism', somehow, I hope that my students will 'become' feminists. I expect knowledge and identification. The irony is that if I teach 'feminism' like another discipline, what gets transmitted is a vast array of discourses which may, or may not, coalesce into the body of knowledge, know-how and cultural competence which we call a gender role. Each coherent discourse is likely to influence a listener. A parent can never hope that her children will be limited to her own influence and that her own chosen discourse will be transmitted intact. As Ross Chambers puts it in his *Room for Maneuver*, this kind transmission has often been thought of in terms of (good or bad) 'influence':

In literary theory, the term traditionally used to designate the kind of change that is brought about by reading is *influence*. But oddly, 'influence' has largely been conceived as a relation between authors and/or texts. Influence as the kind of change that cultural texts of all sorts (not just literary ones) can bring about in desire is a topic that has been left to moralists, who have of course understood the deflection of desire as a deviation from legitimacy, and so have fulminated (in former times) against the pernicious influence of the theater or of novels, or (in our own times) against the supposed depredations of TV or pornography. (Chambers, 235–6)

Dominant ideology is said to be transmitted by (or reflected in, but is there a difference?) the media and public institutions, but these hegemonic spaces are also infiltrated by minority voices which will insist on their marginality and difference. It has become obvious by now that no History is powerful enough to totally silence such fragmented accounts of difference. Trinh Minh Ha's *Woman, Native, Other* thus analyses the relative influence of the grandmothers' voices over successive generations of female children.

I am not conjuring up the figure of the grandmother as an appeal to some mythic feminist ancestor: I do not necessarily assume that all grandmothers are marginal nor that all marginal discourses are inherently liberatory simply because they can be idealized as a form a resistance. Narratives emanating from a 'grandmother' (one gender role among others) cannot be reduced to a form of innocent and beneficial knowledge which all communities of women should work at preserving undiscriminately in the name of a feminist tradition: perhaps no discourse should be transmitted 'intact' (by 'intact' I mean protected from commentaries, free from rewriting and criticism).[4] According to Trinh Minh Ha, remembering should not be confused with sacralizing:

Mother always has a mother. And Great Mothers are recalled as the goddesses of all waters, the sources of diseases and of healing, the protectresses of women and of childbearing. To listen carefully is to preserve. But to *preserve is to burn*, for understanding is creating. (Minh Ha, my emphasis, 121)

I suggest that Bretécher's little girl is potentially infiltrational because she must 'burn' two competing discourses about women. Were she tempted to 'choose' (to preserve) one at the expense of the other, they might add up to a schizophrenic body of knowledge. Perhaps no one definitely chooses among several discourses. Perhaps one discourse becomes (temporarily) a conscious or unconscious dominant construct. The little girl does not have a 'choice'[5] between her mother's feminist discourse and her culture's sexist assumptions: parent's or society's teachings cannot be altogether obliterated or forgotten or rejected. Besides, dreaming of harmonious syntheses is probably unrealistic: competing discourses functioning like textbooks or imagining themselves as manuals of social practices will give their readers contradictory suggestions or orders. Infiltration generates or is an unstable terrain, not an adequate foundation for rock-hard certitudes.

I once heard a woman say that women's 'intellectual' or 'conscious' yearnings (professional or political ambitions) are in permanent contradiction with their real or unconscious needs (the joys of a traditional nuclear family). I wonder if that woman was not alluding to the fact that each (female) child is always subjected to conflicting attempts at endoctrination. And I suspect that infiltration will result in a permanent feeling of incompetence and confusion if the competing ideological forces, each of which promote their own version of the 'ideal' woman, are not identified as discursive formations, as scripts and scenarios.

I have no doubt that a 'feminist discourse' is necessary to counteract or at least expose supposedly neutral masculine constructions. But the previous statement is informed by my own historical position as an adult in the last decade of the twentieth-century. Of course, a part of me hopes that little girls will not 'buy into' patriarchy and that they will be influenced by their feminist mothers. But am I not expecting from the child some form of mystic revelation or religious conversion (as a 'woman', she should see the feminist light)? Are madness, or métissage, as literary themes, some of the ways of expressing the failure to embody two contradictory gender roles?[6] On the other hand, if the relationship between the subject and the role is conceived as a temporary and tactical link, if both teachings are 'burned', the little girl may have a chance to play the infiltrator: to preserve a difference, a départenance from normative and prescriptive dictates (be they feminist or anti-feminist norms). Départenance preserves and welcomes the possibility of interruptions which I would like to identify as the signature of infiltration, the moment when the game denaturalizes gender roles. When the mother interrupts, she reinscribes the children's voice within a limited territory: their game is not coterminous with 'culture' or 'society'. Although she is theoretically more powerful than the children, she is now ascribed the role of the parasite who infiltrates herself into a circumscribed order of discourse. But in the same way, the children's game is itself a form of infiltration and interruption: their discourse departs from and interrupts the 'Real' just like the little girl interrupts and dissociates herself from the little boy. The introduction of such interruptive interventions ironically destroys the illusion of cultural continuity created by the beginning of the story.[7]

## Departening a role?

Once this dream (or nightmare) is shattered, discontinuity infiltrates my own account of children's games: I find it more difficult to analyse the little girl's position as 'reactionary' or 'anti-feminist'.[8] After the mother's intervention, it is no longer clear that the little girl unthinkingly and happily embraces the traditional values to which the game alludes. In fact, it is no longer clear whether as a 'woman', she has already internalized what 'society' (or at least one of its loud dominant discourses) expects from her, or whether she is playing a forbidden role because, as a 'child', she systematically rebels against the values her parents endeavour to inculcate in her. Because she instantly modifies her performance when the mother shows up, I learn that her positioning is ambiguous: I can no longer determine what role she plays vis-à-vis her role. Her (relative) autonomy from the discourses she produces is a solution to an immediate and specific problem.[9]

If her relationship to gender role is tactical, then she is not making a political statement, at least not in the conventional sense of the term.[10] The little girl succeeds, not in promoting a traditional female role but in keeping the economy of play alive: a space which a figure of authority can interrupt but not control.[11] She invents a discursive borderland[12] where there is no magic coincidence between what she says and what she believes, between the game and her desire, between a 'role' and an 'identity'.

The female child is confronted with at least two different sets of discourse which would dictate the contours of her role as a woman: the mother symbolizes a certain feminism, and the language of advertising is a metonymy for a certain dominant ideology ('Heureusement j'ai ma nouvelle Xtra spécial machine'). Her radical departure from the original scenario (Mrs Extra White) demonstrates that she can identify each of the logics involved and reproduce them at will. The children denaturalize the role by inserting it into a set of propositions which can be temporarily accepted within the limits of a game of impersonation. The little girl has 'listened carefully' as Minh Ha puts it and she is now ready to 'burn' and create. The ideological content of her impersonations of a gender role (the game and the 'lie') is an insufficient criterion to ascertain whether her position is that of a revolutionary or of a counterrevolutionary: what she does 'preserve' is not a slogan (women have a right to go back to a 'traditional' feminine role or women have a right not to be forced into 'radical' feminist positions), but the space of the game, where roles are not dictated by authority. Of course she is 'influenced', by her mother and by other discourses, but she is conscious of repeating a memorized script, a scenario which she has not created or written. The flexibility with which she quickly switches to another script, like a viewer zapping from channel to channel, suggests her familiarity with interruptions, the efficiency of her vigilance and her cultural competence. She is not promoting one specific gender role, but the possibility of playing (a role).

## Playing and representation

To say that children's games cannot be confused with an unconditional adherence to the values represented in the game, is not to say that the ideological content of their play is irrelevant. Play is not a privileged realm outside discourse or outside representation: it so happens (and historically, this is no coincidence) that the little girl's 'game' is enacting a set of standards against which feminist thinkers have protested. I do not take Bretécher's story as a suggestion that adults should never interfere with their children's discourse and that only total abstention is the guarantee of the children's freedom. On the one hand, I fail to imagine how a parent (or any socialized user of language placed in the situation of a teacher) could actually conceive of absolute abstention. On the other hand, in this text, the children's 'freedom' of choice is guaranteed (always to a certain extent) not by their ability to create a new discourse ex nihilo, but by the skilfulness with which they react to changes in their situation: they are capable of carrying out a *mise en abyme* of some preexisting discourses among which they choose and which they (lazily)[13] rewrite. It would be impossible for the mother not to transmit any educational message, not to influence her children, but it is as illusory to imagine that her interventions would be decisive and definitive one way or the other.

Sooner or later, the mother will have to take a stance: for example, I imagine that few parents consider themselves immune from the debate about toys: should a parent encourage or explicitly forbid the use of ideologically loaded toys such as guns, or dolls? Of course, parents' control over representation is limited in this instance too: if I outlaw toy-guns and revolvers, I may discover, not only that my territory of influence is limited to my physical presence (as happens to the mother in the story) but also that I have no power over the child's imagination. I may exert discretionary buying power, I may refuse to be an adult consumer of toy-guns but if the child by-passes my edict, it will be less obvious (and less obviously desirable) to resort to authority over a child who invents a gun or a doll out of a piece of wood or an old rag.

Literature has used and abused the character of the imaginative child whose toys speak for him or herself, whose toys denounce poverty and lack. Toys which are not distributed through traditional commercial channels are usually endowed with some special ideological aura: they are supposedly on the side of innocence, of simplicity, of the 'natural'. Interestingly enough, the 'natural' toy can be used both as a critique of capitalism and materialism per se (children don't need, and tire easily of these extra sophisticated toys) and as a critique of the evils of capitalism ('poor' children are deprived of the joys experienced by the 'rich' owners of these sophisticated toys). For instance, in nineteenth-century French texts, the little toy-maker is portrayed as the victim of his or her social condition: literary 'imaginary toys' usually function as a celebration of the mind's ability to transcend economic conditions. In Hugo's *Les Misérables*, Cosette (hardly a rebel) manufactures what the narrator identifies as a pathetic rag doll without asking for Madame Thénardier's permission. The hero of Baudelaire's prose poem 'le Jouet' goes even further: his live rat becomes a source of envy for the rich little boy shielded from the streets by the bars of the gate. Even if the children's strategy is presented as a tragic substitute, poverty does not altogether eliminate the idea of the toy or the toy itself.

More recently, as television commercials push the latest, most sophisticated and 'realistic' gadgets, some parents may find the complicated contraptions in bad taste and complain (or hope) that their children will get bored with these unimaginative toys. But the reason why parents resist new cultural artifacts may be the same reason why children are attracted to them.

Furthermore, all this does not explain how an 'imaginary' doll differs from a 'real' doll: rather than recognizing that we (as parents and consumers) have the power to impose the classic 'doll' (the one we used when 'we' were young)[14] as a 'true' representation of the miniature child, we would rather suggest that the world of toys is divided between real dolls and fake makeshift dolls. I suspect that when I conceptualize certain dolls as 'fake' or 'imaginary', what I call 'imagination' is a form of representation of the real, which subverts parental authority (when the independent or incorrigible child transgresses the law) or rises above poverty (when he/she compensates for his or her parents' financial powers).[15]

But the distance between the toy and the way in which it is used only reproduces the vexed issue of the ideological 'content' of the toy: how do we theorize the difference between little boys playing with 'real' guns because they believe (or do they?) that they are toys, and little boys playing with real 'fake' plastic guns, or fake 'fake' pieces of wood? How do I explain, for example, that I have forgotten the names of most of the protagonists of *Les Misérables* (I must have been twelve or thirteen when I read the book) but not the distressing discovery I made about myself: I lacked the most 'charming' of all instincts: the desire to play with dolls:

Comme les oiseaux font un nid avec tout, les enfants font une poupée avec n'importe quoi. ... La poupée est un des plus impérieux besoins et en même temps un des plus charmants instincts de l'enfance féminine. Soigner, vêtir, parer, habiller, rhabiller, enseigner, un peu gronder, bercer, dorloter, endormir, se *figurer que quelque chose* est quelqu'un, tout l'avenir de la femme est là. Tout en rêvant et en jasant, et tout en faisant de petits trousseaux et de petites layettes, tout en cousant de petites robes, l'enfant devient jeune fille, la jeune fille devient grande fille, la grande fille devient femme. Le premier enfant continue la dernière poupée. (Hugo 1985, 321)[16]

[As birds make nests out of everything, children make dolls with anything. ... The doll is one of the most pressing needs and at the same time one of the most charming instincts of female childhood. To nurse, to clothe, to adorn, to dress and undress, to teach, to scold a little, to pamper, to put to sleep, to imagine that something is someone, here is woman's whole future. While day-dreaming and chatting, while making a trousseau and baby clothes, while sewing little dresses, the child becomes a young girl, the young girl becomes a big girl, and the big girl becomes a woman. The first child replaces the last doll. (my translation)]

Rather than making me indifferent to such definitions of 'instincts' and feminine 'needs', 'Un Couple' reminds me that historical contexts are not negligible, and also that if a grown-up's position functions like a form of arbitrary authority, the child's imagination may be used as a counter-practice. Ascribed to a feminine territory, the little girl may decide to infiltrate and explore other creative possibilities, to use her imagination as a way of escaping censorship or constraints. Even if Hugo's voice sounds anachronistic (his story is not plausible anymore, no 'powerful' grown-up is expected to thrive on such a tale in 1992), a feminist mother's voice will always be part of a competitive clatter of discordant voices, Victor Hugo's and Simone de Beauvoir's included. Her narrative is in competition with other contemporary narratives and the power of 'tradition' (commercials, schools and their canonical canons, other mothers, other children). The other stories will function either as other laws or will exert their own power of seduction over the children.

It seems that one of the viable positions is to produce a discourse which will make the child aware that the relationship one entertains not only with toys (and with what toys represent) is never transparent or unproblematic. How does the child see the relationship between the doll and the role of the 'little mother'? How does the child, male or female, situate him or herself with regard to fire-arms and with regard to the figure of the 'little soldier'?[17] Making sure that such questions are raised is neither impossible nor useless. Taking a stance in this context is a way of adding one's voice to a polyphony or perhaps a cacophony of opinions which will infiltrate the child's universe. Some little girls and boys will be playing with 'dolls' at the same age as they start reading *Les Misérables* and watching *Terminator 2*. Are children not already making choices when we hope to be inventing their future reality? And if, out of mental fatigue, I start imagining that there is some sort of magic shortcut which ensures that burning all dolls will protect little girls from becoming reproductive machines, I wonder if I am not inviting ironic reversals.

### Feminism and opposition?

If I reconcile myself with the impossible disappearance of representation, I may also be concerned about the implications of my predilection for 'gaming,' 'playing' and imitating. It may be argued that advocating 'games' is an irresponsible political move because it does not take into account the fact that, historically, certain discourses are hegemonic or marginal. But Bretécher's position does not ignore the history of feminism: it deliberately takes for granted that feminism has reached a point where it is plausible to assume that traditional patriarchal constructions (housewives know how to clean their messy husbands' clothes) are no longer exclusively dominant. If the beginning of 'Un Couple' is at first a source of irritation and impatience, I am forced to acknowledge that the myth has neither disappeared nor even lost all power. Bretécher suggests however that the seventies have produced other oppositional discourses which now coexist with more traditional visions of gender roles. One of the problems of feminist theory today is that it is becoming difficult to demonize the other side. What does one do when one finds oneself in a relative position of strength and weakness, when infiltration has already occurred within one's own positioning?

Bretécher's 'Un Couple' recognizes that 'feminism' inscribes itself within a history of shifting power relationships between dominant and marginalized discourses. Confronted with the ironies of the story, I feel compelled to constantly verify the status of my own discourse. If and when a feminist moment coincides with a powerful moment (when I realize that I have indeed had some 'influence'), how do I respond to the punctual break down of categories? How do I reconcile myself with the possibility that feminism (which strategically needs a territory, a base, an identity, a community, a constituency) no longer benefits from a description of its position as extremely marginal? Does feminism belong to what Spivak calls the 'emerging dominant' discourses'?[18] If a silenced voice is heard by a sympathetic community which relays its discourse, if this community is also heard by unsympathetic communities, competition replaces exclusion: hegemonic voices are no longer pretending that feminism does not exist. I wonder if the detractors of feminism will suddenly prove more and more efficient because they are using discourses in a way that minorities are not used to countering.

I find it difficult to accept (but indispensable too) that for the little girl, the mother's discourse functions like a new dominant discourse, an oppressive canon. Her personal history leads her to interpret the adult's constructions as a reference, as the Law. Our own personal history may tell us that the mother's discourse is marginal and fragile. This is partly due to the fact that the mother in this text has no authority over us. We may even read her position as doubly marginal in the sense that not only is her 'feminist position' a minority discourse within patriarchal structures, but her rather intransigent and unimaginative reversals represent a negative caricature of 'other' feminists. I am willing to bet that no feminist theorist will heartily suscribe to the simplistic vision of a mother who would accept nothing less but the final and absolute reinscription of women as Volkswagen drivers and of men as housekeepers.

The text questions the distinction between dominant patriarchy and marginalized feminism: it insists that a minority utopian counter-discourse (the gender role which the mother would like to produce and reproduce is still highly improbable) can, and will, function exactly like hegemonic ideologies. I am still in love with the dream of innocent and idealized women's visions. But a Pyrrhic victory may result from my failure to acknowledge that infiltration has already occurred. I find it hard (and tempting) to blame little girls (or young generations) for their lack of interest in the 'cause,' their misinterpretation of the 'struggles': am I not resenting their more advanced capacity of infiltration? Is it true that I do not wish to be reminded that infiltrators are most efficient in the place which is already ambiguously infiltrated?

## Utopias

If feminist discourse has infiltrated our culture to the point that I cannot always tell it apart from a chorus of voices, it does not mean that no position is ever recognizable and that it is irrelevant to choose between different feminist scripts: the little girl's freedom of choice does not consist in creating her identity ex nihilo. She can still however circulate and navigate between a number of discourses which still punctually function as discrete entities.

Infiltration as a subject's position or as a description of the relationship between competing values and discourses does not mean that an ideal no man's land exists where little girls may retreat. The fact that the infiltrator's performance is limited to a relatively small number of gender roles (the traditional housewife, the *femme-enfant*, the vamp, the liberated woman, how many can we really list?) makes me very sceptical of certain attacks against traditional feminism. For example, when Annie Le Brun accuses feminists of narrow-mindedness and of a serious lack of imagination, it seems to me that the alternatives she proposes are not very desirable:

Méprisant depuis toujours les maîtres qui ont des moeurs d'esclaves comme les esclaves impatients de se glisser dans la peau des maîtres, j'avoue que les affrontements habituels entre les hommes et les femmes ne m'ont guère préoccupée. Ma sympathie va plutôt à ceux qui désertent les rôles que la société avait préparés pour eux. (Le Brun 1990, 41)

[I have always despised masters who act like slaves and slaves eager to get into the master's shoes ['skin' as the French says]. Consequently, I admit that I have never been very interested in the regular confrontation between men and women. I have more sympathy for those who desert the roles which society has prepared for them.]

At first, Le Brun's tirade exerted a powerful attraction over me (as she puts it, 'je l'avoue'). I was drawn to her implicit conclusion that the solution is not to invert binary pairs and that nothing would be gained if 'slaves' became masters. I was also sensitive to the argument that men too are limited by, and suffer from, the 'rôles que la société avait préparés pour eux'. I was put off however by the

dismissive tone and the impression that the 'I' seems to position
herself above the uninteresting 'affrontement' between men and
women. I also noticed that 'slaves' (the word is but a very reductive
and inadequate description if it is meant to account for every subject
who feels oppressed and wants to change his or her relationships
with other individuals or groups) were blamed for their desire to 'se
glisser dans la peau des maîtres', and it occurred to me that this
image had seduced me into ignoring the implications of the
metaphor: what does it mean for the body of the slave to infiltrate
him or herself under or into (as the French says) the master's skin. If
it were possible to describe such a mutant, to describe a body as a
slave with a master's skin, would 'reversals' and 'binary oppositions'
still function?

I find Le Brun's metaphor of fusion and merging even more
productive than the allusion to military 'desertion' which is here
presented as a positive alternative. I am not so sure anymore that it is
possible to identify feminist territories, but I am even less convinced
by the vision of an 'outside' of 'société'. Is it not, at best, idealistic to
suggest that men and women are equal in front of possible 'liberation' from gender roles and that there is a space outside the constant
symbolic negotiation between the individual and the collectivity?

The little girl does not see herself as a 'soldier'. She does not
desert, she (temporarily) 'gets under the skin' of one of several
plausible master-discourses. In Bretécher's imaginary universe, nobody escapes into an idyllic future nor retreats into a utopian pre-
phallocentric order.

Which is not to say that her position is ahistorical: she can only
infiltrate efficiently some of the scenarios recognized in a given
historical and cultural context. The little girl belongs to the last third
of the twentieth-century, at a moment when the search for utopias is
criticized by feminists themselves.

Since the beginning of the century, the search for gender utopias
has generated important feminist models. Some long for a pre-
patriarchal social structure and celebrate ancient matriarchies. Of
course, such utopias assume that power, when exerted by women, is
different from and more desirable than, power yielded by men. As
we shall see in a following chapter, Renée Vivien's poetry and prose
are thus haunted by the wish to eliminate everything pertaining to a
male principle imagined as the source of aggressiveness, ugliness,
violence, hatred, in favour of a female 'principle' conceived as its

attractive opposite. When I read about Mytilene, the city of Women, which Sappho's translator offers as an ideal model, I am usually tempted to read this mythical construction as an unpractical demand for a model which remains extremely marginal in its conception. But thinking about Vivien through Bretécher's satires, it occurs to me that Vivien fails to explain how the 'women' of Mytilene ever 'became' women of Mytilene (to use Beauvoir's expression). In other words, Vivien does not imagine how this feminine discourse ever came about or became exclusively hegemonic, nor how it acquired the power to define a specific feminine role.

The same questions have been asked of feminist theorists whose rereadings of psychoanalysis purported to displace the all-powerful Phallus. Luce Irigaray's successive and evolving attempts at defining the identity and role of the lesbian (*Ce Sexe qui n'en est pas un*), of mothers and daughters (*Le Corps à corps avec la mère*' or 'L'une ne bouge pas sans l'autre' in *Ce Sexe*) have thus generated heated debates among feminists who criticized Irigaray's 'essentialism' and her 'idealization' of the maternal.[19] In her 'Difference on Trial: A Critique of the Maternal Metaphor in Cixous, Irigaray, and Kristeva', Domna Stanton remarks, however, that the discourse on 'maternal difference' was by no means the exclusive province of French feminism and that North-American feminists such as Adrienne Rich, Nancy Chodorov and Sara Ruddick repeatedly made use of the same category (Stanton 1986, 176). Towards the end of the seventies and the beginning of the eighties, the 'maternal' had become a form of hegemonic utopia dominating not only other 'feminist theoretical discourses' but also other cultural representations of women.

Other temporarily dominant utopias have been criticized. Judith Butler's *Gender Trouble* dismantles those oppositional models which hope to define the feminine as a pre-history of language (Kristeva's semiotic)[20] or as existing in some imaginary pre-gendered space. For instance, she explores Gayle Rubin's hypothesis that before the intervention of 'compulsory heterosexuality', 'each child contains all of the sexual possibilities available to human expression' (Rubin 1975, 189, cited by Butler 1990, 74). We should thus postulate the existence of a 'before', some infinite and plural identity upon which the masculine and the feminine impose their strict gender grids. But as Butler remarks, 'The bisexuality that is said to be 'outside' the Symbolic and that serves as the locus of subversion is, in fact, a construction within the terms of that constitutive discourse, the construction of an 'outside' that is nevertheless fully 'inside,' not a possibility beyond culture, but a concrete cultural possibility that is refused and re-described as impossible'(77).[21] Her formulation explains the paradox of an infinite freedom which is always dependent on (rather than served by) what Rubin calls 'human expression'. Not only is there no 'outside' of language or expression but language has the magic capacity to pretend that this 'outside' exists, thus sending oppositional desire on a wild goose chase for the 'real' other.

The little girl can choose from a limited array of ready made discourses. She plays with the already known, the already formulated. Theoretically speaking, I am tempted to say that she gives up on utopia (in the etymological sense of a 'nowhere') and prefers to infiltrate prefabricated constructions. She provides an answer to some of Butler's questions: 'If we accept the Foucauldian and Derridean criticisms of the viability of knowing or referring to such a 'before' how would we revise the narrative of gender acquisition?'(Butler 1990, 75). I wonder if the infiltrator's advantage could not be described as a way of renouncing this revision or rewriting of the narrative. It may be possible to observe the way in which a proliferation of discourses can be alternately adopted and rejected while insisting on preserving the immediate possibility of distance and interruption.

Once again, my desire to move away from the utopias of the seventies does not necessarily mean that I always agree with the criticism levelled at these feminist theories: I am not so sure that 'the laugh of the Medusa' or the 'mechanic of the fluids' are any less defendable, from a theoretical point of view, than say, the mirror stage or the Oedipal triangle. And I simply do not have an opinion anymore about whether or not these discourses constituted a bad strategy when they were first popularized (to a certain extent) or repeated by different speaking subjects, when they first infiltrated academic and popular culture. But what I find interesting if that these revisions are criticized by voices which do not need to define themselves as being 'outside' feminism. These voices feel that they have the right, or the freedom, or the time, or the energy, or the space to remain 'within' in order to change 'it' of which 'I' am.

## Performance? A minority role

For example, I am trying to propose a new definition of a gender role after reading or being infiltrated by some of Derrida's and Foucault's ideas. As a result, I do not much trust in a revision of role which would revive Diderot's paradox of the comedian. I want to avoid presenting the little girl as the empty vessel capable of 'expressing' a 'feeling' which she would not 'really' experience: even the most radical feminists have failed to invent this ideal utopian identity which would exist 'outside' gender roles. When the little girl 'plays a role', she is not an actress invited to impersonate a fictional character: to say that, like a professional actor, she can always propose different 'interpretations' of the role is not necessarily liberatory. The so-called freedom or latitude which would exist 'between' a woman's role and the real person's 'interpretation' is always controlled and policed by those who have the power to measure my 'interpretation' by the standards of this abstract and collective role. There is no pure and original moment before 'women' and 'women's roles' have not mutually infiltrated each other, although the illusion that it is possible to have a 'woman' on one side and a role on the other is still such a powerful metaphor that I have problems reimagining scenarios.

If I have enough power to impose a discourse, then my performance may be perceived as a role. My performance will infiltrate the role until nobody is able to distinguish between the two, until people still think that they can distinguish between the representativity of a role and the singularity of a performance when in fact, they are taking one for the other and vice versa. For example, the actress Catherine Deneuve represents 'Mariane' which is itself a supposedly abstract and representative allegory for France. In other terms, a performance cannot theoretically be distinguished from a role. I could, however, describe the creation of the category performance as the desire to account for a role whose power I do not fully accept: the performance would be what I call a minority role. The performance could be imagined as a weak role (weak as in powerless but it is no coincidence that the word sometimes means bad, mediocre), a role which the spectators always compare to their own version of the role (a forgotten powerful performance).

That a performance can become a role does not necessarily mean that the individual acquires power, since it implies that the role becomes powerful, which means that the subject's position regarding the role is treated as irrelevant: if (some day), I decline a glass of wine during dinner, I will be asked why, as a 'French person', I do not drink with my meal. My decision (which I do not even identify as a performance rather than a role) is interpreted as a corrupt version, a 'weak' interpretation of the role which all French people are supposed to play when they eat in public. I will lose my power of representativity, I will not be exemplary. But at the same time, the monolithic power of 'representativity' will have been slightly displaced since the difference between 'us' and 'them' (the French) has been infiltrated by the presence of one statement which can be added to the million possible definitions of the French: one narrative about 'the French' and 'wine' has just been added to a repertory of discourses. Some day, one of the witnesses of the embarassingly predictable episode may be able to testify: 'I know of one French person who does not drink wine with her meals'. From the total sum of possible statements, a reversal between the relative position for performance and role may some day occur: the performance modifies the role when the discourse of one individual acquires exemplarity. It is always possible that I modify a role through my performance while there is always a role to constrain my 'weak' performance.[22] The hope to 're-interpret' a (gender) role could thus be redefined as the temptation to present one's performance as a majority or dominant role.

Finally, what I learn as an infiltrator is that the very distinction between the performance and the role limits my freedom, even though I was hoping that the performance was a space of latitude, the very guarantee of my freedom. My freedom from the role, the amount of my 'creativity' vis-à-vis a preexisting role will always be limited and at best relative as long as I have to operate within the parameters of the opposition between the (collective) role and the (supposedly individual) performance. Yet, the distinction is more powerful than my imagination and refuses to go away once I have declared it useless and oppressive.

'Un Couple' has taught me to view the distinction between performance and role as a space of infiltration: the effects or manifestations of infiltration could be called 'interruptions' and 'instability' or 'playing'. Whether I choose to read the little girl's discourse as a game and the text as a theoretical playground (this is not 'serious'), or whether I focus on the consequences of interruptions (the mother's interruption reminds me that my performance can always be interrupted by your arrival), I deprive my audience of the privilege, the power or the violence to catalogue my perform- ance as part of the repertory of statements which they would like to use as reference, system, role, identity, etc. I make it difficult to let the performance/role become some illusory, yet powerful 'identity'. In a sense, I introduce hybridity or the 'metonymy of presence' (Bhabha, 1986).

## Le monde est vieux

Infiltration is thus linked to simulation, to doubling and hybridity, and also to the desirability of certain stories: it strikes me that from the beginning of this analysis, the protagonists of my infiltrating experiment are busy talking or listening to each other, and more specifically, telling or listening to stories.[23] I would like to suggest that 'playing' (a role) can be reformulated as a narratological tactic: when a figure of authority tries to impose a role upon me (a simplified way of saying that 'I' am being created as the lack of distance between my role and my performance), I may oppose this violence by forcing the powerful figure to listen to a (different) story. This definition of 'play' contradicts the usual connotation: 'playing' is a form of imitation, a mimetic activity reserved for little animals and human beings, innocent, and irresponsible creatures.

In a chapter entitled 'Toward a Theory of Play', Patricia Yaeger wonders why a 'feminist theory of play' (Yaeger 1988, 211) tends to encounter vehement resistance. Her analysis of Clifford Greetz and Sigmund Freud's definition of play, shows that games are often interpreted as a very specific form of imitation which serves a very specific purpose: only the powerless imitate the powerful in an attempt to compensate for their vulnerability. We assume that the 'child' is 'only' imitating a discourse which he or she will later be able to adopt as his or her own. The only reason why a child does not produce this discourse him or herself, does not 'sign' the performance, is (or so we tend to think) that they are still too weak or too insecure. But, as Yaeger puts it:

in this view, play allows children to rehearse the serious games of their parents and to negotiate symbolic transformations of unruly states. In playing, each child adjusts herself to social expectations and does not change those expectations to fit her needs. (Yaeger 1988, 212)

Thus defined, play is not a subversive activity, it is situated on the 'outside' of some social scene which stands for 'reality', 'adulthood', 'responsibility', 'presence'. Again, theatre comes to mind as the privileged metaphor: 'play' is akin to 'rehearsing' which takes place before the real performance, the 'premiere'. Strangely enough, what we metaphorically consider as the 'original', the first 'real' performance is always preceded by rehearsals which don't count as performances, which we would rather forget. I would like to suggest that the little girl's game reverses (or brings our attention to the reversible structure of) the order of the rehearsal–premiere sequence. Her way of 'rehearsing' or 'imitating' a discourse heard on TV or at her mother's house underscores the fact that the 'real' and the 'serious' are an accumulation of narratives which one may cite and repeat. In other terms, it is difficult to theorize the difference between what grown-ups call 'games' and what they call being serious. I wonder if 'playing' teaches us how to produce some 'real' performances when we grow up or if the 'real' allows the possibility of 'play' as repetition.

Furthermore, the metaphor of 'rehearsing' is particularly inappropriate in this case because it implies that playing is a painful and tedious process of absorption and memorization of a discourse. Obviously, the little girl has already mastered the art of imitating, she is already infiltrated by the gender roles discourse, or else, she has already infiltrated the adults' game show.

The little girl chooses among a set of narratives which the powerful implicitly offer her as education. In so doing, she reverses the relationship between the adult and the child, the real and the imitated, what is serious and what is play: unsuspecting, the mother is made part of the game, she undergoes the effect of infiltration as she becomes the recipient of a story rather than the director who advises the actors. In an ironic reversal, the little girl 'amuses' the mother, telling her what she wishes to hear. The mother becomes the child who enjoys a bed time story and the little girl becomes the exhausted mother who trades a story for the promise of a moment of peace and quiet. The point of the story is to put the mother('s suspicion) to sleep and the little girl must make sure that she captivates her audience and satisfies her desires.

Her expertise as a story-teller, as an inventor of scenarios, allows her to negotiate the intrusion of 'real' authority into her game. But all of a sudden, it becomes clear that the game itself was about telling stories and inventing scenarios. In other words, playing prepares children for real life, but not because they become undistinguishable from a memorized role: playing is a 'rehearsal' but the rehearsal of a practice rather than of a role. As a result, adulthood is re-constructed as a 'game', as a discursive space where one takes punctual and rapid decisions toward a role. Not only is there a similarity between the child's and the adult's activity, there is also a similarity between what the little girl protects and the tactic she uses to protect it: the common denominator is a narrative. The little girl tells stories so that she may continue telling stories. The child has learned how to use discourse, when to use what discourse, how to be acutely aware of the point of the story.

The little girl's competence and skill reside in her knowledge that her story will please the adult. When her mother interrupts, the little girls invents a fable designed to seduce a grown-up just like La Fontaine's orator resorted to stories to captivate his audience: in 'Le pouvoir des fables', a speaker from Athens desperately tries to mobilize his public's attention. He needs to convince fellow Athenians that Philip is putting them in terrible danger. But to his humiliation and dismay, he sees his public distracted by another performance, that of children: 'Tous regardaient ailleurs; il en vit s'arrêter/A des combats d'enfants et point à ses paroles'(282, v.46–470). Like the little girl, the orator changes his tune. He interrupts his traditional speech (which I equate with the little girl's first traditional fantasy) and he regretfully resorts to 'contes d'enfants' himself (a revolutionary emergence of a new genre within a political speech). Apparently, he assumes that if his public is interested in 'combats d'enfants' there must be something childish or chidlike about them. In fact, when the orator alludes to 'contes d'enfants', I wonder if he distinguishes between a story written for a child and a story written by a child. It is interesting that the orator is bent on distracting the public from children's fights ('combats d'enfants') so that they can turn their attention towards grown-ups' fights. The little girl also struggles to distract the mother's attention from a 'jeu d'enfants' which would be serious enough to spell trouble for the two of them. Her position as a threatened story-teller is exactly similar to that of the orator: it seems imperative that she concoct a narrative which will instantly seduce her audience.[24]

As a result, she shatters the myth according to which grown-ups make 'better' or more 'serious' audiences, because their attention span is longer, because they are not as likely to be amused or abused by a childish fable. The little girl's successful tactic exposes the grown-up as a child with power. Reformulated from the infiltrator's point of view, this last statement reads as follows: 'suivant que vous serez puissant ou misérable', you will be more likely to believe that the reality (or illusory nature) of the absolute distinction between children and grown-ups is a comment on their respective powerfulness or powerlessness at a given moment. And if that is indeed the case, La Fontaine's lesson loses much of its seemingly self-evident clarity. Another 'lesson' is suggested by the outcome of the anecdote: like the moralist who wishes to enlighten his readers, I may be tempted, as a 'feminist', to indulge in the systematic production of feminist fables, or feminist fairy tales for the benefit of twenty-first-century children. But Bretécher's text reminds me that adult moralists, who intend to educate children (or any subject supposed to be ignorant, innocent, backward and primitive) are not themselves very different from their public: 'Le monde est vieux, dit-on: je le crois (the narrator of the fable concludes) cependant/Il le faut amuser encore comme un enfant' (283, v.69–70).

## Notes

1   This is a quotation. 'A celui à qui je dois tout' [To the one to whom I owe everything] is the dedication in Bretécher's first album, *Les Frustrés*, published in 1975. A footnote accompanies the declaration: 'Ça ne coûte pas cher et ça fait plaisir à des tas de gens' [It's cheap and it makes tons of people feel good]. I offer this fake dedication as an example of successful infiltration: it both plays on the strength of identities and rejects them, it stands for the impossibility to ever stabilize the difference between a role and an identity.

2   'Un Couple' was published in the third volume of *Les Frustrés*, in 1978. In *Le Vingtième Siècle des femmes*, one entry is devoted to Claire Bretécher. It is pointed out that she is one of the very few women cartoonists and the only one to have received national recognition. She started publishing in 1973, in the *Nouvel Observateur*, and according to the authors of the article, 'Comme Sempé, elle devient une référence à mi-chemin du culturel et du sociologique. Roland Barthes la sacre "meilleur sociologue français"' [Like Sempé, she becomes a standard reference, somewhere between the cultural and the sociological. Roland Barthes awards her the title of 'best French sociologist' (my translation)] (Montreynaud 1989, 574).

3   By 'textual overbidding' I mean a form of oppositional thinking which satirical cartoonists like Reiser and Franquin often use as a last pessimistic strategy. The phenomenon of textual overbidding typically criticizes a system and falls short of proposing visible and immediate solutions. I suggest it is typical of, and particularly well suited to, discourses which rely on surprise or shock or scandal such as political cartoons or what the Surrealists have called 'black humour' (humour noir). See my

L'Humour noir selon André Breton, and 'Franquin et Reiser: Vers une éthique de l'humour noir comme surenchère'.

4 'Grandmothers' are (also) fictional or real characters playing grandmothers. Their role is no more rigidly fixed than any of the other so-called women's roles and no 'natural' alliances with other roles are to be expected. When exile further complicates (or perhaps brings into relief the complexity of) relationships across generations, it is not a safe assumption that grandmothers, daughters and granddaughters will always form coalitions or support groups. I am thinking for example of the literature written by the generation of Beur writers for whom the figure of the Grandmother is often as threatening as the figure of the tyrannical Father for women writers of the 1970s . The powerful grandmother often emblematizes a problematic 'tradition' and she is often described as the rival or enemy of the female narrator. See Ferrudja Kessas's Beur's Story, or Aïcha Benaïssa's Née en France: l'histoire d'une jeune beur. See also the series of interviews conducted by France Alibar and Pierrette Lembeye-Boy among Caribbean women in Le Couteau seul..., la condition féminine aux Antilles.

5 See Patricia Williams's The Alchemy of Race and Rights for an interesting reexaminiation of the apparently impeccable notion of 'choice' in the case of a convicted rapist who was supposedly given the 'choice' between a jail sentence and castration. As Williams puts it: 'The vocabulary of allowance and option seems meaningless in the context of an imprisoned defendant dealing with a judge whose power is absolute' (33).

6 See for example the literary treatment of various forms of hybridity resulting in madness in Myriam Warner-Vieyra's Juletane or André Schwarz-Bart's La Mulâtresse Solitude.

7 See Spivak on the relationship between what she calls 'substantive problems' and 'the structure of our practice': 'This recognizes what I now call interruptions – all of a sudden becoming aware that, in fact, there is an infinite regress on the margins of your substantive work. It's a genuine interruption in that it is discontinuous with the substantive concerns, but it is itself interrupted by bringing oneself back to the substantive investigation' (Spivak 1990, 44).

8 If a woman, and preferably a 'young' woman, chooses a traditional feminine role, one hastens to cite her as exemplary: she either symbolizes the shortcomings of feminist teachings, or she is the 'proof' that feminist thinkers are wrong because they cannot convince (even) their 'natural' public. Let us assume for a minute that a public speaker is bent on ridiculing what she imagines to be the theories of 'gender feminists,' and spends twenty minutes quoting meticulously (and out of context) all the declarations which, she thinks, will succeed in proving that feminism has 'failed'. One would expect such a person to declare herself a non-feminist or an anti-feminist. But the chances are in fact that the author of such a text would not dare renounce some of the aura and power of 'feminism' and that she would endeavour instead to redefine the role of the 'feminist' in order to fit 'feminism' within her own discourse, or to fit herself into 'feminism'. For example she could accuse 'other' feminists of being mistaken 'gender-feminists' when the only feminism worth mentioning was embodied by this one (supposedly representative) voice. In this case, I was even surprised that the speaker deemed it necessary to name her own brand of feminism since, after all, it seems like such an efficient strategy to consider all 'gender-feminists' as Others and present them as the caricatural mirror image of her own (true) Feminism. For example, even if in other regards I totally disagree with Annie Le Brun, I think that she is much more clever and strategically efficient when she fulminates against Cixous, Kristeva, and all the members of the Des Femmes publishing company, calling them 'neo-feminists'.

9 See the mother's facial expression when Colas starts telling his story, then successively, the little girl's, Colas's again, and finally the mother's.

10 We expect politicians to tell us *what* they believe rather than what their position is regarding the issue of 'believing'. We want to know if they are for or against reproductive rights for women, if they are for or against tax increases. It occurs to me however that the little girl's position is not unlike Judge Clarence Thomas's pre-nomination declarations that his opinions about abortion rights would not change the fact that he could be an impartial judge. The fact that the little girl's position gives her so much latitude towards the end of the story may provide a different explanation for why listeners were concerned for what appeared as a 'lack' of political statement.

11 As Michel Serres's (1980) work on the parasite has demonstrated, no event, no communication, no dialogue is ever safe from the intrusion of 'noise'. In a sense, the two children are in the same situation as the two protagonists of La Fontaine's famous fable 'Le Rat de ville et le Rat des champs' which serves as a pre-text for *Le Parasite*. It could be said that the (more sophisticated or older) little girl is inviting the (younger and less politically apt) little boy to feast on the remains of cultural artifacts and discourses left behind by the media and the parents. Their story is a satire (a warmed up rehash), a doubling and repetition of 'real' commercials and conversations. Like the 'rat des champs', the little boy is not aware at first that the feast is stolen from an unsuspecting figure of authority and it takes the interruption for him to learn that the consumption of certain cultural discourses is illegal.

12 For different ways of conceptualizing liminality, see Gloria Anzaldúa's *Borderlands: La Frontera, the New Mestiza* and Mary Louise Pratt's 'Arts of the Contact Zone'.

13 I am willing to concede that the children are no great writers, that they do not have much imagination because I am clinging to the hope that 'opposition' does not need to come from the Romantic Rebel, or from God's inspired messenger without whom the 'people' would be lost and powerless (see the difference between the children's recreations and Hugo's 'Mages' for example).

14 I put the second 'we' between quotes because it occurs to me that it may not be the same as the first 'we': when an adult remembers his or her own childhood, a nostalgic narrative colours the relationship between 'I' as a speaking subject and 'I' as a remembered 'child'. In *Imagined Communities*, Benedict Anderson points out that one needs a narrative to 'recognize' oneself as a photographed infant: 'How many thousands of days passed between infancy and early adulthood vanish beyond direct recall! How strange it is to need another's help to learn that this naked baby in the yellowed photograph, sprawled happily on rug or cot, is you ... Out of this estrangement comes a conception of personhood, identity (yes, you and that naked baby are identical) which, because it cannot be "remembered", must be narrated' (Anderson 1991, 204). Perhaps the parents who 'remember' their supposedly more authentic toys are suffering from a case of 'imagined childhood'.

15 Not to mention that the toy can also be used differently from what the parent expects. See the beginning of Toni Morrison's *The Bluest Eye*; the little black girl, confronted with a supposedly generic (white) doll, does not react as a passive and ideologically helpless consumer: 'What was I supposed to do with it? Pretend I was its mother?'(Morrison 1970, 20). Having exhausted the most obvious possibilities (holding it, sleeping with it, etc.) the child decides to take it apart, like a literary critic or a scientist or a mechanic searching for new models of knowledge: 'I had only one desire: to dismember it. To

see of what it was made, to discover the dearness, the desirability that had escaped me, but apparently only me' (Morrison 1970, 20). See also Sebbar-Pignon's article 'Mlle Lili ou l'ordre des poupées,' a witty and lucid analysis of little girls' 'curiosity' for what is inside the doll.

16 For an interesting analysis of the same kind of enlightening remarks about the 'natural' relationship between little girls and dolls, see Elizabeth de Fontenay's 'Pour Emile et par Emile' a reading of the fifth book of *L'Emile*. The author suggests that Rousseau contradicts himself when he claims, on the one hand that little girls like dolls because they represent motherhood, their natural 'destiny' ('la poupée est l'amusement spécial de ce sexe; voilà très évidemment son goût déterminé sur sa destination' Rousseau 1964, 459) but, on the other hand, that dolls are the symbol of feminine vanity ('les filles aiment mieux ce qui donne dans la vue et sert à l'ornement; des miroirs, des bijoux, des chiffons, surtout des poupées' Rousseau 1964, 459). 'Mais on ne comprend plus,' Fontenay concludes, 'la poupée consitue-t-elle un amusement «spécial» en ce qu'elle préfigure la maternité, fin naturelle de la femme, ou bien en ce qu'elle signale l'amour-propre le plus perverti?'(Fontenay, 1785).

17 One can also imagine the opposite experiment: I could decide to give a doll to a little boy in an attempt to modify his (supposedly 'natural'?) tendency to adopt an already internalized masculine 'role'. But the principle remains unchanged: in *Les Misérables*, the narrator does not seem to realize that his essentialist and pseudo philosophical digression about 'women's instincts' leaves a rather significant detail unattended. Colette (who is perhaps a less one-sided character than I thought) does not use just any material to manufacture her fake doll, she recycles a 'little saber', an object whose masculine connotations are supposedly obvious.

18 See Spivak's 'Teaching for the Times': '"we" – that vague, menaced, and growing body of teachers of culture and literature who question the canon – are not oppositional any more. We are being actively opposed' (Spivak 1992, 3).

19 For an analysis of the criticism leveled at Irigaray, see Christine Holmund 'The Lesbian, the Mother, The Heterosexual Lover: Irigaray's Recodings of Difference': 'Debate as to the value of Irigaray's analyses of identity, equality, sameness, and difference centers for the most part on her visionary re-creations of an undefinable, nonunitary female identity based on difference. Does Irigaray's version of difference become yet another model predicated on sameness, as Linda Godard charges? Does her new model of female identity duplicate without transforming phallocentric representations of 'Woman'? Does she ignore the differences among women as Domna Stanton maintains? Are Elizabeth Berg and Debra Terzian right to say that Irigaray speaks not as a woman but as a phallic mother or a man?'(Holmund 1991, 296).

20 See the first part of the third chapter entitled 'The Body Politics of Julia Kristeva' (Butler 1990, 79–93).

21 One of the ways of redefining a given gender 'role' as a forbidden excluded 'outside' consists in stating that the role in question does not exist: one could say for example that a given role is a form of hybridity or a *métissage* (a perverse or creative mixture) which should be defined as variations of other roles authorized by hegemonic discourses or minority dominant sub-groups. For example a bisexual may be described as a temporarily confused straight person, or as a gay individual who betrays his or her 'real' nature. A transvestite will be reduced to a man dressed as a woman. In the 1920s, lesbians were women functioning like or perhaps trying to 'pass' for men. The

characteristics of 'impossible' roles would be that they are always conceived as failed performances of other roles (even if the limits of 'real' gender roles can only be defined somehow in terms of play).

22  I purposely chose what I consider a non-violent episode to illustrate this point. But such structures are potentially harmful: when a woman is not feminine 'enough', when 'effeminate' men are automatically perceived as gay, in other words, when a minority performance is compared to other so-called 'roles', one can usually expect and fear the underlying presence of a whole battery of rather tasteless jokes, remarks, innuendos or even persecutions.

23  For a study of the ways in which power and oppositional practices function when two protagonists engage in a dialogue, see José Rabasa's 'Dialogue as Conquest'.

24  The orator knows that in order to compete with the spectacle offered by 'fighting children', he must become a spectacle himself, he must make a scene. The effectiveness of such a tactic (I spectacularly adopt a certain role in order to obtain something from my audience) may explain why it usually encounters such violent resistance. Women who make a spectacle of themselves are dismissed as 'hysterical' or 'grotesque' (as Mary Russo puts it in her title): 'There is a phrase that still resonates from childhood. Who says it? The mother's voice – not my mother's perhaps, but the voice of an aunt, an older sister, or the mother of a friend. It is a harsh, matronizing phrase, and it is directed toward the benavior of other women: "She" [the other woman] is making a spectacle of herself' (Russo, cited by Nancy Miller 1991, 23).

# The cleaning lady as ethnographer: working, giving and writing

Stereotypically speaking, the 'woman of letters' is an exception to the rule, a sort of privileged mutant who has freed herself from the restrictions imposed upon 'women' by infiltrating the world of writing. At the other end of the spectrum of female roles, stands a symmetrical and negative character: the female housecleaner. I wonder how these two figures interact and how they create or re-invent models of infiltration. Do the female writer and the female housecleaner redefine the ways in which gender roles differ from themselves or will they tend to re-appropriate and reinforce the distinctions imposed on them by dominant discourses?

Because the woman of letters is considered privileged and success-ful, her relative empowerment redraws the boundaries of her gender, thus creating new liminalities. In the same way as Bretécher's mother and little girl reinvent the distinction between playing and imitating, the woman of letters and the housecleaner install new, infiltratable boundaries. By analysing these two emblem-atic female identities, I may be drawing closer to the imaginary centre, scrutinizing a supposedly higher degree of coherence: I imagine that the difference (or rather the relationship) between the housecleaner and the woman of letters corresponds to the close-up view of an already infiltrated soil. In this chapter, I will first analyse the supposedly original distance between two female roles, before focusing on a specific example of infiltration: Françoise Ega's *Lettres à une noire* (*Letters to a Black Woman*) will provide an intriguing model of ethnographic housecleaning which I would like to propose as a successful redefinition of the difference between public and private, working and labour, gift and servitude.

Women of letters have always been able to infiltrate the literary circles of their times at the risk of being ignored, ridiculed or assimilated. Fictional representations of women of letters are not rare anymore and perhaps never were. Yet, if I try to conjure up the vision of a great writer, the first image that will come to mind will probably be a black and white photograph of Baudelaire, or the formidable silhouette of Victor Hugo. Not that I particularly appreciate Victor Hugo's work anymore, but part of the literary history that I want to infiltrate in this book has taught me that all the women who write are 'Precious Damsels', exuberant and slightly ridiculous imitators.

Of course, women of letters have become an object of study; they are the focus of a large body of theoretical and historical studies produced by the feminist movement for the last two decades. The systematic search for literary foremothers would now make it more difficult to deny the existence of women writers in any given period: it is becoming impossible to sustain the claim that women cannot write or that they are somehow essentially incapable of becoming successful writers. Yet the 'woman of letters' is not exactly the same as a 'writer' nor really different from a 'writer'. In the first chapter of her book, *Woman, Native, Other*, Trinh Minh Ha reviews the numerous myths which make of the 'woman of letters' a suspiciously ambiguous phenomenon, playing an unstable role, constantly engaged in a process of self-definition and self-creation. The woman of letters is supposed to have developed a voice of her own. She has managed to make herself heard in a domain traditionally dominated (and idealized) by men: literary creation, writing, but also the circulation of texts, publication and distribution networks. Because of the relative control she exerts over language and means of distribution of the written word, she belongs to the privileged: she speaks when other women remain silent. She is part of the 'elite' in the etymological sense of those who have been chosen, elected. As Minh Ha puts it, 'Writing, reading, thinking, imagining, speculating. These are luxury activities, so I am reminded, permitted to a limited few' (Minh Ha 1989, 6).[1] Because writing is often conceptualized as a luxury, a gratuitous activity, the 'woman of letters' falls under the category of the 'artist', coopted by the intelligentsia (defined as a masculine universe) and cut off from the world of labour.

According to Trinh Minh Ha, the texts written by the 'woman of letters' will thus be plagued by guilt:

guilt over the selfishness implied in such activity, over themselves as housewives and 'women', over their families and friends, and all other 'less fortunate' women. (Minh Ha 1989, 7)

Because she is a successful infiltrator, and aware that she is resisting other infiltrators, the woman of letters is thus condemned to harbour simultaneous and contradictory concerns: at times, she will worry that she has been too successful in infiltrating the world of the privileged and the powerful, whereas at other times, she will deplore the fact that she cannot quite live up to the standards of excellence of some imaginary universal writer. In both cases, she will interpret her difference as inferiority. The nagging fear of falling short of the mythical stature of the canonical writer, the master of language and guardian of all 'great' literature could be seen as the typical infiltrator's syndrome: having overcome power's resistance to let them in, the infiltrators are bound to internalize their presence 'inside' as a form of usurpation. There is no métissage, rather parasitical presence, a fraud. On the other hand, once they 'pass', infiltrators become part of what will be infiltrated by others.

Trinh Minh Ha draws the pessimistic portrait of a doomed woman writer: on the one hand, she is the creator of a hybrid (alien, gooey?) text, which forcefully proves the point that women can indeed write and think and read and imagine, but which does not have the power to convey this message to those 'less fortunate' women who might benefit from the knowledge. The books written by the 'woman of letters' tend to be inaccessible to the women who do not belong to the 'elite', who have not been chosen. Even when the woman of letters explicitly expresses her desire to share the power that has led her to write,[2] her texts apparently fail to perform the kind of 'reproduction' which Bourdieu talks about (Bourdieu and Passeron 1970).

One must admit that Minh Ha's vision of a vicious circle is particularly poignant and by the end of the chapter, the disillusioned reader may well be convinced that we are all helpless prisoners in a system within which the class and gender of each subject have already been added up into coherent paradigms so that forever, the guilt-ridden parasitical woman of letters and the oppressed and silent housecleaner will stare at each other, powerless to start a dialogue. The 'woman of letters' (whom we imagine to be white, western, educated, free from severe financial worries, endowed with a room of her own and with the equivalent of the five hundred pounds which Woolf considered indispensable to her independence) will come to represent the negative image of the housecleaner which we will tend to portray as the victim of deterministic social and historical conditions: probably illiterate, perhaps a foreigner or a woman of colour.

If the 'woman of letters' is usually imagined as a symbol of the privileged and successful woman, then, the housecleaner is probably the best representative figure of the dominated and exploited woman. In *The Predicament of Culture*, Clifford emphasizes the literary importance of the 'servants' who are part and parcel of the representation of bourgeois families. He notices that they tend to symbolize the whole working-class:

In Western writings servants have always performed the chore of representing 'the people' – lower classes and different races. Domesticated outsiders of the bourgeois imagination, they regularly provide fictional epiphanies, recognition scenes, happy endings, utopic and distopic transcendences. (Clifford 1988, 4, note 1)[3]

If the woman of letters is stereotypically plagued with guilt, then, the housecleaner becomes the archetype of the victim: she is innocence personified. But since the housecleaner does not produce any text, it is traditionally incumbent upon the woman of letters to represent her, and to make her speak as a fictional character. The servant thus remains silent. Deprived of access to a discourse, she becomes a subject-matter, a literary character constructed by someone else's writing. Or rather, our definition of what the housecleaner 'really' is often results from our encounter with the text by the woman of letters.

Surely, at this point, one may argue that writing is not simply a luxurious and gratuitous activity and that it can or should be used with emancipatory projects in mind. Minh Ha reminds us that it is tempting to establish an opposition between what she calls 'art for art's sake' and '*engagé*' writing respectively. The criticism levelled at so-called 'art for art's sake' forms of writing is that it is a futile practice, a socially parasitical activity, both produced by and addressed to a self-identified exclusionary bourgeois elite. Sartrian '*engagé*' literature, on the other hand, has come to represent a form of writing which claims to be the vehicle of a political message and which seeks to improve the social conditions of some people, even if the texts thus produced are not necessarily capable of speaking the language of the economically underprivileged communities they pretend to address. Even if such a simplistic opposition obviously deserves closer scrutiny, the myth does function in our collective imagination. Needless to say, when one imagines a 'woman of letters', the first stereotype which springs to mind is an intellectualized abstraction, the figure of a woman who has nothing to do with traditionally female housecleaning chores, and who would 'naturally' be inclined to produce luxury literature, ream after ream of sentimental poetry or self-indulgent autobiographical introspection. The woman of letters' text would thus ignore not only the existence of the housecleaner but her dependence upon her labour which frees her from such contingencies. One might invoke Renée Vivien's poetry for example and regret that her writings never mention or take into account the fact that her exceptionally favourable financial situation always allowed her to delegate ordinary manual labour in order to devote her time to the high pursuits of poetry.

It seems, however, that the woman of letters' situation exemplifies the dilemma of the infiltrator as a case of 'damned if you do (it too soon), damned if you don't (do it enough)' where 'it' represents the performance of a separate voice. Texts written by women always run the risk of evoking the problematic erasure of the woman who cleans their house: both the writer and the housecleaner can be constructed as sharing the same gender. But they are separated and made different by a relationship of power. As a result, the presence of the two women on the social and intertextual scene further undercuts the traditional distinction between purely 'literary' and 'social' writing. Here is the dilemma: if, like Vivien, a woman erases the working woman from her work, she will be accused of betraying other women, but if she decides to dip her pen into social ink, if she chooses writing as the means of social and political struggle, then she runs the risk of being stereotyped as another contradictory figure. If her text represents other women as victims, if her writings portray a housecleaner and denounce her exploitation, then, her identity as a 'woman' will suddenly be remembered and she will be accused of complicity with the system and of bad faith. A woman who writes about the fate of the housecleaner will not be permitted to forget that her very writing supposedly participates in that oppression simply because she could be cleaning her own house instead of writing. Somehow, male writers are not supposed to be torn between writing the next chapter of their book and ironing their own shirts. Literary history has never been preoccupied with (certain) material details: to my knowledge, nobody has ever found it relevant or meaningful to wonder if the woman who washed Balzac's socks was his wife or a servant. When a woman of letters decides to delegate housecleaning and other so-called feminine chores for the sake of 'art', when her writing purports to criticize and hopefully put an end to other women's oppression, then the contradiction becomes glaring.[4]

Perhaps the guilt (another word for self-conscious infiltration?) generated within the woman of letters by this paradoxical situation makes her more sensitive to the issue and contributes to increase the number of literary portraits of servants. But male writers also seem fascinated by the female servant and often summon her as the archetypal victim of an unjust social order. Richardson's Pamela obviously comes to mind, and in nineteenth-century (metropolitan) France, writers were apparently fascinated by the phenomenon of the domestic worker, this undefinable 'supplement' to the bourgeois family. Baudelaire's 'servante au grand coeur' (Baudelaire 1961, 112) and Flaubert's 'un coeur simple' [A Simple Heart] are now part of the most traditional literary canon. More recently, non-European women writers have also focused on the figure of the servant and have added new layers to the intertextual sedimentary terrain. The 'servante au grand coeur' and Félicité have little in common with the Sagouine's powerful and witty monologues.[5]

Although each domestic worker is different from one another, although the reasons for their otherness are different in every case, they are always outsiders: their otherness may be reassuring because it cannot be eradicated The female servant is the other of the (bourgeois) family or the male bachelor for whom she works. Often, she is also a stranger, a foreigner with an accent, or an exotic body. Her otherness is often represented as racial difference. Each culture produces its own foreign housecleaners: if a French humourist imitates a foreign accent and pretends to be called 'Conchita' when impersonating a character who does not want to talk on the phone, the implicit reference to the Portuguese housecleaner immediately becomes representative and meaningful. Yet, this absolute 'other' is also accepted as a professional infiltrator.

The relationship between infiltration and certain forms of 'passing' may be interestingly highlighted by the fact that the servant is often constructed as the white woman's racial other. Should we read Madame de Duras's Ourika in parallel with Sembène Ousmane's 'La Noire de…'.[6] What do Maryse Condé's Tituba and Simone Schwarz-Bart's Télumée have in common?[7] Of course, the female slave working for the planter's wife cannot be amalgamated with the young working class domestic servant who lives with her employers in nineteenth-century Europe, and the twentieth-century 'cleaning lady' who works for an institution like a university or a hospital or who takes care of several individuals' houses is yet another case. But all these women have one thing in common: their presence within the house modifies the distinction between the interior and the exterior, between the public and the private domain, between the stranger and the member of the family. Clifford points out that the domestic worker is a 'troubling insider' who 'turns up inside bourgeois domestic space. She cannot be held at a distance' (Clifford 1988, 6).

Given that the 'woman of letters' and the 'housecleaner' are both caught in the web of social and historical constructions, given the imaginary and ideological void encountered by a woman who would seek to adopt a role beyond the binary opposition, given the difficulty to imagine to what literary genre such a woman's writing might belong, I would now like to turn to Françoise Ega's *Lettres à une noire*, which precisely approaches the issue from a radically different perspective.[8]

This novel provides refreshing and revolutionary paths out of the seemingly unavoidable contradictions faced by a woman who must choose between writing and working. *Lettres à une noire* simply will not allow the reader to rely on preconceived definitions of 'woman', 'writing' and 'working'. The book moves between social classes, nationalities, and racial communities. It breaks down ideological barriers and exposes our own prejudices. Françoise Ega, the author of *Lettres à une noire* is also known as 'Maméga'. Maméga is the main character and narrator of the novel. A black woman born in Martinique, she now lives in Marseille with her husband, who would like to find a decent and stable job in Provence after spending several years in Africa as a member of the military. In this text, the woman of letters does not come from a white middle- or upper-class background. She is a black woman who is also a housecleaner. The dichotomy between the woman of letters and the domestic is blurred from the very first pages of the book. *Lettres à une noire* also undercuts the opposition between fiction and reality in a very complex manner: this epistolary novel is also an autobiography in which the 'I' is called Maméga, and tells the story of an employee who cleans houses for 'ladies' in Marseille. As the title indicates, the book consists of a series of letters, addressed to a Brazilian woman called Carolina.

## The housecleaner as ethnographer: the limits of labour as observation

The first model which comes to mind to describe Maméga's writing, is that of the ethnographer: in a sense, Maméga writes about the 'Martinican housecleaner' in the same way as Marcel Griaule described the Masks of the Dogon in 1938, in the same way as Placide Tempels described Bantu Philosophy for a Western audience.[9] An ironic version of the colonizing ethnographer, Maméga describes a group of people to which she does not belong, a professional category which is foreign and other. I call Maméga a 'woman-of-letters-housecleaner' but this ambiguous role is not a predetermined given: it is a chosen and slowly constructed identity. Clearly, at the beginning of the book, Maméga has a view of what a 'genuine' housecleaner looks like. For her, the typical housecleaner is a young Martinican woman, who has recently emigrated from her native island, and who is temporarily employed by one of the middle-class Marseillais women whom she calls the dames (the 'ladies'). When Maméga talks about housecleaning, she does refer to her own experience but her status as a housecleaner is quite remarkable in that she has chosen to adopt this role because she wants to write about it. Maméga becomes a narrator and a housecleaner at the same moment, and this double event is caused by a specific crisis. One incident triggers a simultaneous desire to become a housecleaner and to write a diary where she will record her observations on the social conditions experienced by the Martinican housecleaner. Paradoxically, the moment when Maméga steps out of her house is also the moment when she starts writing. Both practices are originally fused as one unique response to a serious situation:

Il y a huit jours que j'ai commencé ces lignes. ... Je suis indignée. Une fille de mon pays m'a raconté de telles choses sur sa vie chez ses patrons que j'ai juré d'en avoir le coeur net. Je gagne de l'argent et je fais le point: je suis femme de ménage depuis cinq jours. (9)

[Eight days ago, I started writing these lines. ... I am outraged. One of the girls from home told me such incredible stories about her life with her bosses that I swore I would get to the bottom of it. So, I earn money and I take stock of the situation: I have been a housecleaner for five days.]

Like an ethnographer accumulating data before writing his or her narrative, Maméga moves from one job to another. She is successively employed by half a dozen 'ladies' and she accepts other temporary positions. Throughout the book, Maméga insists on the absolute necessity to see for herself, to participate. To her husband, who resents her absence and worries about her chronic state of exhaustion, she patiently explains that unless she observes what is going on herself, she does not have a right to testify.

Naturally, this insistence on the exclusive value of 'participation' poses a number of political and theoretical problems. Maméga's position could be compared to that of a recognizable school of traditional anthropology which valorizes lived experience and authorizes its discourse by reference to the real, the authentic. Perceived from the point of view of post-structuralist academic discourse (within which the discipline of anthropology as a whole, since Malinowski and Lévi-Strauss, has suffered from a severe crisis of legitimacy), Maméga's discourse may sound naive or even reactionary because it seems to presuppose that only 'authentic' experience justifies a testimony and, conversely, that a testimony is justified as long as it is based on experience. As Clifford remarks, 'Many ethnographies ... are still cast in the experiential mode, asserting prior to any specific research hypothesis or method the 'I was there' of the ethnographer as insider and participant'(Clifford 1988, 35). And the author adds: 'Of course it is difficult to say very much about experience. Like 'intuition,' it is something that one does or does not have, and its invocation often smacks of mystification'.[10]

One should note, however, that Maméga's decision to work as a housecleaner is not to be confused with a desire for abstract or academic knowledge. Her choice has nothing to do with those early twentieth-century anthropological discourses which insisted on the legitimacy of 'theory' (as opposed to 'field-work'). Historically, such discourses have tended to reinforce the value of the overall system within which they were embedded.[11] Maméga is aware that her study is replete with political and ideological significance: her desire to work and to write, born of a moment of 'outrage', is not to be interpreted as an impossibility to 'act' for which writing seeks to compensate. The letters to Carolina are not a substitute for active intervention. When Maméga first hears the outrageous story from Yolande, a fellow Martinican, her first impulse is to obtain a redress of grievances from the tyrannical boss. Her successful struggle is narrated in the fifth letter: at first, Maméga is infuriated by Yolande's passivity and encourages her to rebel against her employer. She criticizes her for allowing a white family to exploit her like the indentured servants who used to toil for years before they could pay back the price of their passage: 'Comment, vous vous laissez faire! Qu'est-ce que c'est que ce trafic humain! Avez-vous un contrat de travail? Etes-vous à la sécurité sociale? [Do you mean that you let them get away with it? What is this trafficking in human beings? Do you have a work contract? Do you receive social benefits?] (13). But when she realizes that Yolande is sick and helpless, she storms into the employer's house and, to the astonishment of both Yolande and her employer, she practically kidnaps the young Martinican servant. Throughout the book, she thus records active moments of intervention. Maméga literally intervenes: she introduces herself into a territory from which she is normally excluded, and by refusing to be treated like an Other, she blurs the distinction between inside and outside. Her 'outrage' is both the cause of her intervention and a self-chosen identity. When Yolande's employer, whom she threatened with work inspectors, finally explodes: 'Non mais de quoi vous mêlez-vous? D'abord, qui êtes-vous?' [Can't you mind your own business? And who are you anyway?] Maméga retorts: 'Une négresse indignée. C'est pas visible non?' [An outraged black woman. Can't you see for yourself?] (19).

Given the effectiveness of this tactic and the success of the intervention, one may wonder why Maméga needs to resort to infiltration and become a housecleaner herself, or why she insists on writing a book about her own experience. Maméga could tell the story of her interventions and the book could have constituted an impressive collection of success stories, of what de Certeau calls 'accounts of particular games' (23) instead of an autobiographical account. Maméga's decision to become a housecleaner is in itself a strategy of intervention in the sense that she now forces her way inside the white bourgeois family, but her decision to privilege 'personal' experience raises not only theoretical but tactical and ideological problems.

Maméga wants to make the point that nobody should allow the employer to abuse his or her privileges without rebelling against such tyranny. The 'filles de son pays' (the girls from home) should not put up with modern forms of slavery. When she interferes in Yolande's life, she demonstrates that the housecleaner always retains a degree of freedom and that when work conditions are too degrading, it is always possible to leave regardless of previous (illegal) arrangements. But as soon as she is hired as a housecleaner, her own position becomes rife with contradictions: when she willingly chooses a form of servitude against which she wants others to rebel, Maméga unfortunately panders to her employers' prejudices. As a competent and conscientious housecleaner who does not rebel against her employer, Maméga reinforces the stereotype of the submissive Martinican woman. Maméga's husband, who, from the beginning, has been hostile to the experience, bitterly underscores the contradiction:

Mon mari a rouspété: j'aurais dû rester chez moi: 'Pourquoi aller grossir les rangs de ce bétail humain?' (13)

[My husband has been complaining: I should have stayed at home: 'Why swell the rank of this human cattle?']

The 'outrage' which motivated the first intervention seems badly channelled into a quest for 'authentic' experience: at one level, the desire for observation and participation is incompatible with the message of overt resistance which Maméga seeks to convey. The reader may be disturbed by the nagging feeling that Maméga's chosen tactic contributes to the perpetuation of stereotypes and prolongs the situation of oppression she wants to overturn. Although she condemns her fellow Martinicans' resignation, she herself must transgress her own principles of decency and human dignity in order for her experiment to be significant and conclusive in her own eyes: as an observer, patience and submissiveness become her priorities even though such an attitude would be otherwise unacceptable.

Je suis un cobaye volontaire, je rengaine mon envie de mettre mon tablier contre le mur et je recommence à bosser. (15)

[I am a volunteer guinea pig; I refrain from hanging my apron up on the wall and I get back to work.]

Si je le dis à la maison, mon mari va crier: 'Reste chez toi' et il mettra ma mobylette en panne! Si je reste chez moi, je ne pourrai jamais voir jusqu'où peut aller la bêtise humaine. (14)

[If I talk about it at home, my husband will scream: 'Stay at home' and he will mess with my moped. If I stay at home, I can never find out how far human stupidity can go.]

Clearly, Maméga's role as an observer consists of putting up with the intolerable and to explore extreme conditions. As an experimenter, she displays a degree of indifference to her own oppression which seems incompatible with her previous feelings of 'outrage'. Even when her work becomes degrading and humiliating, Maméga remains capable of distance; she can laugh at her own misery. This individual capacity for distance, however, is politically problematic because for the 'ladies' who hire her, Maméga's behaviour is not an easily interpretable text. Her employers are never aware that a rebel is hiding behind the hard-working housecleaner with unfailing good spirits. Her political stance and her indignation remain invisible, and one may wonder if it is not tragically ironic that Maméga, who wants to put an end to other housecleaners' resignation, should be forced to adopt the performance of a model employee.

Her presence as an observer (a supposedly neutral outsider) cannot but contribute to the formation of a role: she becomes a representative housecleaner. By shaping her employers' expectations of what a 'typical' Martinican housecleaner can be, her discourse and performance constitute ambiguous strategies which perpetuate the very system she claims to be observing. For example, I find it troubling that she should be proud of the compliments she receives for her hard work. Of course, as she explains to Carolina, she is not unhappy to counteract another powerful stereotype, that of the lazy black person: 'enfin un témoignage où il n'est pas question de nègres roupillant, un plumeau dans les jambes!' [at last a testimony which does mention a nigger dozing off with a feather duster between his legs!] (23). But even if the stereotype of the lazy black boy is still widespread, it does not correspond to the specific social context which frames Maméga's narrative: in Marseille, the 'bonne antillaise' (the Caribbean servant) is particularly attractive to potential employers precisely because of her well established reputation for being an undemanding hard worker. Maméga's performance may thus not be the most strategically judicious choice.

## The oppositional resources of Maméga's role

*Writing as labour*
Because of the contradictions between Maméga's political objectives and her position as an observer, the relationship between her writing and her labour becomes a paradoxical space of opposition which I would now like to explore. For her employers, Maméga's work remains an incomprehensible and reactionary text, but her letters, her writings, provide us with a different interpretive possibility.

Lettres à une noire gives new meaning to Maméga's apparent passivity. As readers of the text, we are able to perceive the character of the submissive, hard-working Martinican housecleaner as a complex and unpredictable construction. Let us assume for a moment that, as readers, we identify with the employer of a professional house-cleaner. The book provides me with new elements to interpret my reality and encourages me to reconsider what I thought was a clear and unproblematic behaviour on the part of my housecleaner. As I watch my housecleaner's relentless fight against dirt and dust, it suddenly occurs to me that I may have hired the writer of an epistolary novel in which I will become a character. And when I warmly congratulate her on her effectiveness, I may be the object of a study which seeks to discover just how far 'human stupidity' will go. As a reader of Maméga's novel, I suddenly learn a different lesson: I realize that my faithful housecleaner may be a subject, may be an outraged 'observer' for whom submissiveness and devotion are nothing but a form of work and research, a way of accumulating anthropological evidence. If I am one of the *dames* who prefer to hire Martinican women because they will not cause any trouble, it may dawn on me that I was grossly mistaken, and that Martinican women belong to a community which may not allow me to exploit one of its members and get away with it. Maméga's text thus enables the reader to reinterpret his or her own experience and that of the narrator. The housecleaner's narration provides us with a meaning which would have remained hidden if the woman of letters, as usual, had been one of the *dames*.

But Maméga's tactic goes even further: although her narrative seems to hold the somewhat simplistic view that 'authentic experi-ence' is the only legitimate guarantee of objectivity and truth, her position *vis-à-vis* her own writing is in fact much more subtle: she is aware that the relationship between her labour and her testimony is complex and original. On the one hand, her writing endows her labour with political meaningfulness since her letters allow the reader to appreciate the genuine oppositional value of her role as a model housecleaner. On the other hand, Maméga knows something more: not only does her text claim that servitude does not exist until some-body decides to document and narrativize it, but her book also points to its own inadequacies as a book. The book seems to know that it will not suffice on its own, that it is futile and incapable of bearing testimony. Maméga reaches the limits of her own possibilities of exploration when she accepts a position as a seamstress in a brothel. And confronted with the spectacle of another fellow Martinican who, this time, plays the role of the Ma-dame, Maméga feels that her writing is powerless:

Tant que l'on n'a pas vu cela, Carolina, on ne peut pas croire tout à fait à cet esclavage volontaire. (115)

[As long as one has not seen it with one's own eyes, one cannot really believe in this self-inflicted slavery.]

Maméga warns her fictional and real reader that her testimony is incomplete, that nobody will 'believe' her. Even if she succeeds in writing about slavery, something will still be missing, an excess of reality remains which the narrative cannot account for: for Maméga, it is not enough to denounce prostitution, nor is it enough to name, to formulate, the problem in terms of 'self-inflicted slavery'. She insists that her readers should see for themselves.[12]

For Maméga, writing follows a 'vision' (not as the Romantic poets understood it, but in the sense of personal involvement). Her writing is supplementary to her labour, but in a sense, her labour is also supplementary to her writing. Like the prostitutes, Maméga tolerates a form of self-inflicted slavery because originally, her decision to work as a housecleaner is not motivated by dire economic need. Simultaneously, writing is for Maméga a form of labour: because she is not a full-time and economically privileged woman of letters, writing is just as time- and energy-consuming as manual labour.

Les femmes de lettres, je crois, ont des bureaux avec des lumières appropriées. Le bruit ne pénètre pas dans leur sanctuaire. Moi, je t'écris à la lueur de la grosse ampoule de la cuisine pendant que les enfants rabâchent les leçons pour demain. (111)

[Women of letters, I think, have desks with appropriate lighting. No noise penetrates their sanctuary. Whereas I am writing to you by the light of the big naked bulb in the kitchen while the children are repeating their lessons for tomorrow.]

The writer's tool (the typewriter) is constantly pawned and then retrieved when the financial situation of the couple improves a little (often thanks to Maméga's housecleaning). Maméga's children monopolize her pencil and paper. Friends and family want to persuade her that writing is not work because she does not make any money: 'Quant à mon mari, il me trouve ridicule de perdre du temps à écrire des sottises, alors, il cache mon stylo' [As for my husband, he finds it ridiculous that I spend my time writing nonsense, so he hides my pen] (11). Even her friend Solange reminds her that 'mots, ni en vinaigrette, ni en sauce blanche [elle] ne s'en servira' [words, [you] can't put them into a salad dressing or a white sauce] (214). And yet, Maméga's humour successfully demonstrates, in one little sentence, that in spite of the other characters' scepticism, there is hardly any difference between the kind of work she performs as a professional housecleaner and her writing which requires so much discipline: she knows that both activities are manual labour. As she puts it, 'j'ai deux mains et il faut m'en servir' [I have two hands and I have to use them], then adds ironically: 'je ne tape qu'avec six doigts, c'est peut-être pour cela que ma paperasse ne me nourrit pas' [I type with only six fingers, maybe that is the reason why my scribblings do not feed me] (186).

### Labour as gift

Not only is writing considered as a form of labour instead of a gratuitous activity reserved to some intellectual elite, but the nature of the housecleaner's 'labour' is also redefined by Maméga's ambiguous status: her position as participant-observer radically alters the meaning of her production as a housecleaner. *Lettres à une noire* turns labour into a form of research, a freely chosen activity which cannot be reduced to a system of exchange where somebody's energy is accounted for in terms of an arbitrarily determined salary. Here labour becomes what Michel de Certeau calls 'popular tactics', a form of 'diversion':

The actual order of things is precisely what 'popular' tactics turn to their own ends, without illusion that it will change any time soon. Though elsewhere it is exploited by a dominant power or simply denied by an ideological discourse, here order is tricked by an art. Into the institution to be served are insinuated styles of social exchange, technical invention, and moral resistance, that is, an economy of the 'gift' (generosities for which one expects a return), an aesthetics of 'tricks' (artists' operations) and an ethics of tenacity (countless ways of refusing to accord the established order the status of a law, a meaning or a fatality). 'Popular' culture is precisely that; it is not a corpus considered as foreign, fragmented in order to be displayed, studied and 'quoted' by a system which does to objects what it does to living beings. (26)

The most blatant example of 'diversion' and 'gift' in *Lettres à une noire* ironically occurs at the very moment when Maméga thinks that she has to give up on her ethnographer-housecleaner position. February

18, 1963 is a meaningful date in Maméga's history. That day, she finally decides to respond to a newspaper ad which reads: 'On demande une femme de ménage deux heures par jour'. [Housecleaner needed, two hours everyday]. In her letter, she tells Carolina that this time, working will not be a political activity or a way of collecting social data: 'Carolina, je n'ai pas été là par amour du prochain, mais bien pour ramener mes six cents francs en deux heures' [Carolina, I did not go there for the love of human beings, but to bring back my six hundred francs in two hours] (77).

Since the very beginning of the book, Maméga regularly alludes to particularly tight economic periods when her husband's salary does not ensure the bare necessities. When this happens, the complexity of her status as participant-observer disappears and her political and ideological beliefs and hope are reduced to a 'faith' in money: 'lorsque j'ai le porte-monnaie creux, je ne crois qu'aux billets de banque qui me permettront de faire mon marché tout de suite' [when my wallet is empty, I only believe in green bills which will let me buy groceries right away] (76). When her family lacks the minimum, Maméga's creative practice reverts to a most traditional conception of labour. Maméga is confident that she can function according to the inhumane capitalist laws of exchange and her belief in the power of money suddenly replaces the 'outraged' black woman's faith in social change. Her disgust for modern forms of slavery is replaced by another fear: Maméga is afraid of lacking food. On that day in February 1963, the letter addressed to Carolina mentions that it is urgent for Maméga to transform her labour into much needed 'bread' for her children and husband. Whenever extreme poverty threatens Maméga's family, the theme of 'bread' resurfaces, a symbol for survival, a metaphor both for lack and bounty, an international sign of recognition among the poor of every country with whom Maméga always feels bonded:

Mon homme dit 'Pourvu qu'il y ait le pain chaque jour, le reste viendra après'. Je crois, Carolina que tu connais ces paroles. Dans ta favela, tu n'as jamais pu penser à autre chose qu'au pain de chaque jour. Je crois que c'est ce qui me rapproche de toi, Carolina Maria de Jesus. (11)

[My man says: 'As long as we have bread everyday, the rest can wait'. Carolina, I assume you know what he means. In your favela, you have never been able to think about anything else but your daily bread. I think that this is what makes me close to you, Carolina Maria de Jesus.]

When Maméga responds to the ad in the newspaper, nothing is further from her mind than 'diversion' or reappropriation. On the contrary, it looks like the system has sucked her into a traditional role. But a formidably ironic twist unexpectedly modifies her situation. While Maméga works for the person who had advertised in the paper, the 'lady' tells her her own story and this pathetic narrative reverses the relationship of power between the two women. Maméga had responded to the ad because she badly needed to eke out her meagre income but she becomes the recipient of a tragically trite story ('ses enfants ne s'occupaient pas d'elle et elle n'avait que la retraite des vieux travailleurs' [her children did not take care of her, she only collected a small retirement pension] 75). The 'Granny', the 'petite vieille', as Maméga irreverently calls her, is too weak to clean her own house and, obviously, the two hours' worth of labour which she requested in the newspaper ad are quite inadequate for the amount of work to be done. It would take much more than two hours to finish the job but the 'Mémé' only requested two hours because she cannot afford more than six hundred francs. In the story, she does not see herself as the giver but as the receiver: the idea of incurring an impossible debt terrifies her, and as soon as the amount of money she can afford to spend has been earned by her housecleaner, she desperately tries to force Maméga out of her house. An almost farcical scene follows as the little old lady uses every rhetorical strategy she can muster (including lapsing into pidgin French) to persuade the 'stubborn woman [who] had invaded her home' to leave at once because 'Deux heures lui suffisent' [Two hours are all she needs] (76). Obviously, the notion of 'need' should be interpreted according to the protagonist's means. She obviously 'needs' more time even though her financial situation will not permit her to hire Maméga for more than two hours. But Maméga refuses to understand what is implied in the statement and chooses to take the words at face-value: 'Pensez-vous, deux heures! Il faudrait des journées, Mémé! Voilà trois mois que vous ne faites rien dans l'appartement' [Two hours? You cannot be serious! It would take days, Granny! You have not done anything to this apartment in three months] (76). Maméga refuses to follow the old woman's logic and will not be persuaded to reason in terms of exchange: the equivalence between what the woman really 'owes' her and what she 'needs' is exposed as unrelated. Even though Maméga answered the ad because she needed to exchange her labour for money, she suddenly acts and speaks as though the laws of capitalist exchange were not valid anymore. A form of 'diversion' has taken place thanks to the old woman's narrative:

'Ça y est, j'ai terminé Mémé: gardez les six cents francs pour un bon pot au feu! Je viendrai vous voir de temps en temps. ... Mémé, je ne pourrais jamais manger ce que j'achèterais avec vos pièces de monnaie. Et dire que vos enfants sont des dames qui crânent quelque part sans se soucier de vous!' Voilà pourquoi, Carolina, j'ai du pain sur la planche pour un mois durant. (77)

['Look Granny, I am done: keep the six hundred francs for a good beef stew! I'll come and visit once in a while. ... Granny, I could never eat what I would buy with your coins. And when I think that your children are 'ladies' who are busy showing off somewhere instead of taking care of you!' And this is why, Carolina, I have a lot on my plate for another month.]

Maméga needed bread and instead, she brings back a story to transcribe and, as the French says, some 'pain sur la planche' ('bread on her board' i.e. even more work to do). She has earned metaphorical 'bread' instead of six hundred francs. Her labour has been 'diverted' and has been converted into generosity, gift. She has spent time and energy but the 'bread' she was hoping to bring back ironically turns out to be more work to do, more energy to spend. She also brings back the old woman's tale which will now become part of her book and enrich its ethnographical dimensions since the story tends to prove that even the category of the employers, of the 'ladies' cannot be fantasized as one coherent, one-dimensional group. Maméga brings back exactly what she thought she needed ('du pain') but this 'pain sur la planche' constitutes an excess compared with what she expected. Literally and metaphorically, she gets a little less and a little more than she had bargained for: as a housecleaner, she discovers that she still has something to give, at the very moment when she thought that all she could do was take. As a woman of letters, she formulates the now self-evident truth that the 'ladies' are sometimes 'little old ladies' who could be victimized even by their truly powerless housecleaners. Maméga has 'invaded the house' of the little old lady just like she had stormed into Yolande's life, but this time, her determination serves to impose a new economy, this economy of gifts which de Certeau finds in the margins of our society and which resembles an 'illegitimate' form of potlatch:

the potlatch seems to persist ... as the mark of another type of economy. It survives in our economy, though on its margins or in its interstices. It is even developing, although held to be illegitimate, within modern market economy. Because of this, the politics of the 'gift' *also* becomes a diversionary tactic. (27)

## The 'diversion' of the letter: illegitimate reading and the book as perruque

Maméga forces us to redefine the opposition between writing and labour, and, in the same way, her text invites us to reconsider the relationship between the reader and the writer. The system of address used by Françoise Ega does not correspond to any simple model. *Lettres à une noire* is an ambiguous space where specific and recognizable conventions are both used and subverted. In the same way as the housecleaner reappropriates the significance and the product of her labour, the woman of letters manipulates and reappropriates the value of writing. At first, the text produced and signed by Maméga may seem very conventional: the narrative is strictly linear, subordinated to the constraints of realism, the text does not formally problematize its relationship with an extra-textual reality, nor does it question its own definition of subjectivity or representation. As far as this book is concerned, the *nouveaux romanciers* may well never have written and no anxiety of influence links Ega to her immediate precursors. *Lettres à une noire* also departs from the French tradition of *écriture féministe* which dominated the seventies: one would be hard put to formulate a common denominator between Maméga and Cixous or Catherine Clément's writings except perhaps that all three authors are interested in traditionally silenced groups. I do not want to suggest that no alliance is possible between feminist intellectuals and Ega's fiction, but the point of view from which the housecleaner-writer addresses feminist issues is obviously quite different from that of the theoreticians.

One aspect of Ega's book remains original in spite of its conventional features: its system of address. *Lettres à une noire* perceives itself as a book with no legitimate audience, a book which will not be read by the person to whom it is addressed, the person for whom it is being written. This diversion of the activity of reading is operated by means of a simple manipulation of the literary genre chosen by the narrator: as readers of the book, we are made aware that we are not the intended audience, that we are eavesdropping on a conversation where we are not welcome. *Lettres à une noire* belongs to a recognizable literary genre (as the title indicates, it is an epistolary novel).[13] But something is wrong in this correspondence. The narrator sends letters to a certain Carolina, a young Brazilian woman about whom we know very little except that she is extremely poor and that she writes. Most of the conventions of the epistolary genre are scrupulously respected: the 'I' writes to a specific correspondent and we read the letters over the narrator's or the presumed narratee's shoulder. Typically, the reader is cast in the role of the voyeur or of the interceptor. Maméga never receives any answers but the monophonic aspect of the correspondence is not original in itself.[14] What is highly problematic however is the way in which the text positions its implied reader: Carolina is both too real (as an extra-textual person) and not real enough (as an imaginary reader) to constitute a convincing fictional correspondent. Contrary to what happens in Montesquieu's *Lettres persanes* or Rousseau's *Nouvelle Héloïse*, Carolina, the recipient of the letters, is not a character created to meet some intradiegetic need for internal coherence or verisimilitude. Carolina does exist, but strangely enough, she only exists in the real world, 'outside' the novel or at least outside the epistolary exchange. Reading *Paris-Match* on the bus, Maméga had discovered the existence of a Brazilian woman writer who was portrayed in the act of writing her texts by the dim light of an oil lamp in her 'favela'.[15]

Maméga's decision to address her own diary to this woman is motivated by the feeling that the Brazilian writer resembles her, that their experiences are similar. One may of course argue that the 'real' existence of Carolina is irrelevant: like the 'I' of the narrator, Carolina is a textual entity and it does not matter whether she is real or not. But Maméga is not writing to just any 'real' person. Her choice is not only significant but politically meaningful, and it also complicates the book's system of address. Maméga chooses as her only possible 'reader' precisely a person who will never read *Lettres à une noire* because her social conditions make reading impossible. In a classic epistolary novel, the fictional correspondent exists solely for the purpose of justifying our reading of the letters: correspondents 'exist' within the book and provide us with a fictional pretext for reading their mail. In the case of a monophony, a realistic explanation is usually given to the 'real' reader as to why the fictional correspondent remains silent, but the silence of the protagonist has to be accounted for because it is envisaged as a flaw in the system, an exception to the rule. The absence of the fictional correspondent does not abolish the imaginary pole of the reception. In *Lettres à une noire*, however, the 'I' does not respect this conventional system of address: the narrator addresses the letters to a woman but she knows in advance that the woman will never read them. What Janet Altman calls the 'epistolary pact' is not respected because the correspondence does not originate in a mutual desire for exchange:[16] a long 'correspondence' between Maméga and Carolina is remarkable because it is a case of failed epistolary connection. Two women produce literary texts which are potentially addressed to each other, yet neither writer will ever read what the other writes. The paradox consists in sending a letter which says: 'I write to tell you that you will not read this and that I will not read what you write'.

The letters are neither purloined nor stolen. Instead, the non-reception is predicted by the narrator; at the very beginning of the book, Maméga declares:

Mais oui Carolina, les misères des pauvres du monde entier se ressemblent comme des soeurs; on te lit par curiosité, moi je ne te lirai jamais; tout ce que tu as écrit, je le sais ... (9)

[Yes Carolina, all over the world, the poor suffer from miseries which resemble each other like sisters; people will read what you write out of curiosity, I, on the other hand will never read it; everything that you have written about, I know it ...]

Maméga is aware that she is sending letters which are tautological for Carolina: her correspondent already knows what the letters talk about, nothing unknown to Carolina. Carolina does not need *Lettres à une noire* to find out about poverty and racism. In spite of her anthropological approach, the narrator's objective is not to document a form of exotic oppression of which Carolina needs to be informed. The letters do not claim to enlighten an ignorant public. The Brazilian woman could easily function as an exotic other: after all, Carolina was the subject of an article on 'black Women' in *Paris-Match*. For the French magazine, she was the very symbol of otherness. But paradoxically, this 'other' cannot become Maméga's reader because for her, she is a figure of the same, she is too similar to the narrator. The 'I' knows that Carolina's 'curiosity' will not be aroused by her tale and Maméga never tries to seduce her reader by promising her a curious or interesting story. The narrative contract of seduction is precluded by the fusion which has already taken place between Maméga and Carolina, and of course, this fusion is tragic because it results from a shared experience of poverty which cannot be redeemed by a fruitful communication or exchange. Maméga produces a text which is addressed to the one person who can never benefit from it:

Carolina, tu ne me liras jamais; je n'aurai pas le temps de te lire, je vais vite, comme toutes les ménagères trop occupées, je lis des condensés, ça bouge trop autour de moi. (10)

[Carolina, you will never read this; and I will never have any time to read what you write, I hurry, like every overworked housewife, I read readers' selections, there is too much agitation around me.]

Not only is reading useless, it is also impossible. According to Maméga, reading requires 'curiosity' (which implies some sort of otherness and distance between the reader and the text) and 'time' (and for housewives, time is always a luxury). If our intuitive understanding of the opposition between the housewife and the woman of letters implicitly posited a conflict between her 'labour' and her 'writing', Maméga's rewriting of the epistolary contract undercuts and reformulates the paradigm: the overworked housewife's ultimate choice is not between her labour and her writing but between writing and reading (which is here interpreted as the activity of the privileged, of those who can enjoy time and curiosity).

In *Lettres à une noire*, all the characters agree that it is ludicrous for Maméga to write to Carolina and to publish a book to which only metropolitan French readers will have access. The old woman sitting next to Maméga on the bus cannot be persuaded that Maméga's letters are not addressed to a 'boyfriend': somehow, love letters seem to constitute the only legitimate genre for a housecleaner going home at night. At home, Maméga's children insist that it is 'ridicule d'écrire à une personne qui ne me lira jamais' [ridiculous to write to somebody who will never read what I write]: 'Voui! Pourquoi tu lui dis des choses à Carolina? Elle ne parle pas français' [Yeah, why do you tell Carolina all these things? She can't speak French] (24).

In spite of the general hostility generated by the incommensurable distance between Carolina and the letters, the flawed system of address obviously serves a purpose: the unbridgeable chasm separating the two women is a significant and powerful metaphor. It aptly symbolizes the difficulty with which minority groups can engage in a dialogue without being overheard or interrupted by dominant voices. Brazilian and Martinican women may perceive their experiences as 'similar' but they cannot speak to each other and they cannot hear each other. As Arthur Flannigan-Saint-Aubin puts it: 'the relationship between Maméga and the other (non-European) women that populate her universe are all modulations of her relationship to Carolina' (Flannigan-Saint-Aubin, 1992, 61).[17] Maméga echoes the recurrent and anguished question raised by post-colonial authors (how can one write in the language of the colonizer or from within a system which makes the colonizer the privileged reader of my text?), but she slightly modifies the terms of the problem. Her question seems to be: 'Can I only write to the woman who is like me, who shares my misery but who will never read my book, and are all my texts doomed to be read by those to whom they are not addressed?'

Carolina is at the same time the only possible correspondent and the most impossible correspondent, the one who will not read, the one for whom the book has no purpose. The manipulation of the system of address and the diversion of the epistolary genre lie in the denunciation of this paradoxical dissymmetry. If we imagine writing as a form of production and reading as a form of consumption, Lettres à une noire becomes an open-ended system where the product never reaches its intended consumer. Subverting the conventions of address of a literary genre thus introduces radical changes within a codified system of exchange. Another way of formulating the difference brought about by Lettres à une noire would be to say that the novel redefines the relationship between reader and writer by undercutting the traditional model of the writer–producer versus the reader–consumer. When suggesting that housewives and cleaning ladies will not be able to read the book, Maméga makes the point that reading is also a form of work which requires time and availability: as de Certeau points out, reading is also a form of production. In Lettres à une noire both writing and reading belong to the category of work. The woman writer is no longer perceived as the privileged counterpart of the housecleaner because their activities are similar: they are both engaged in a form of work which subverts the traditional relationship between production and consumption. In fact, Maméga's book could be said to function like the worker's perruque. As de Certeau puts it:

Accused of stealing or turning material to his own ends and using the machines for his own profit, the worker who indulges in *la perruque* actually diverts time (not goods, since he uses only scraps) from the factory for work that is free, creative and precisely not directed toward profit. (25)

Like the worker involved in the creation of a *perruque*, Maméga creates 'gratuitous products whose sole purpose is to signify [her] own capabilities through [her] work and to confirm [her] solidarity with other workers and [her] family through *spending* [her] time in this way' (26). But the French word *perruque* also refers to a 'wig' or a 'toupee' and *Lettres à une noire* also functions like a *perruque* in that sense: the toupee is what covers baldness and what denounces it as an undesirable lack as well. The *perruque* allows a bald person to move around as though he or she had hair but it is a supplementary garment whose presence is due to an absence.

In fact, both Maméga's book and her labour function like a toupee. Let us examine for example Maméga's ambiguous relationship with what is supposed to be the oldest form of female work. When Maméga accepts a position as a seamstress in a hotel owned by a Martinican woman, she asks what she will be expected to do, and the 'patronne' explains:

Ici, c'est un peu spécial, je ne veux pas prendre une couturière qui me procurera des histoires! ... Il s'agit de couper les draps usagés en deux et d'inverser les morceaux afin de prolonger leur existence. Cela fait deux ans que je n'ai pas fait faire ce boulot, j'en ai un plein placard. (112)

[Here, it is a little special, I don't want to hire a seamstress who will get me in trouble! ... Your job will be to cut up worn out sheets through the middle and to sew the edges back together so that they last a little longer. I have not been able to do it for two years and I have a whole closet full of them.]

On the one hand, Maméga sides with the woman whom she identifies as the oppressor (the black Martinican woman who despises her white prostitutes partly because her power over them allows her to get revenge from a husband who left her for a white woman). When she sows the sheets together, Maméga becomes a pawn in the business she strongly disapproves of. Her position as an infiltrator is even more problematic than when her hard work perpetuated the myth of the ideal black housecleaner. Clearly, an even more pressing moral issue is at stake for Maméga: 'De la porte vitrée, je vois les dames qui vont et viennent avec des messieurs, toute la matinée, cela a duré' [Out of the French window, I see the

ladies coming and going with gentlemen. All morning, it lasted]
(112). Shielded from the prostitutes and her clients by a glass panel,
a transparent but symbolic barrier which isolates her from the other
women, Maméga is both watching and actively helping the system to
perpetuate itself. She will prolong the existence of sheets which,
without her intervention, threaten to fray and disintegrate. But the
transformation undergone by the used sheets at the hands of
Maméga resembles the form of writing adopted in her letters to
Carolina. She cuts the sheets through the middle and brings the edges
back together by means of a hem, a suture. Symbolically, she brings
the margins back to the centre, and pushes away from the centre the
part of the sheet which bears the marks of tear and wear. But a trace
remains of her activity: the sheets have not disappeared but they are
now marked by a suture which is the signature of Maméga's
intervention. Like the *perruque*, her work makes it possible for the
sheets to be used as sheets instead of filling up a closet, but they
remain marked by Maméga's labour. The glorious mythological
weaver, Penelope or Arachnea, is here replaced by a humble
seamstress. Maméga's work is a bricolage, an expedient means which
will allow the sheets to last a little longer even though the system is
showing signs of wear and tear. It is a *perruque* because it reveals the
existence of a problem while offering a temporary solution. Her
sewing is the place where writing and labour coexist or coincide
without altogether abolishing the distinction. Similarly, her book is a
form of ironic recycling which reminds the reader of the economic
implications of the parallel she establishes between writing and
labour. Like Andy Warhol, Ega uses scraps of knowledge and
information, 'leftover things',[18] leftover time, leftover meaning.
Writing is neither a form of apolitical art nor a form of engagement
which can be substituted for action, writing will not achieve
anything if it is dissociated from labour. But labour, when diverted
by popular tactics, when turned into a form of gift, is capable of
subverting the economy of production–consumption. It becomes a
form of art, a gratuitous activity which will not be easily exploited.

The opposition between writing and labour cannot and perhaps
should not disappear. The suspicion that writing remains the province of a privileged intellectual elite is probably still a valid theoretical and historical starting point. Those who write may still legitimately worry that they are sometimes guilty of speaking for the
'others' and usurping their right to represent themselves. I assume

that it is still judicious to suspect that the proletarian domestic worker experiences labour as a painful form of alienation. But Maméga's tactic also suggests that oppositional 'schemas of action' can be invented where writing would retain all the characteristics of manual labour and where labour could become a gift, a form of energy reinvested in a different artistic activity. This type of work-writing could not easily be recuperated and coopted by any hegemonic structure.[19]

## Notes

1 See for example Hélène Cixous' famous 'La venue à l'écriture': 'Tu peux désirer. Tu peux lire, adorer, être envahie. Mais écrire ne t'est pas accordé. Ecrire était réservé aux élus. Cela devrait se passer dans un espace inaccessible aux petits, aux humbles, aux femmes' (Cixous 1977, 20–1).

2 See for example the interview with Caribbean writer Simone Schwarz-Bart and her husband in which Schwarz-Bart expresses the hope that her book will encourage young people from the Caribbean to write so that Caribbean 'cultural patrimony' may be saved from extinction (Schwarz-Bart 1979, 18).

3 Clifford's book opens on a quotation from a poem by Williams Carlos Williams. The poem tells the story of a young female servant called Elsie. The poet is at the same time voyeur and ethnographer as he watches the silent servant who obviously represents otherness. The poem is a meditation on the ambiguous status of this 'troubling' presence and on the repercussions of this presence on the writing of the poem: 'There is violence, curiosity, pity and desire in the poet's gaze. Elsie provokes very mixed emotions. Once again a female, possibly colored body serves as a site of attraction, repulsion, symbolic appropriation' (Clifford 1988, 5). For different approaches to the relationship between the servant and the text, see also Chaney & Castro (1989) and Offen, Pierson and Rendall (1991).

4 Minh Ha quotes hassie gosset who wonders what could be the point of writing when 'a major portion of your audience not only cant (sic) read but seems to think reading is a waste of time? [...] plus books like this are not sold in the ghetto bookshops or even in airports'; see 'Who Told You Anybody Wants To Hear From You? You Ain't Nothing But A Black Woman' in *This Bridge Called My Back: Writings by Radical Women of Color* (175), cited by Minh Ha (1989, 7).

5 *La Sagouine* (by Acadian writer Antonine Maillet) departs from the romantic vision of a helpless and submissive victim: the issue raised in these books is the complex relationship of power which develops between the employer and the employee. Obviously, power is not unilaterally yielded by the employer and the servants know how to set limits to the employer's authority.

6 Ourika is not a servant even though she represents the racial other who lives in the midst of a white family. She will finally die of grief in a convent after becoming aware of her ambiguous position as insider/outsider. Part of the novel is devoted to the white family's members who curiously observe Ourika as she gradually comes to realize that

her intimacy with the rest of the family is founded on a series of lies about her origin, her identity and her race. See also 'La Noire de ...', the penultimate short story in the collection entitled *Voltaïques* (1962), where the heroine's death is also presented as the only plausible fictional outcome to the extreme degree of alienation experienced by the Black domestic servant doubly exiled from Africa and from her own community.

7 Tituba's first years as a slave are spent at the service of her husband's mistress and Télumée is Madame Desaragnes's cook and personal servant (Condé 1986 and Schwarz-Bart 1972).

8 Françoise Ega's novel was published in Paris, in 1978 as *Lettres à une noire*. All references to this edition will now be indicated in parentheses. All translations are mine.

9 See Griaule's *Masques Dogons*. For an analysis of Tempels' much criticized *Philosophie bantoue*, see Christopher Miller's *Theories of Africans* (11–14). The author makes reference to several 'sustained critics of Tempels' (Pauli Hountondji's *Sur la Philosophie africaine*, V. Y. Mudimbe's *L'Odeur du père* and Fabien Eboussi Boulaga's article, 'Le Bantou problématique' Miller 1990, 13 n. 20).

10 Clifford's allusion to a form of 'mystification' strangely echoes a passage in the preface to Maméga's *Letters to a Black Woman*. The preface is signed by 'Emile Monnerot, Martiniquais, Psychiatre des Hôpitaux, Chef de secteur, Directeur de travaux cliniques à l'U.E.R. de Médecine de Marseille' [Emile Monnerot, Martinican, Doctor in Psychiatry, Head of Department, Director of Clinical Research in the Medical School of the University of Marseilles]. (I could not help wondering if this elaborate self-promoting description was motivated by an identity crisis or a compulsive desire to legitimize one's own discourse.) Monnerot (who wrote the Preface to Maméga) establishes a parallel between Maméga's book and Griffith's *Black like Me*. According to Monnerot, both experiments are similar: Maméga became a housecleaner in the same way as Griffith had his skin 'medically darkened' (6). But Monnerot suggests that 'In Maméga's case however, no fraud has been committed' (6). The psychiatrist seems to consider that Maméga's experience is pure and honest whereas Griffith's attempt is marred by mystification because he transgresses a racial barrier. Monnerot's intolerance of so-called 'fraud' does not do justice to the revolutionary potential of Maméga's character. When Maméga adopts the role of the 'housecleaner,' her experiment is an incursion into the realm of otherness which closely matches Griffith's attempt at reverse passing. Is Monnerot suggesting that it is somehow easier for a black woman to become a 'real' housecleaner than for a white man to become a black man? I would rather emphasize the fact that their tactic is similar and that the value of their conclusions may precisely be limited by their shared and implicit belief in the authenticity of the 'real'.

11 See for instance Mudimbe's *The Invention of Africa*. The author suggests that in spite of the apparent differences between all the texts written about Africa during the colonial period, they all share the same episteme. Even when they criticize colonialist practices and philosophies, they tend to reinforce its values. The most striking example, according to Mudimbe, is Tempels' *Bantu Philosophy*.

12 As Gayatri Spivak puts it: 'I am not suggesting that there is a hard reality out there ... But I would also not want to identify such reality with the production of signs. Something else might be going on' (Spivak 1990, 33).

13 It is probably significant that the epistolary novel be associated with women (in the sense that the writer of the fictional correspondence is often a woman), with eighteenth-

century literature (it is historically dated and perhaps slightly old-fashioned), and usually considered as one of the best vehicles for 'love stories' (implicitly opposed to more serious political writings). Furthermore, with the exception of Mariama Bâ's *So Long a Letter* (which, as the title indicates, is not exactly a correspondence), epistolary novels are not well represented in African or Caribbean Francophone literature. For an analysis of the place of epistolarity in African literature, see Mineke Schipper's study: '"Who Am I?" Fact and Fiction in African First-Person Narrative' and the chapter intitled 'Senegalese Women Writers' in Christopher Miller's *Theories of Africans* (1990, 246–93).

14 See for example Madame de Grafigny's *Lettres d'une Péruvienne* (the reader has access only to Zilia's letters to Aza) or Riccoboni's *Lettres de Mistriss Fanni Butlerd* where the writer excludes her unfaithful lover's voice from her correspondence.

15 Mamega remembers reading about Carolina in an issue of *Paris-Match* devoted to Black women. The book in question is by Carolina Maria de Jesus whose diary has been published (and widely edited) as *Child of the Dark; the Diary of Carolina Maria de Jesus*. New York, Dutton, 1962 (originally published as *Quarto de despejo*. Sao Paulo: Livraria F. Alves, 1960). My warmest thanks to Lemuel Johnson for directing me to this book and for pointing out the amount of discrepancies or recuperative rewritings in the translation. For the French reader of Ega's text, Carolina Maria de Jesus exists both as origin and as absence, an ambivalent central yet erased position which, in itself, could be seen as the metaphor of infiltration.

16 See Janet Gurkin Altman's *Epistolarity: Approaches to a Form*: 'If pure autobiography can be born of the mere desire to express oneself, without regard for the eventual reader, the letter is by definition never the product of such 'an immaculate conception,' but is rather the result of a union of writer and reader' (88). In a related note, Altman adds: 'the truly epistolary novel is governed by a desire for *exchange* with an *addressee* who is specifically *other*' (112). Here, the addressee is a figure of the 'same' and exchange is perceived as impossible.

17 See also his 'Reading Below the Belt: Sex and Sexuality in Maryse Condé and Françoise Ega'.

18 For Andy Warhol (1975), 'leftovers' are 'things that were discarded and that everybody knew were no good' (54), and his interest in 'recycling' leftovers is linked to his perception of waste as funny ('I always thought there was a lot of humor in leftovers' (55)). Mamega is also involved in 'recycling' but her stance is more ironic than amused: she does not recycle useless and broken objects but whole categories of human beings who have been left over by capitalism, forms of writing and literary genres which are left over by 'great literature', and intersections between labour and writing which do not belong to any definition. Andy Warhol's work belongs to what Andrew Ross calls the 'reorganization of cultural taste that took place in the course of the sixties' (1989, 170) and Françoise Ega's 1978 book does not exactly fit within the same historical or cultural universe. But her form of writing shares with Warhol's outrageous experiments the suspicion that literature and art 'had something more directly to do with products, consumers, and markets' (Ross 1989, 170) than with the 'aesthete's windless realm of great art'. The difference being of course that for Ega, social solidarity is never perceived as a ridiculous farce.

19 A French version of this text is included in *L'Héritage de Caliban/Caliban's Legacy*, edited by Maryse Condé (Pointe-à-Pitre, Guadeloupe: Jasor, 1992): see 'Lettres à une noire de Françoise Ega, la femme de ménage de lettres', 213–32.

# Infiltrating concentration camp logic

> Lorsque j'ai été prisonnière, d'abord dans une prison française, ensuite dans un camp en Allemagne, j'ai connu des compagnes qui prenaient des notes, et parfois pour la première fois de leur vie. Je préférais consacrer mon énergie à des choses plus importantes, ne pas non plus provoquer le sort en encourant des risques supplémentaires, sans compter que je savais déjà que je n'aurais pas envie de conserver certains souvenirs. Il y a des moments où l'amnésie semble préférable à tout. (Montferrand 1991, 15)

> [When I was a prisoner, first in a French prison, and later, in a camp in Germany, I met women who took notes, sometimes for the first time in their lives. I chose to devote my time to more important things, not to tempt fate by incurring more risks than was necessary, not to mention that I already knew that I would not want to preserve certain memories. Sometimes, amnesia seems more desirable than anything else.]

## The ambivalence of 'counter-history'

For Bretécher's children infiltration is a form of play, for Maméga infiltration is a way of redefining labour and writing. In Michèle Maillet's *L'Etoile noire* (*Black Star*) infiltration is a matter of life and death. In this novel, the imaginary centre to be infiltrated is Nazi ideology. Nazism, by definition, absolutely needs to impose two myths: purity exists, and the centre is purity. In such a system, infiltration is both a survival technique for those who have been declared impure, but also the ultimate transgression. The infiltrator contests the very idea of a waterproof and pure core, he or she

undermines the ideological foundation of the system. Michèle
Maillet's book is surrounded by the barriers of a concentration camp,
an extreme example of exclusionary practices where belonging or
being cast out can make a difference between survival or death.
What, one may wonder, is the role of infiltration when categories
are of such vital importance? What can the infiltrator do to survive
and undermine the system? What solutions do Sidonie and Suzanne
(the two main protagonists of the story) propose to ensure that their
notebook ('cahier') will survive even their own deaths?

Because categorizing and story-telling are shown to have such
potentially devastating or liberating capabilities, I find it difficult to
provide a synopsis at this point. I could have said that L'Etoile noire is
a book about concentration camps. In fact, this is how the novel was
first recommended to me. But after reading L'Etoile noire, I wonder if
I can produce any literary blurb without being haunted by the
remorse of generating precisely the kind of discourse the book seeks
to oppose.

If I try to summarize the plot, I end up with a skeletal caricature:
the novel takes place during the Second World War. It is the story of
a young Martinican black woman, who is employed as a house-
keeper by a Jewish family, the Dubreuils, when she is arrested,
deported, and sent to a death camp where she finally dies. Such a
summary may give my readers the almost unformulated impression
that they are already familiar with the book, its meaning, and its
characters. The linear sequence of events I have just listed, arrest,
deportation, imprisonment, and death in a concentration camp, as
well as the identity of the characters (black, Jewish, French and
German) already seem to belong to one coherent and familiar history
lesson. We may even be consciously or unconsciously wondering, at
this point, if L'Etoile noire will turn out to be a rather predictable tale.
In retrospect, I remember that I did not rush to the library or to the
bookstore to secure the 'book on concentration camps' which my
friend had recommended. Perhaps, without being aware of it, I felt
that I had already read 'similar' books.

I was, however, quite conscious of the fact that my anticipated
boredom was taboo, even scandalous. Well before asking myself
whether the book was worth buying for its 'originality', or its
specifically 'literary' interest, I was aware that such criteria might
result in irresponsible value judgements. I knew I needed another
critical discourse. This chapter is, in a way, an attempt to infiltrate

the critical and literary categories which do not let me distinguish between different forms of silence: the silence of utter powerlessness and the silence of active infiltration. Have we replaced what was and could have remained absolute silence[1] with a literary canon, a literary genre which makes each testimony a familiar series of episodes? Is there such a thing as the infiltrator's story, or at least, is there any hope of letting an infiltrated history circulate?

We could read L'Etoile noire as an example or possible model of non-official or 'counter-history', that does not celebrate the victory of any power, be it temporary and non-hegemonic. But this text is founded on a first paradox: the novel kills its main character and narrator, Sidonie, who dies at Mathausen. Her voice is kept alive however, depriving her Nazi persecutors of the last word. To complicate matters, Sidonie's story is both familiar and exceptional because it is one of the very rare accounts produced by a black female victim of death camps.[2]

I am tempted to analyse the problematic intertwining of defeat and victory, silence and testimony, exemplarity and exception in L'Etoile noire from the vantage point of what has been called 'new historicism', and more specifically, in the light of the critique which this theory has elicited. Although it goes without saying that it would be absurd to describe L'Etoile noire as an example of 'New Historicism' or of any other academic '-ism', an analysis of the ambitions and limitations of New Historicism provides a productive theoretical starting point.

In an article entitled 'Re-Membering the Deformed Past', Aram Veeser reminds us that 'New Historicists' endeavour to recapture narratives repressed by official History, i.e. 'the history of victors'. Official History is one possible fiction whose characteristic feature is to propose and impose a series of 'de-formations' which exclude oppressed minority groups:

New Historicism thrives precisely on remembering the history of [such] de-formations. The history of the victors (the only history that has made its way into print) presents itself as strong and whole. New History relates an alternative history, presents transcripts that are not only 'hidden' but also crooked, misquoted, gibbous, and defaced. It digs out the powerful anecdotes that incubate within booming triumphalist histories. (Veeser 1991, 4)

In her attempt at reconstituting, reinventing and remembering the voice of a young Martinican woman who could have remained one of the anonymous victims of Nazi camps, Maillet's gesture is not altogether different from that of New Historicists. It is also to be noted that, in a post-colonial context, this story departs from one the most prevalent models of resistance narrative to be found in Francophone Caribbean or African literature: Sidonie is not the rebel turned dictator, she does not fall prey to what I would term a Christophe Complex.[3] But because L'Etoile noire is not the ambivalent success story of a victim metamorphosed into a victorious hero[ine] (and potentially new authoritarian leader for the 'people'), the novel may be faulted for its defeatist standpoint. From beginning to end, L'Etoile noire remains the story of a helpless victim reduced to absolute powerlessness.

I am not criticising the novel on the ground that each story should contain a political lesson, but it seems that an unresolved tension does subsist between the desire to unearth 'repressed narratives' (the testimony of 'victims' for example) and the 'real' or 'social' or 'ideological' outcome of such archaeological fictionality. It may be taken for granted that there is a reason for writing the 'story of victims'. It may also be safely assumed that such re-formations have in mind the interests of victims rather than the glorification of the official history which contributed to their silencing. This raises the question of the advisability of a strategy emphasizing the powerless- ness of those who have 'lost' their struggle. Theoretically, what discourse could best serve the interests of those who died at Auschwitz? Is the memory of victims adequately represented (pre- served? honoured?) by any (hi)story whatsoever?[4] If one looks to history for 'lessons' or 'guidance' (stories as pedagogy in Walter Benjamin's sense), is it safe to assume that novels like L'Etoile noire constitute useful 'repertories of schemas of action', as Certeau puts it, or some 'cultural patrimony' (this time, in Bourdieu's terminology) for individuals who find themselves confronted with comparable sets of circumstances?[5] As a story-teller who manages to add her voice to the dominant discourse, does Sidonie impart a form of knowledge that would increase (or decrease) our chances of survival? Do I (sometimes, often) contribute to the oppression I want to oppose by offering a tragic and hopeless plot to potential victims, (myself included)? Veeser writes that some historical narratives

have insistently highlighted the 'atrocities' visited on the lower class bodies, have lovingly detailed the 'colonial torture' lavished on the starkly victim- ized, 'broken, hapless underlings' who people New Historicists prose. Nor can New Historicism, according to Eagleton, offer 'ressources of hope' to the 'Jew, colonial subject, youth peasant and so on', who supply the 'mutilated' bodies that are a New Historicist 'item de rigueur'. (Veeser 1991, 3)

I am quite aware that Veeser's generalization is somewhat problematic and I am sure that New Historicists may be very reluctant to recognize their work as described in the above paragraph. Maillet's novel, however, consciously adopts the victim's point of view and manages to temporarily silence the victors. Veeser's questions are therefore pertinent.

Two implicit accusations are levelled at such stories: they are suspected of obscene or pornographic intentions (tortures are 'lovingly detailed')[6] and they simply teach submissiveness and hopelessness ('New Historicism transmits to the subaltern the fatal inability to act' (Veeser 1991, 4, my emphasis)). In the case of L'Etoile noire, one could wonder for example whether Maillet is indulging in an indecent fascination for the tortures undergone by the characters, or if Sidonie's utter powerlessness to protect her children and herself is likely to demoralize or completely paralyse other survivors or victims.

Such questions in turn raise problems about the legitimacy of a reader's response to 'historical' texts. Answering the first part of the accusation requires for example that I bring into play the author's intentionality and I wonder if many readers would insist on putting Maillet's text on trial for that reason. As for the second reservation, the 'demoralizing' effect of the story, I wonder if it does not imply a definition of reading to which I do not subscribe. After all, is it possible for a narrative to 'transmit' anything to the subaltern, let alone 'the fatal inability to act'? What does 'transmission' represent in this case? Does a narrative systematically 'transmit' waves or information like a radio system does? In order to believe in the possibility of such 'transmission', one would have to recognize that texts are endowed with an immense amount of power (a narrative could indeed either paralyse or goad its readers into action). We would have to assume that our reading is a form of enslavement, that interpretation entails no latitude, no uncertainty. A female reader, for example, would have no choice but to treat the characters as projections or mirrors of herself, to model herself upon one of the 'historical' characters represented in L'Etoile noire, to identify with the victim's fate and be made desperate by such a tragic blueprint.

I obviously do not assume that such perfect 'transmission' is possible, but Veeser's and Eagleton's criticisms suggest that if the triumphalism of official history always at least partially serves the interests of the 'oppressors', it does not necessarily follow that (historical) justice will be served by replacing the victor's story with that of the victim. First of all, if the victim's story does manage to get printed, 'transmitted' on a large scale, it could be said that it has itself become a new dominant discourse. Perhaps the historical notion of 'victors' does not have to be extra-textual and the canon of history might be able to accommodate several successive 'victor's histories'. More importantly, I cannot rule out the possibility that some readers will interpret the victim's story as an unconscious validation of the victor's ideology. The representation of victimization may constitute the best propaganda for forms of totalitarian power which theoretically justify racial or social systems of exclusion (even the would-be 'passivity' of deported Jewish families has been counted against them).

L'Etoile noire, however is not the ideal story of an ideal subaltern. In fact, the reader soon realizes that Sidonie's struggle against Nazism is made up of a succession of ambiguous moments, and also that her voice cannot be isolated. In the second part of this chapter, I would like to show that Sidonie often becomes the unwilling accomplice of a form of oppression which she fails to theorize or understand because she is never given a chance to examine the categories of identity to which she is forced to subscribe. As a result, her own discourse becomes the tool of her oppression and that of her allies. Because Sidonie's discourse can also be seen as a palimpsest of the specific kind of oppression she undergoes, it seems appropriate to follow this trail of ambiguities. Rather than hoping that Sidonie's narrative will provide the long-awaited perfect model of counter-history, the story of the Second World War according to Martinican women, I will now analyse how Sidonie is trapped by her own role as a historian and how her political positions make her the instrument of the power which oppresses her.

### Sidonie, the dead author of counter-history

As a writer of her own history, Sidonie must situate herself vis-à-vis other discourses which want to provide her with a given identity. Before being turned into a writer by unforeseen circumstances, Sidonie is primarily a reader. In L'Etoile noire, the moleskin notepad on which the traces of her ordeal are inscribed takes the place of another book, a novel she had just begun before being arrested and which, symbolically had to be left behind, unfinished. Before producing history, Sidonie had consumed history books written by others:

> Le livre que j'ai en cours est resté à mon chevet: un roman inspiré des amours de Napoléon et Joséphine, que ma mère m'a donné avant mon départ, il y a sept ans et que j'ai retrouvé récemment. Peut-être ne le finirai-je jamais. (45)

> [I left the book I had started on my bedside-table: it was a novel inspired by the love-story between Napoleon and Josephine, which my mother had given me before I left, seven years ago. I had rediscovered it recently. I may never finish it.]

The unfinished history book is an adequate emblem of all the ambiguities of history as original text, as model and reservoir of heroes and heroines. For if indeed, identifying with victims may be demoralizing, suggesting that a dominated group identifies with the values of a dominant group may prove even more destructive. For a Martinican black woman, claiming Joséphine's success as 'her own' means sharing the historical prestige of a figure born on the same island, but also identifying with 'l'impératrice Joséphine des Français rêvant très haut au-dessus de la négraille' [Empress Joséphine of the French dreaming high, high above negridom] as Césaire puts it in *Cahier d'un retour au pays natal* (Césaire 1995, 74–5). One wonders what the mother had in mind when she chose such a gift for her daughter, and it soon becomes clear that her selection was by no means innocent. Josephine's (love)-story was indeed meant as a set of instructions, as a model to be followed. The fictional/ historical character of the young Martinican woman destined to marry one of her most powerful contemporaries functions as some kind of subliminal echo to the parents' often repeated advice. For it was made clear to Sidonie that when in France, she was supposed to marry a white man:

> Mon père voulait voir l'avenir à sa façon, changer la vie comme il pouvait. L'avenir à sa façon, c'était sa fille, c'était moi. «Épouse qui tu veux Sidonie, mais ne nous ramène pas un Nègre ou un coulis, car tu n'entreras plus ici». (38)

> [My father insisted on seeing the future his own way, on changing life as he could. The future as he saw it was his daughter, myself. 'Marry whomever you like, Sidonie, but don't bring us back some Negro or some Gook, for you will not set foot in this house again'.]

When Sidonie is arrested, the German officers allow her only a few seconds to gather her belongings, and at an instant's notice, she must make some decisive choices. For example, she abandons this so-called historical novel which sees history as an exotic love story and she chooses instead to pack a brand new notebook. I suggest that the decision to trade an already written book for a collection of blank pages coincides with the loss of an entire set of familiar and reassuring identities. Sidonie must give up on her own personal history, to become a blank book herself. When she faces the first blank pages, all the elements of her own fairy tale have already vanished. Yet, before the intervention of the German patrol, Sidonie could have drawn a relatively optimistic portrait of herself. At the beginning of the novel, she describes herself as a brilliant student, the privileged member of a respectable light-skinned middle-class family, protected by the powerful Dubreuil family who would have legally adopted her but for her mother's intractable opposition, and who left Martinique with her protectors supposedly to start medical school (40–1). For Sidonie, success was guaranteed by a multi-faceted identity of which she was not really aware.

Sidonie's emergence as a historiographer coincides with the moment when the problematics of identity (of her identity) becomes unavoidable. For her, the war really begins when a set of circumstances forces her to pay attention to a discourse which had surrounded her all along but which she had absolutely refused to heed. This discourse is about the construction of collective and individual identities. At the beginning of the novel, Sidonie cannot imagine why anyone would want to arrest her, but she does recognize a familiar refrain, sentences she has heard before:

Jude, Negerin, tut nichts, selbe Schweinerei!
C'est l'un des civils qui a parlé. Je devine le sens des mots que je reconnais vaguement: juif, nègre, cochon. La même cochonnerie, la même engeance. Ce discours, je l'ai déjà entendu, vaguement. Je n'y ai jamais prêté attention. (14)

[Jude, Negerin, tut nichts, selbe Schweinerei!
One of the civilians said this. I guess the meaning of the words which I vaguely recognize: Jew, nigger, pig. Same trash, same riff-raff. I already heard that speech, vaguely. But I never paid any attention.]

Her lack of 'attention', her indifference, have already been mentioned several times before her encounter with the militia. Now, she cannot disregard the implications of such discourse any longer.

Sidonie must take a stance vis-à-vis her identity and the construction of identity in general. Paradoxically, the moment when she most wants to 'pass', to infiltrate, is also the moment when she discovers that she is not tactically or ideologically trained to do so. She can no longer dismiss the fact that others will define her, that everybody is caught in a system which thrives on labels and distinctions. The moment when Sidonie starts writing the notebook coincides with the moment when she discovers that her indifference towards identity politics has to be expressed in the past. About Madame Dubreuil's Jewish identity, she writes: 'pour moi ça restait abstrait. Pour d'autres, ça ne l'était pas; peut-être ont-ils été dénoncés? Je savais qu'elle était d'une autre race que la mienne, mais autour de moi je ne rencontrais que des gens d'une autre race que la mienne, alors' [for me, it was always abstract. For others, it was not; Perhaps someone reported them? I knew that she and I did not belong to the same race, but everyone I met belonged to a different race] (16). For Sidonie, her skin colour was ultimate otherness and the rest of the world was undifferentiated. She 'knew' she was black: 'Mais je n'ai jamais beaucoup pensé à ma couleur; question de chance, sûrement; de circonstances, de temps et d'habitude' [But I never gave much thought to my colour; probably a matter of luck, of circumstances, of timing and of a way of thinking] (26). I suggest that Sidonie's narrative is first and foremost a coming to terms with the fact that she cannot deny the importance of how identity is constructed, imposed, and used in a context of extreme violence and domination. Willy nilly, her writing begins as a discovery of identity politics, and of her own powerlessness to control identity formations.

In their introduction to The Nature and Context of Minority Discourse, Abdul JanMohammed and David Lloyd write that 'the task of minority discourse in the singular' is 'to describe and define the common denominators that link various minority cultures' (JanMohammed and Lloyd 1990, 1). Because these minority sub-cultures always entertain conflictual relationships with the dominant culture, the authors urge different groups to form alliances, to bring their differences together in a form of coalition which would unite differences under the banner of solidarity. In a sense, this is exactly what L'Etoile noire is doing: it is inviting readers to discover, or re-discover, or realize that they 'knew' (like Sidonie) that black people from the French Caribbean and French Jews from the metropole had died in the same death camps. But the novel also explores the

difficulties and dangers of conceptualizing such alliances: the metaphor of the 'common denominator' is both luminous and theoretically difficult to circumscribe. Given the history of western 'universalism' and its related glorification of the 'Same', the search for
'common denominators' is bound to be problematic because it may
model itself on reactionary patterns. During the Second World War,
the dominant culture was itself looking for common denominators
among 'minority cultures' the better to oppress them as a united
'inferior' group. What Sidonie discovers for example, is that all the
various aspects of her identity are now erased because a dominant
discourse has created a monolithic class of 'inferior people':
'J'appartiens désormais à un groupe indistinct dans lequel Hitler a
classé les Juifs, les Tziganes et les Noirs' [I now belong to an
undifferentiated group within which Hitler has put Jews, Gypsies
and Blacks] (25).

As a result, in order to oppose the totalitarian power feeding on
resemblances, Sidonie is led to claim differences within this supposedly coherent and inferior group. For example, she distinguishes
among black people according to their distinct historical and national
entities. She refuses to lump together all the black communities who
lived in Paris at the beginning of the war:

pour les Allemands, et aussi pour certains Français – il n'y avait même
aucune différence entre ces musiciens [Noirs américains], les Africains des
troupes coloniales françaises, et les Martiniquais, Français, comme mes
enfants, depuis des siècles. (25)

for the Germans, and also for some French people, there was no difference
between these [Afro-American] musicians, the Africans who served in the
French colonial army, and Martinicans, who had been French, like my
children, for centuries.]

Ironically, the list of different black communities is reminiscent of a
passage in Césaire's *Cahier d'un retour au pays natal* (Césaire 1995, 90–1)
in which the narrator defines *négritude* as a community defined by the
sharing of similar forms of oppression. Sidonie, a contemporary of
the *Cahier*'s narrator, adopts a different, post-*négritude* strategy. Instead
of turning the discourse of indifferentiation against the powerful in
an attempt to replace the 'same' with 'common denominators', she
chooses to insist on differences between Martinicans and Africans. At
this end of the twentieth century, Sidonie's point of view is perfectly
understandable. It has become commonplace to emphasize the fact

that the African diaspora is now split into communities which do not share exactly the same culture, the same history nor the same desires. For a few decades now, Caribbean peoples have been willing to claim their African heritage while insisting that their identity has been shaped by their own history. If I find Sidonie's discourse problematic, it is not because she insists that one should distinguish between Afro-American musicians and Senegalese 'tirailleurs' but because she keeps swaying between the discourse of 'differences' and the discourse of 'common denominators' without being aware that neither theory is inherently enabling or disenabling and that dominant voices can use both constructions to oppress minority groups.

Nazi identity politics is itself self-contradictory (and this is what makes it theoretically porous) since in order to form a large, supposedly monolithic, group of 'inferior' people, in order to erase differences between them, it is necessary to confine each individual within some imaginary territory of identity which is constituted as a difference from other communities. Before being recognized as indifferently inferior, people are first classified as black, Jewish, homosexual, etc. Sidonie, as a narrator, chooses strategies which the text, governed by a logic of its own, cannot really celebrate. This reluctance to embrace identity politics may be one of the most 'modern' aspects of L'Etoile noire, in the sense that the narrative, produced in the 1990s, clashes with the logic of the narrator, who belongs to a different historical context. L'Etoile noire echoes some of the theoretical hesitations that productively agitate the fields of cultural and post-colonial studies. In La Force du préjugé: essai sur le racisme et ses doubles, Pierre-André Taguieff suggests that it may have become necessary to rethink the opposition between 'racism' and 'anti-racism' if we are to address the specific types of social conflicts emerging in our contemporary multicultural urban societies. Taguieff meticulously scrutinizes the implications of discourses founded either on differences or on resemblances between entities and he comes to the conclusion that neither theory is in itself a solution to racial, economic or political conflicts. Maillet's text as a whole points in the same direction by suggesting that Sidonie's world view is never powerful enough to constitute a valid defence against those who oppress her. In a sense, whether she chooses to valorise differences or unity does not make any difference, and the same holds true for those who exercise power in the concentration camp. They can justify their practices just as easily by means of a discourse which seeks to differentiate between groups or by means of theories of amalgamation. Barbarism does not need to be theoretically or ideologically consistent to generate terror, and conversely, a critique of ideology may not suffice to generate visions among the oppressed. Taguieff's last chapter is entitled: 'Métapolitique républicaine: universalisme ou barbarie? Universalisme sans barbarie' (Taguieff 1990, 480–92). The author concludes that both the search for common denominators and the celebration of differences may result in specific forms of 'barbarism'. On the one hand, as 'Max Horkheimer notait en 1961: «Est barbare l'attitude qui consiste à ne pas traiter *a priori* un homme comme un particulier, comme une personne, mais à le définir en général et d'abord comme un Allemand, un Nègre, un Juif, un étranger ou un Méditerranéen»' [Max Horkheimer noted in 1961: "Barbarism consists in refusing to treat a man like an individual, a person a priori, and in defining him generally and primarily as a German, a Black, a Jew, a foreigner or a Mediterranean"].[7] On the other hand, in the wake of recent postcolonialist and feminist studies, it seems at best naive to invoke a reconciliatory form of 'humanism' which also partakes in forms of barbarism. As Taguieff puts it:

La barbarie particulariste de la différence et de l'exclusion ne doit pas faire oublier la barbarie universaliste de l'inégalité et de l'uniformisation. (Taguieff 1990, 486)

[The particularist barbarisms of difference and exclusion should not make us forget the universalist barbarisms of inequality and uniformisation.]

Sidonie's narration seems trapped between and victimized by both forms of barbarism. For example, at the very moment when she insists on differentiating between communities of black people (when she does not adopt the 'common denominator' strategy), she reintroduces the logic of undifferentiation herself. She blames the Nazis for failing to distinguish between different black communities, but her reason for insisting on difference is not that she wants to celebrate and value new emergent or re-discovered cultures (African, Afro-American or Caribbean people have developed separate cultural identities as a result of historical circumstances) but because she considers that the group to which she belongs is different from difference. As a Martinican woman, 'française depuis des siècles' [who has been French for centuries], she wants to take advantage of the privileges attached to her French nationality. Sadly, as she claims her status as a French citizen, as her discourse veers towards nationalism, she excludes herself from the black community and the coalition of differences invoked earlier, and she denies other black people the rights and status she claims for herself and her children.

Sidonie cannot make good use of the principle of the 'common denominator' suggested by JanMohammed and Lloyd as a strategy for minority groups. Her attempts at imposing her own conception and politics of identity (perhaps because they follow a long period of indifference) result in a succession of seemingly haphazard and ill-chosen tactics. Not only is the discourse of differences generated by Sidonie as a response to Nazi undifferentiation powerless and ineffective, but it is also a sordid ideological trap which makes her an accessory to her enemies. When Sidonie seeks to differentiate herself from the group which appears to be the specific target of Nazi identity politics, she implicitly sanctions the way in which this group of others is treated. Sidonie's discourse is indifferent to those black peoples who have not been granted French nationality. It also betrays the Dubreuils and it refuses to address the fate of Jewish people as long as they can be described as others. For example, when the German officers burst into her house, unaware that she is trying to avoid the unavoidable, Sidonie 'suddenly' hopes that she has discovered a mistake, a crack in a system which she imagines to be logical and rational:

Soudain, je saisis clairement l'absurdité de la situation: une rafle. C'est une rafle, et ils me prennent pour une Juive. Une Juive noire. Et ils se demandent si ça existe.
Alors j'ouvre la bouche pour la première fois, presque calmement, sûre de moi:
– Nicht Jude. Catholique, je suis catholique! (14).

[Suddenly I clearly see the absurdity of the situation: a roundup. It's a roundup and they think that I am Jewish. A black Jew. And they are wondering if it exists.
So for the first time, I open my mouth, almost calmly, confidently:
– Nicht Jude. Catholic, I am a catholic!]

This naive theory of the mistake is the opposite of infiltration. It suggests that some situations are not 'absurd' and that Sidonie is the victim of an individual error. Politically, it is also a disastrous move, since, in order to be right, to differentiate herself, Sidonie must side with the enemy and betray whoever identifies (or is identified) as

Jewish. My criticism of the 'mistake theory' is not a moral judgement on what 'real' people do in desperate situations. I am suggesting instead that *L'Etoile noire* explores and redefines barbarism as the moment when the distinction between strategy and tactic becomes irrelevant.[8] The novel as a whole does not seem to imply that Sidonie temporarily chooses to adopt the enemy's position as a way of winning her own battle: her tactics are ineffective. Most of the time, when she plays the game of identity politics, when she proposes her own version of who she is, her discourse is simply ignored, her own constructions are dismissed as implausible. For example, in the same way as the Nazis will not let her betray the Dubreuils, she will not be allowed to sever the bond between herself and her children. She is willing to declare them 'others' to protect them but her fables do not convince the militia: 'Les enfants pas à moi. Ils sont en visite, en vacances. Je ne les connais pas' [The children, not mine. They are visiting, they are on vacation. I don't know them] (15).

The logic of undifferentiation is not a last resort. It constantly resurfaces in Sidonie's interpretations of the real. She does not hesitate to ascribe labels to whole groups of individuals, refusing to acknowledge differences within the group. For example, whereas the novel as a whole is able to draw a parallel between Jews and blacks, Sidonie does not know how to link her own situation of oppression and that of homosexual prisoners who, like her, have been absorbed into an undifferentiated and 'inferior' mass. Sidonie never alludes to the fact that the Nazi regime passed laws to establish discursive and legal resemblances between a Jew, a black, and a homosexual. In *L'Etoile noire*, the narrator would have us believe that a homosexual is always despicably associated with betrayal and usurped power:

La blockowa du Strafblock est une Tzigane qui a trahi les siens et s'est mise au service des nazis. Pour elle, l'arrivée d'une jeune et jolie fille est une aubaine qui lui permet d'assouvir ses vices. Avoir nommé cette pervertie responsable du block des punies est odieux. Aux souffrances physiques s'ajoutent la honte et l'humiliation. (240)

[The blockowa of the Strafblock is a Gypsy who has betrayed her people and is now serving the Nazis. The arrival of a young and pretty girl is a chance to satisfy her vice. It is a disgrace that such a pervert should have been assigned to the disciplinary ward. To physical pain are added shame and humiliation.]

This unmitigated example of homophobia is all the more striking as Sidonie's discourse is not systematically tainted with manichean crudeness. Earlier, she has made the ideologically elegant point that one should not confuse Nazi politics and the blockowas (who were often coerced into collaborating: 'nous l'oublions souvent, nos tortionnaires sont elles aussi des prisonnières' [we often forget that our tormentors are prisoners too] 187). On the other hand, Sidonie does not make any allusion to those prisoners who were wearing a pink triangle, and the violence of her own discourse reproduces the theories of those who declared homosexuals inferior, evil, sick or damned. In *L'Etoile noire*, homosexuality is called a 'vice', a 'perversion', it is a weapon used to oppress the weak. Nothing, in Sidonie's frightening tirade, indicates that she makes a distinction between sexual violence and homosexuality, insinuating that heterosexual rape does not carry its share of 'shame and humiliation' or that each and every homosexual relationship is a matter a brutal and violent domination.

It is also obvious, however (and for the reader, the double evidence is generative of tensions) that *L'Etoile noire* as a whole seeks to include and not to exclude. By documenting the fate of French black West Indians and by adding them to the list of concentration camp victims, the novel functions as a search for 'common denominators' as advocated by JanMohammed and Lloyd. But it also invites the reader to remain vigilant and suspicious of what can be done with identity politics. Obviously, it is not enough to decide whether one wants to celebrate 'common denominators' or differences within minority groups. *L'Etoile noire* seems to suggest that any totalitarian power may appropriate both theories to oppress individuals rather than to help them build alliances. Ironically, the text as a whole provides the readers with the means of criticizing its main character who is victimized by her own complicity with the discourse of Nazi power. The narrator alone cannot fight the system which condemns her to death, and in order to exist, *L'Etoile noire* needs to add another dimension to Sidonie's story, another form of discourse, a complementary narrative strategy, another definition of solidarity.

### Suzanne, interpretation and silence

*L'Etoile noire*, however, is not only Sidonie's story. This text offers an interesting and viable model of oppositionality, provided I focus not only on the narrator's discourse but also on another specific feature of the novel: the way in which history is produced and strategically transmitted by two different female characters. After exploring the ways in which Sidonie writes her diary as well as the complex mechanisms which allow this narrative to reach its implied narratees, I suggest that L'Etoile noire is not only an example of 'counter-history' but also the product of a collaboration, or alternation, between two women, Sidonie and Suzanne.

Suzanne first appears as a secondary character. The two women met by chance at the beginning of their deportation, they did not know each other, and apparently, they have very little in common. Suzanne is a white woman, a teacher, and we never find out anything else about her. She does stand out among the crowd of other terrified prisoners, however, because she alone chooses to help Sidonie when all solidarity seems to have disappeared due to the extreme suffering undergone by the travellers. Throughout the book, Suzanne remains in the background but she is indispensable to the narrative because both women are responsible for the production of the book as we read it. A little conventional notice inserted at the end of the novel (no page number) justifies the presence of the manuscript ('C'est ainsi que se termine le petit carnet de Sidonie. L'écriture, de plus en plus ténue, y est presque illisible. Ce carnet a été renvoyé par les soins d'une codétenue à la mère de Sidonie qui l'a reçu après la guerre' [This is the end of Sidonie's little notebook. Her handwriting gets fainter and fainter to become almost invisible. After the war, Sidonie's mother received the notebook which had been sent back to her by a fellow-prisoner]). In this third part, I would like to show that although Sidonie is the single narrative voice, Suzanne actively contributes to the notebook because she makes both the transmission and the production of the story possible.

Sidonie is a historian, she needs to formulate a politics of identity. Suzanne on the other hand does not write anything. She remains silent but she protects her friend's narrative and ensures its circulation. She does not seem involved in the problematic definition of 'identity' and this characteristic distance is related to her specific oppositional function, which is to transmit a voice spoken by another woman. For Sidonie, Suzanne remains mysterious because she does not correspond to the categories of identity used to describe other prisoners: 'Et Suzanne? Pas juive, pas noire, pas tzigane' [What about Suzanne? She is not Jewish, she is not black, she is not a Gypsy] (140). In a universe codified according to identities, Suzanne does not make sense and Sidonie seems to be wondering what she was accused of. In an insane universe where the label imposed upon the subject by the powerful becomes a matter of life and death, Suzanne remains strangely outside the logic of identity. She is the 'maillon entre nous et les autres. Son destin est le nôtre et celui de tous' [the link between us and the others. Her fate is ours and everone's] (53). Suzanne's refusal to belong to that system is indeed perceived as a form of transgression since she is arrested and deported. But unlike other prisoners, she has not been arrested for what she *is* (or what others say she is) but for what she *does* and for what she *knows*: she speaks German perfectly. This is the extent of her 'guilt' and not until after her arrival at the camp does she reveal this to Sidonie:

Ils vont venir me chercher. Avec quelques autres, je leur sers d'interprète. Ils ont eu besoin de moi, tout à l'heure, quand tu dormais.
Je ne comprends pas bien ce qu'elle est en train de me raconter:
– J'ai dormi? Tu parles allemand?
– Oui, et c'est pour cela qu'ils m'ont arrêtée. Pas à cause de ma peau, à cause de ma langue. Ils ont cru que j'étais une espionne … Remarque … (121)

[They are going to come for me. With a few others, I serve as an interpreter. They needed me, a little while ago, while you were asleep.
I am not sure I understand what she is telling me:
– Did I sleep? Can you speak German?
– Yes, and that is why I was arrested. Not because of my skin colour, because of my tongue. They thought I was a spy … Having said this …]

In Suzanne's case, the system is not content with imposing a supposedly 'impure' or 'inferior' identity on her. Her mastery of the German language cannot be reduced to some undesirable physical or mental feature. In order to blame Suzanne for her knowledge of German, it becomes necessary to invent a non-identity centred discourse. According to Nazi logic, if she speaks German, then she must be a spy ready to use German for unspeakable infiltrational manoeuvres. I would add that she is indeed dangerous for a totalitarian system because her knowledge of languages allows her to control the transmission of meaning between foreign communities. The spy is the infiltrating other who is mistaken for the same, she who seems at home in a foreign land, she who talks to 'foreigners' without them immediately noticing her otherness.[9] Understandably, she represents a serious threat for a system thriving on classifications and hierarchies. In a fascist territory obsessed with inclusion and exclusion, dominated by the concept of 'belonging' to the chosen race, the spy must be mercilessly eliminated because she exposes the fragile foundations of identity politics. Suzanne is not arrested because she is (described as) undesirable but because her presence blurs the convenient national(ist) assumptions according to which the French speak French and the Germans speak German. Interestingly, Suzanne neither recognizes nor denies that she is a spy ('Having said this ...'.). She simply acknowledges that she speaks German fluently, that she knows the enemy's language.

Suzanne's perfect knowledge of the other's language, which makes her so threatening, also puts her in an ambiguous and duplicitous position: like the 'common denominator', her knowledge is a double-edged weapon which can easily turn against her. As a spy, Suzanne could have transmitted information to her allies and helped organize networks of resistance by sabotaging German operations. But as a prisoner, Suzanne is now forced to do the same transmission work within the camp: she becomes the accomplice of those who have arrested her, she must relay their orders, translate their words. In a sense, she is now helping them to control and police the camp, and her linguistic ability makes the camp a more organized and efficient space, confining her own voice as well.

En tiers au milieu des autres, tel peut se trouver dans une position délicate et ambiguë, s'il n'est pas – ou est trop – concerné. Porteur, par exemple, de bonnes ou de mauvaises nouvelles, interprète, il profite parfois immensément, d'une situation qui, aussi souvent, se retourne, et peut donc se trouver impitoyablement chassé, exclu comme parasite. (Serres 1990, 78)

[A third among others may be in a delicate and ambiguous position: either too involved or not enough. For example the bearer of good or bad news, the interpreter, sometimes benefits immensely from a situation which may also change drastically. He will then be mercilessly expelled, excluded as a parasite.]

In L'Etoile noire, Suzanne's capacity for resistance thus seems doubly limited. On the one hand, her knowledge of German is easily made use of by the Nazis, on the other hand, the fact that she chooses to remain silent, and does not write her own story, does not seem to offer much in the way of possible compensations. But I suggest that even these two infiltrational characteristics have potentially subversive effects. For example, because Suzanne does not write, she can devote more time and energy to observation and interpretation. She always seems to know more than Sidonie does about what is going on in the camp. Her strength consists of being able to anticipate what will happen to them and to adopt specific strategies to protect her friend, ensuring her survival, and consequently, that of the narrative. Throughout the book, Sidonie is amazed by Suzanne's ability to predict the immediate future:

Suzanne, hier soir, m'a parlé. Comment fait-elle pour en savoir toujours plus long que moi? (181)

[Last night, Suzanne talked to me. How is it that she always knows more than I do?]

Suzanne is a more efficient interpreter. She reads signs that remain invisible for Sidonie. And each successful moment of interpretation allows her to adopt the best possible strategy for a specific problem. For example, when Suzanne, Sidonie, and her twins are packed into a bus shortly after their arrest, Suzanne makes a point of not sitting down. She remains standing in the aisle and only later does Sidonie understand that her decision was motivated by foresight. Suzanne has positioned herself in the only place where she can shield the children from other passengers who cannot keep their balance when the bus swerves around a curve. Sidonie wonders: 'Comment a-t-elle deviné que les choses allaient se passer ainsi?' [How did she guess it would happen that way?] (55). When the prisoners arrive at the camp, Suzanne warns Sidonie: 'Je crois que nous n'aurons pas de lit ce soir. Nous allons passer la nuit ici'. [I think we will not get a bed tonight. We are going to spend the night here] (129). And once again, Sidonie asks herself: 'Comment sait-elle cela?' [How does she know?]. When another prisoner offers Sidonie some water for Nicaise, her dying child, Suzanne immediately understands that the gesture is not to be interpreted as a gift. She translates the other woman's ambiguous signals, she re-interprets a discourse which Sidonie thought she had understood:

– Wasser, Wasser, agua... Eau. Ta fille...
Je comprends, elle m'offre de l'eau. J'ai à peine esquissé le geste de tendre le bras vers l'objet si précieux que la main de l'ombre s'est déjà repliée, et que celle de Suzanne s'est interposée.
– Non, n'accepte pas.
– Mais Nicaise, Nicaise en a besoin...
– Ce sera pire si tu acceptes...

Je ne comprends pas. Je sens un étau de fer se fermer sur l'une de mes
chevilles...
– Elle va te prendre tes chaussures. Sidonie, Sidonie, ne la laisse pas... (130)
[– Wasser, Wasser, agua... Water. Your daughter...
I understand, she is giving me some water. I have barely tried to hold out
my hand towards the precious object when the ghost's hand withdraws
while Suzanne's interferes
– No, don't accept.
– But Nicaise, Nicaise needs it...
– It will be worse if you accept...
I do not understand. I feel one of my ankles caught in an iron vice.
– She is going to take your shoes. Sidonie, Sidonie, don't let her...]

Suzanne knows that the woman does not intend to give but to trade,
that she will only let Sidonie have a little water if she is willing to
part with her shoes. Sidonie, obviously, is in no position to make an
informed decision because she does not understand the 'ghost's'
logic.

Suzanne thus takes responsibility for the two women's survival,
day by day. She predicts what is about to happen while Sidonie is
responsible for giving meaning to the past. Suzanne does not have a
story to tell, she is on the side of silence and at first, a reader may
legitimately wonder if a subject can be oppositional who does not
provide her own representation of 'historical events', who does not
try to leave a trace in history. One of the original features of L'Etoile
noire is the suggestion that such a silent subject does have a role to
play. Even if Suzanne is not an author, she can still choose among a
number of stories written by others and act at the level of the
circulation of the narratives. Suzanne's skills and energy protect
Sidonie's writing and they also partake in its distribution. Sidonie's
story should of course remain untold and the system insists that
writing is forbidden. But Suzanne functions as the guardian of
writing: she warns Sidonie when she is unaware of impending
danger because she is wrapped up in her diary. She makes sure that
other prisoners do not denounce Sidonie, and she also helps her find
a safe hiding place for the notebook. Sidonie knows that Suzanne
guarantees the possibility of writing: 'En général, je ne peux écrire
que lorsque Suzanne fait diversion ou me sert de paravent' [Usually,
I can write only when Suzanne creates a distraction and acts as a
screen] (194).

Paradoxically, Suzanne also protects the production of counter-stories by her skilful interruptions. She knows when Sidonie should stop writing in order to be able to keep the story alive in the long run. Sidonie's voice and Suzanne's silence are eminently complementary. Their collaboration could be described as a form of alternation, where each takes a turn so that different strategies of resistance are foregrounded or backgrounded depending on the context. Their respective positions combine and double as one sophisticated system of opposition. Here is an example of a series of significant 'interruptions' which invite the reader to reconsider stereotypical distinctions between action and theory or between passive and active resistance.

One of the historically interesting aspects of L'Etoile noire is its echo of Césaire's Discourse on Colonialism. Sidonie's imagination links fascism and colonization in striking visionary parallels between slavery and her present situation. The analogy is not original in itself but the notebook manages to link the resemblances to broader issues about history and education, about writing and the past, about silence and remembrance. In a sense, Sidonie's experience as a black victim of Nazism allows her to write a history of the Caribbean which she had not been able to formulate beforehand. Her counter-history of the concentration camp is intertwined with a counter-history of Martinique. For Sidonie, raised in a middle-class Martinican family before the beginning of the Second World War, slavery was not even part of the narrated past: neither her parents nor the French colonial educational system took the responsibility to write that page of history.

Et je pense à mes parents qui pendant vingt ans m'ont appris, répété, affirmé que l'esclavage était oublié, envolé, aboli. Ils allaient jusqu'à faire comme si cela n'avait jamais existé. (27)
Les livres d'école ne parlaient pas de l'esclavage. Pourquoi? (38)

[And I think about my parents, who, for twenty years, taught me, repeated, insisted that slavery was forgotten, gone, abolished. They went as far as acting as though it had never existed.
Textbooks never talked about slavery. Why not?]

Only after she is deported to Ravensbrück does she discover that she can write the history of slavery, that she 'remembers' what it means to be a slave. For Sidonie, being locked up in a train, forced to perform exhausting and humiliating tasks, being tattooed is not altogether unfamiliar. Another voyage, another time are somehow conjured up: the middle passage, slaves dying of exhaustion in the canefields, slaves being branded upon arrival. As we read Sidonie's story, a series of flashbacks takes us away from the gruesome 'reality' of the immediate present, of the concentration camp, of the death of Sidonie's child. Sidonie's voice is protected from incoherence and madness by this possibility to retreat into the 'fiction' of a new history, the patient elaboration of her narrative. Sometimes, writing is close to fantasy, to escapism. But Suzanne acts as a safety switch in the sense that she does not allow Sidonie to alienate herself from the present at the expense of her survival. Twice, she interrupts Siodnie's reveries with apparently more basic or more practical concerns: she has found some food, or has managed to procure some crucial piece of information which requires immediate attention.

The novel thus ascribes each character a very specific role. For instance, when Sidonie's son disappears, the text of her diary suddenly moves away from Ravensbrück and a non-identified narrative voice (the passage is in quotes) starts what seems to be an altogether different tale: 'il est quatre heures du matin, les esclaves de Saint-Pierre s'éveillent'. [it is four o'clock in the morning. In Saint-Pierre, slaves are waking up] (118). The allusion to Martinican slaves is no idle digression, the text is rewriting historical connections between a supposedly uncivilized past and our present. And the relationship between slavery and fascism is presented as newly-acquired (self-)knowledge. Writing has taught Sidonie how to both invent and discover her filiations. Suzanne's role however, is to interrupt the potentially dangerous blurring of past and present: 'Sidonie, Sidonie! Tiens, j'ai trouvé du pain. Et surtout, je sais où est ton fils' [Sidonie, Sidonie! Look, I have found some bread. And most important, I know where your son is] (119). A brief, fragile but successful moment of concrete resistance is thus added to Sidonie's narrative. It is to be noted that L'Etoile noire does not tell the reader what Suzanne does. The coherence of Sidonie's narrative voice is maintained until the end even if it means that gaps and unfilled holes in the story persist. We never know what Suzanne does while Sidonie sleeps or writes, but we are made to understand that both the woman who writes and the woman who does not write are complementary elements of the same overall strategy. Sidonie herself formulates a theory of 'alternation' as an attempt to explain the unstable power structure, the strange shifting of power and strength between Suzanne and herself:

D'où lui viennent cette énergie, cette autorité, cette fermeté? Jusqu'à présent, il me semblait que des deux, la femme forte, c'était moi. Peut-être est-ce cela le sens de notre rencontre: l'alternance de notre volonté, la diversité de nos forces? (109)

[Where does she find such energy, such authority, such assertiveness? Until now, I had the impression that I was the strong woman. Perhaps this is the meaning of our encounter: the alternation of our wills, the diversity of our strengths?]

Paradoxically, for the narrative to survive even after the author's death, writing must alternate with other tactics: it is not enough to write a story, it is imperative that the story be protected, transmitted. For instance, Suzanne's last intervention takes the form of another and final interruption: she warns Sidonie that the time has come to stop writing even though the story is not finished, and never will be. Suzanne knows that they are both going to die and that Sidonie must let go of the notebook, allow the information to circulate without her. One last time, Suzanne understands, or 'interprets' signs faster than Sidonie does. She guesses or predicts what the enemy's words mean for them:

Je viens d'apprendre que Suzanne et moi allons changer de camp. On nous envoie à Mathausen. «C'est la fin me dit Suzanne. Mathausen est un camp d'extermination. Mais les Allemands ne gagneront pas la guerre en Autriche. Nous serons vengés. On nous a ordonné de rassembler nos affaires le plus vite possible ...» (244)

[I have just found out that Suzanne and I are going to be transferred to another camp. We are being sent to Mathausen. 'It is over,' Suzanne tells me 'Mathausen is an extermination camp. But the Germans will not win the war in Austria. We will be avenged. We have been told to pack our things as soon as possible ...']

Neither Sidonie nor Suzanne can survive on their own, neither one can do without the other. Without Sidonie, Suzanne would be a dead body deprived of a story, of a tombstone, of the possibility of being remembered. Her skills as a translator would have been squandered. Conversely, if Suzanne had not been able to predict the immediate future, to find out when and how it is possible to survive, if she had not opted in favour of silence, if she had not been content with transmitting the other's words, including the enemy's orders when she works as an interpreter, then, Sidonie's notebook could not have become history. She would not have followed Suzanne's advice to give the precious notebook to Anastasie (a Martinican prisoner

whose presence lends verisimilitude to the reappearance of the
notebook after the war). Her rewriting of history, as well as her
sacrifice, would have been in vain.

An optimistic reading of L'Etoile noire suggests that the relationship
between Suzanne and Sidonie resembles the difference between a
fictional text (which can always be read as a contribution to history)
and a critical piece (which can always be seen as a translation, an
interpretation, a transmission). Like a critic, Suzanne has limited
power over a canon. Like Suzanne (who, after all, is a teacher in
L'Etoile noire), a professor in a department of literature takes the
responsibility to recommend certain texts and encourages students
and colleagues to read them. In much the same way, Suzanne
functions like a pedagogue and a historiographer: by helping Sidonie
to write her story and by helping her distribute her narrative, she
operates a selection which, in the long run, empowers Sidonie's
story at the expense of all the narratives to which she did not
contribute. Her power is that of the translator who lends her own
voice to another author. Even if the translation is never transparent,
she allows readers from other countries to have access to a voice
which would otherwise remain inaudible. Her mastery of the other's
language is a source of subversion even if it condemns her to
unavoidable moments of complicity.

Suzanne's role as a silent historian remains problematic and
ambiguous but her collaboration with Sidonie turns L'Etoile noire into
a complex exploration of the relationship between failure and
success, theory and practice, opposition and fiction. The novel
retains the liberatory aspects of counter-histories while addressing
some of the concerns expressed by critics like Veeser and Eagleton.
Collaboration and alternation, as exemplified by the relationship
between Sidonie and Suzanne, provide the elements of an answer to
people whose history has been suppressed and also to their allies
who do not wish to usurp their right to speak for themselves.
Speaking for the other may appear to be the most logical strategy to
those who refuse to contract 'natural' alliances with the powers that
be. Veeser states for example that:

To avoid a demoralizing stand-off between New Historicists and
postcolonial studies, literary critics will need to adopt the role of the
subaltern. The subaltern, a non-commissisoned officer – occupies a middling place. (Veeser 1991, 10)

But the desire to 'adopt the role of the subaltern' is never innocent since it does not avoid the pitfall of representation: most theorists are painfully aware that if they yield to the temptation of speaking for the victim, what gets told is not the victim's story.[10] One may wonder indeed if there is such a thing as a 'non-commissioned officer'. For Veeser, the 'non-commissioned officier' is comparable to the 'factory foreman' who occupies a 'middling place' between the workers and the management. But the idea that the go-between will necessarily find him or herself on the 'subaltern's' side will probably seem a utopian and unrealistic position to those who have found out the hard way that 'métissage' is not always synomynous with economic, political and ideological empowerment. Suzanne never claims the ambiguous title of 'subaltern' as some kind of trophy of innocence. She never tries to 'adopt' a given identity (she never compares herself to a Jew, a black or a homosexual), nor does she 'adopt' the role of the victim. Her ambiguous status is a demoralizing reminder that, as critics and readers, we may desperately try to speak for the 'subaltern' only to find out that it is impossible to strip oneself of one's privileges, including that of being heard, of having a public. Suzanne does not try to be more of a 'subaltern' than the system forces her to be: she accepts taking advantage of what she knows in order to infiltrate the camp's structure. Perhaps her position of oppositional duplicity and bilingualism will not be totally unfamiliar to those who work within academic circles and who, at night, are visited by nightmarish regrets of failed activism, of betrayal and complicity. Suzanne does choose an in-between position and she is perfectly aware that this entails a certain amount of impure contact with the enemy. She is a mediator, neither innocent nor glamorous. And the notebook remains signed by Sidonie.[11]

## Notes

1 Concentration camp survivors seem to have been confronted with two very different forms of silence. The self-imposed 'amnesia' mentioned by the main character of Hélène de Montferrand's *Journal de Suzanne*, partly explains why the story of what prisoners went through remains unsaid, untold and untellable. To this amnesia was added a generalized form of 'deafness' which Jean-François Lyotard aptly describes at the beginning of *Le Différend*. As Simone Weil puts it: 'Dès que nous sommes rentrés nous avons cherché à parler. Mais nul n'a voulu entendre' [As soon as we came back, we tried to talk, but nobody would listen] ('Le retour des déportés', Montreynaud 1989, 343).

2 Compared with the enormous amount of literature produced by canonical authors during and after the Second World War, one finds very few novels about the specific situation of The French West Indies during that period. It would be interesting to compare L'Etoile noire to Raphaël Confiant's Le Nègre et l'amiral (the title refers to 'l'amiral Robert', the representative of the Vichy government in the French Antilles) in which women's perspectives remain marginal.

3 See Aimé Césaire's La Tragédie du Roi Christophe or the character of Delgrès in L'Isolé Soleil by Daniel Maximin.

4 Among the rich collection of recent texts published on or around this unresolved question, see especially Shoshana Felman's work on testimonial narratives (Felman and Laub, 1992), Colin Davis's study of secrecy in Wiesel's work (Davis, 1994) and Lawrence Kritzman's Auschwitz and After: Race, Culture and 'the Jewish Question' in France (1995).

5 See Michel de Certeau's The Practice of Everyday Life and Pierre Bourdieu and Jean-Claude Passeron's La Reproduction.

6 Can it be said that Foucault, at the beginning of Discipline and Punish gives us a 'lovingly detailed' account of Damien's death? Is there no difference between Discipline and Punish and La Question (a book published during the Algerian war and which sought to expose the methods used by the supposedly civilized French army to 'restore order' in the colony)? Would it be useful to put what we usually refer to as 'pornography' and photographs brought back by journalists who 'cover' armed conflicts in the same category (assuming that I refrain from ascribing moral blame to any given practice)?

7 'Esprit juif et esprit allemand', Esprit. Mai 1979 (5) (quoted by Taguieff 1987, 487).

8 I understand de Certeau's distinction between 'tactic' and 'strategy' to mean that a strategy implies a larger scheme, an overall objective. A strategy may be acceptable even if it goes against the ideals embodied by the overall objective, precisely because one can ascribe a positive value to the new order one has in mind. But in L'Etoile noire, Sidonie's antisemitism or homophobia are not articulated as the only possible strategies given the circumstances.

9 For a relationship between voicelessness and spying, see Marlene Philip's 'The Absence of Writing or How I Almost Became A Spy' in Out of the Kumbla.

10 See for example Spivak's much quoted essays 'Subaltern Studies: Deconstructing Historiography' and 'A Literary Representation of the Subaltern: A Woman's Text from the Third World', in In Other Worlds, Essays in Cultural Politics (197–221 and 241–68). See also Nancy K. Miller's 'Feminist Confessions' in Getting Personal (x–xix). Miller refers to 'a certain overloading in cultural criticism of the rhetorics of representativity (including feminism's) – the incantatory recital of the 'speaking as a's and the imperialisms of 'speaking for's' (Miller 1991, x).

11 I want to thank Callaloo for permission to reprint this chapter which appeared as 'Michèle Maillet's L'Etoile noire: Historian's Counter-History and Translator's Counter Silence', in Callaloo 16.1 (1993): 192–212.

## Reading a recipe book in bed or the de-appropriation of feminine work

> On mange beaucoup et bien. J'engraisse à vue d'ail. (Colette)[1]
>
> Pas de restaurants. Moyen de se consoler: lire des livres de cuisine. (Baudelaire)
>
> [No restaurants. Consolation: read cookbooks]

If my readers intuitively agree that the spy or the passer or the interpreter belong to the category of infiltrators, they may be less convinced that the figure of the cook need to resort to tactical leaking or seepage. Cooking, however, like any other cultural practice, is related to specific genres of discourse such as the cookbook, the recipe, or the feast narrative. But since the processing of food is heavily dependent on the way in which each culture or each community imagines gender, cooking is a strictly mapped territory within which infiltrators are likely to find new paths. Encoding a recipe as an infiltrator requires the knowledge of which categories are celebrated or constantly recreated around food, and a desire to break free from such rules.

Cookbooks are easy to identify, easy to classify, easy to describe. They can hardly be confused with novels or books of poems, in fact, they are neatly separated from the realm of fiction and narratives. Recipes follow strict rules, they belong to a very rigidly defined cultural genre. Like fixed poetic forms, they must feature a number of mandatory elements, although even the most meticulously written recipe will lack the prestige and respect granted to a sonnet. It could be said that in order to write a poem or a cooking recipe, one already needs to refer to an implicit meta-recipe (the 'know-how' or law of the genre). For culinary purposes, however, the meta-recipe does not belong to the rarefied ether of high culture. And yet, a familiarity with recipes is not the exclusive domain of popular culture either. In fact, the genre of the recipe, as we know it in Europe, cuts across social classes. Not that one's self-perceived or imposed class identity is irrelevant, and does not produce difference in writing or reading practices, but, unlike other cultural items, recipes are not thought of either as an exclusively popular pastime or as a strictly intellectual pursuit. In the same way as rock-and-roll and rap music or harlequin romances tend to be associated with popular culture, classical poetry or philosophy supposedly demand initiation rites and the conducive environment provided by college education. If, like some manifestations of popular culture, recipes are sometimes denied the status of art or literature, they will not, however, be perceived as incomprehensible, alienating or aggressively disruptive even by extremely conservative thinkers who assume that it is a moral duty to protect oneself from vulgarity and nonsense. On the other hand, I doubt that intellectuals who object to popular art being treated with disrespect, would view recipes as exclusionary and elitist.

When I think about recipes, I imagine little pieces of scrap paper, or index cards stacked in plastic or wooden boxes, I hear the voices of women, grown-up women, rarely men. I also see publications, magazines, or books, old crumbling books written by seventeenth-century famous characters. A recipe is always potentially detachable, its borders are so obvious. Any reader knows a recipe when he or she sees one because they easily recognize the list of ingredients, the references to local measures of weight, volumes and time. They expect to find a series of action verbs in the imperative which usually constitute the core of a recipe.

### 'Consultable' versus 'readable' texts

Not only is the structure of a recipe visible, but such texts encode the way in which they wish to be read: as soon as we have identified a recipe, it becomes obvious what it wants from us. It would take some severe cultural incompetence or estrangement to imagine that one is supposed to climb on stage and read it out loud like a tirade from a classical tragedy or a poem. We know that recipes are not meant to be performed like plays, or even read like novels, one page after another, until the end of the book is in sight. A recipe is a set of instructions which requires action: we are supposed to engage in a dialogue with the recipe by responding to the orders. Unlike novels, a recipe does not implicitly wonder whether it will have any consequences in the real world: it invites us to 'take', 'shred', 'cut', various objects and I don't think that we spend much time objecting to the fact that we are not being asked to 'think about what we have just done' or to 'take a five-minute break' to 'oppose the authority of the recipe'.

A visible structure and implicit reading instructions are not exceptional characteristics. In fact, I would like to suggest that recipes share such features with a whole set of other texts belonging to what I will call the 'to-be-consulted' category or 'consultable texts'. One does not normally consult a novel, or a poem, but one cannot read a telephone book (unless one is an infiltrator). Recipes have a lot in common with the set of instructions one finds on the package of a brand-new machine, with a calendar, with encyclope-dias, but also with plane tickets and parking tickets. Although I used to perceive these objects as completely unrelated, I now suspect that they constitute a powerful and mostly unquestioned field of prac-tices, a discursive universe whose frontiers will tempt infiltrators as much as national and linguistic borders. The 'to-be-consulted' literature is a universe of printed matter whose sole purpose is to give us orders, even if each genre has its own rhetoric. It would be very easy to rewrite a plane ticket as a culinary recipe. For example: 'go to the airport, make sure to be there two hours ahead of time, put out your cigarette if you smoke, check in your luggage, take a seat, don't keep your brief-case on your lap, etc'. Strangely enough, even if we are generally impatient with authoritarian structures, we may accept these demands quite willingly, probably because the list of orders masquerades as services or favours: customers are free to browse through a mail-order catalogue, a train timetable, and such texts carefully cultivate the impression that they provide us with a piece of information to which we would not otherwise have access. The same remark applies to the new generation of computerized help manuals or 'how to' videos. I suppose I trust and obey recipes because I am convinced that I would fail to cook an acceptable meal without them.

And, as my gratitude and respect for the cookbook increase, two worlds emerge which I slowly recognize as the ideal infiltrational situation: the consultable and readable realms. In the case of the recipe, the distinction between the 'consultable' and the 'readable' text does not emerge out of some cultural void: I suggest that the

split reinforces other major cultural categories, such as the opposition between orality and literacy (to paraphrase Walter Ong's title),
between the feminine and the masculine, between labour and
creation.[2]

Although each generalizing statement is likely to spawn a specific
counter-example, I don't suppose that I have to demonstrate the
following proposition: a published recipe, in the 1990s is (still)
imagined as a text consumed primarily by a female public, and this
intended audience is also perceived as the student listening to the
master, the amateur seeking to learn from the professional or expert.
On the other side of the spectrum, stands the author of the cookbook
and, once again, images are associated with a function: I imagine a
chef, photographed in a public kitchen (in a restaurant or a hotel).
The chef is a man, he is tall, he cannot be skinny, he is probably
white unless the cookbook capitalizes on the appeal of 'exotic'
cuisine, he looks very successful and respectable, and, in case we
have missed these signals, he is decked with the unmistakable white
hat, the powerful symbol of culinary expertise, and a degree in good
taste. The only masculine figure tolerated among pots and pans
without suffering from social giggles and innuendoes, the chef
embodies the distinction between recipe readers, amateurs, housewives, women, and haute cuisine, professionals, powerful artists,
men.

Writing a cookbook has little to do with the daily routine of meal
preparation associated with the archetypal housewife of the 1950s.
Published recipes are also a testimony to the hierarchical barrier
between what Revel calls 'cuisine paysane' (home cooking) and
culinary art. 'Cuisine paysanne' evokes popular traditions, a set of
almost unformulated habits and know-how. 'Culinary art' owes a lot
to the mystically natural 'cuisine paysanne', but it also despises its
lack of sophisticated good taste and self-reflexive philosophy. As
Revel puts it:

l'histoire de la gastronomie est avant tout celle de la gastronomie savante,
car c'est elle qui a laissé le plus de traces écrites. Les grands livres de cuisine
sont évidemment le fruit de la recherche, de l'invention, ou le reflet d'un
changement et non du train-train des moeurs. (Revel 1979, 34)

[the history of gastronomy is above all the history of erudite gastronomy
which has left more written traces. Great cookbooks are obviously the result
of research, invention or the mirror of change rather than of the routine of
daily customs.]

The figure of the 'great chef' is thus strongly connected with the world of written and published recipes. He is the representative of artistic or creative cuisine. The non-professional cook is a woman who spends all morning in the kitchen, whose lesser expertise is a matter of experience and 'peasant' knowledge, and she is the 'natural' consumer of cookbooks written by professionals. When I think of someone reading a recipe, a visual scene forms in my mind: I see a female character, leaning over the counter, following the recipe line by line. She is about to experiment with a new dish, which she intends to serve to her family, or perhaps to her guests.

Even if western cultures do not necessarily recognize themselves in Lévi-Strauss's structuralist analysis, his vision of women as the agents responsible for the transformation of raw food (nature) into cooked meal (culture) is not entirely meaningless. Food-related activities remain assigned according to gender-specific criteria, men and women are given specific tasks according to preconceived rules which only a small (modern? progressive? young?) portion of the population consider interchangeable. If men still light the charcoal at a barbecue, is it because it is 'dirty' therefore 'unfeminine', is it because women have prepared everything else and expect men to chip in at last, is it because the fire is the last element remotely connected to hunting? In *Consuming Passions*, Peter Farb and George Armagelos suggest for example that the way in which food is not only transformed but also exchanged is always gendered:

Eating is intimately connected with sex roles, since the responsibility for each phase of obtaining and preparing a particular food is almost always allotted according to sex. (Farb 1980, 5)

Since the preparation of the meal in the 'real' world is reflected in, or reinforced (if not created) by cultural archives, it is probably not surprising that literature and culture fantasize food along the lines of gender distinctions. While the professional writer of recipes, whose white silhouette occupies the cover of expensive cookbooks, is often fantasized as a man, another world of cooking exists, a world populated by imaginary women, among whom narrated recipes circulate like gossip, as part of daily conversations. In this feminine universe, recipes are hastily jotted down on a piece of paper and they finish their career in a wastepaper basket, or in a file box, examples of the existence of a sub-culture of unpublished recipes. A form of knowledge, which one could call 'oral cuisine', is thus transmitted

between mothers and daughters, between friends, between generations, and collections of unwritten recipes, not unlike the secret
initiation rites of certain sects, weave a network of complicities,
loyalties, competitions between women.[3] Home cooking, even when
shamelessly imitated by published authors of 'culinary art', is still
treated as an essentially popular and feminine province.

A system which distinguishes between the male writer of 'savante'
gastronomy and the supposedly feminine realm of home cooking
begs for infiltrational practices, and in this chapter, I wonder how
the two supposedly different domains are inscribed and kept separate. Keeping in mind that a cookbook also belongs to the category
of the 'to-be-consulted' manual, I want to examine which forces an
infiltrator will encounter when trying to disrupt the clean symmetry
between oral recipes and published cookbooks, great chefs and
female cooks, readable texts and consultable sets of instructions.
More specifically, how does one infiltrate the word of written
recipes when one is a woman and, when infiltration does happen,
how are the parameters of the genre of the recipe and the system of
address modified?

In his preface to Brillat-Savarin's *Physiologie du goût*, Roland Barthes
writes: 'Mythologiquement, la nourriture est une affaire d'hommes;
la femme n'y prend part qu'à titre de cuisinière ou de servante'
[From a mythological point of view, food is men's business; women
only participate as cooks or servants] (11, my translation). As a
result, the cook or servant becomes an infiltrator whenever she is
involved in writing (or rewriting) texts which would otherwise
present themselves as a set of orders and advice addressed to
(female?) readers. We also infiltrate whenever we break the narrative
contract between the recipe and its submissive audience: what
happens if I decide to 'read' recipes like poems or novels or plays
instead of 'trying' them? If one infiltrates written recipes, could it be
that they will stop resembling consultable texts, or parking tickets?

In *The Practice of Everyday Life*, Michel de Certeau insists that we
should move away from the definition of writing as production and
reading as consumption. He argues against the idea that there is a
metaphorical equivalent between the two pairs of concepts (writing
and reading, production and consumption).[4] Infiltrators, however,
may not have enough power or energy to confront this 'binominal
set' head-on and may choose, instead, to take for granted that some
societies not only valorize production at the expense of consump-

tion, but will also view all the activities equated with consumption as equally suspect. Consumption is the passive version of production, and reading is the passive equivalent of writing. The pattern seems logical enough, at least as long as the category of gender does not come into play.

When the housewife tries a recipe, she moves from the book to the real world, from reading to acting, from a practice often confused with leisure and idleness, to the realm of hard work and craftswomanship. When she 'applies' the advice and instructions found in the recipe, the female cook should logically enjoy the consideration granted to those who build, those who make, at least in those circles where the adroit craftsman would be praised and where doubts regarding the social value of the romantic poet would be expressed. But the passage from the beautifully illustrated glossy cookbook to the messy counter smeared with spilled sauces and vegetable peelings somehow does not count as the entrance into the world of production. Even when the meal is finished and handed over to the guests who will not fail to show their appreciation, the cook does not become a cultural producer, not even an artist.

Japanese or Chinese cuisine, emphasizing aesthetically pleasing arrangements and elaborate decoration of dishes, seems excessive and over-sophisticated to our untrained cultural appetites. In a civilized (or colonizing) attempt to tolerate the other's art, we find such dishes 'beautiful', and sometimes we even go as far as promoting this cuisine to the enviable status of fine art. We start describing a food arrangement like a painting or a bouquet, like a sculpture, and we start wondering if we can consume such a work of art without committing some gross sacrilege, or worse, a tactless cultural blunder. Perhaps such meticulous sculptures are not meant to be eaten, they should be admired, framed, put in a museum.

But, when the cook is so successful that her meal is almost granted the status of art, her creation remains a fragile and temporary achievement which exhausts itself in its consumption. While the writer of a book worries that his or her book will remain on bookshelves, untouched, unread, the cook may have mixed feelings about the literal consumption of her work: once eaten, the meal disappears from the realm of the tangible at the same time as the cook's signature is erased. One could argue that, just like a devoured cake, a consumed book does not leave any trace, that the object on the shelf will not exist until someone starts telling stories about it. In

the same way, a meal survives in the guests' memory, in commemorative narratives. Alphonse Daudet's 'Les trois messes basses', or
Michel Tournier's Le Médianoche amoureux are cases in point. But the
book as object is endowed with enough prestige for us to forget the
fact that when it is exposed on a shelf, it does not serve its purpose
as a literary item, as a 'great book'. The devoured dish is never saved,
even as trophy or trace. All that remains is what we call leftovers and
dirt to be cleaned off, further erased. As a result, the meal does not
make it as a work of art. For Simone de Beauvoir, this form of non-
production, of non-creation is the very definition of feminine work
which 'n'aboutit pas même à une création durable'(Le Deuxième Sexe
74) [The worst of it all is that this labour does not even tend toward
the creation of anything durable (Second Sex 509)]. She sees the female
cook as a depressed artist, frustrated by the futility of her attempts,
hoping to find a way of investing her cooking with the glamorous
attributes of more lasting forms of creation. Beauvoir's cook is a
wistful Parnassian poet, forever wishing to confer upon her cakes the
solidity of stone, the eternity of sculptures, of the printed word. Her
efforts are slightly pathetic, and always thwarted.

Contemplant le gâteau qu'elle sort du four, elle soupire: c'est vraiment
dommage de le manger! ... Dès que les choses servent, elles sont salies ou
détruites: elle est tentée, on l'a vu déjà, de les soustraire à tout usage; celle-
ci conserve les confitures jusqu'à ce que la moisissure les envahisse; celle-là
ferme le salon à clé. Mais on ne peut pas arrêter le temps; les provisions
attirent les rats, les vers s'y mettent. ... l'étoffe comestible est aussi
équivoque que les monstres en viande de Dali: elle paraissait inerte,
inorganique mais les larves cachées l'ont métamorphosé en cadavre. (Le
Deuxième Sexe 74)
[She sighs as she contemplates the perfect cake just out the oven: 'it's a
shame to eat it!' ... When things are used they are soiled and destroyed –
we have seen how she is tempted to save them from being used; she keeps
preserves until they get moldy; she locks up the parlor. But the time passes
inexorably; provisions attract rats; they become wormy. ... edible material
is as equivocal as Dali's [meat monsters]: it seems inert, inorganic, but
hidden larvae have changed it into a cadaver. (Second Sex 508)][5]

The access to recipe writing may thus be all the more meaningful as
the cake is eminently perishable. The written trace and the leftover
crumbs have neither the same function nor the same status. The
recipe is no more susceptible to decay than other books, it is what
remains intact after the cake has been consumed. Whoever uses a
recipe is always vying with some indestructible and seemingly

everlasting original creation of which she can only make copies. The text of the recipe precedes her concrete achievement and also outlives it, taking its place. Even if we theoretically value the creative aspect of cooking, the recipe somehow gets the credit in the end.

This phenomenon would not be so problematic if anyone had the option to stop baking cakes and start writing recipes instead, but the two activities are not easily distinguished except by cultural habits which create asymmetrical categories: the text of the recipe and its audience belong to two different worlds. Not only is the chef a professional male involved in the history of gastronomy, but the feminized user of recipes is unlikely to have a history at all, since her amateurish status condemns her to the systematic destruction of all the tangible evidence of her potentially original work.

This imbalance between the producer and the consumer of recipes reminds me of another genre of discourse familiar to students, professors, and readers of Foucault: the genre of the examination.[6] In the case of the recipe, the creator divulges his secrets to a few privileged disciples, he passes his knowledge on to educated consumers who are capable of applying his principles but who are not necessarily called upon as inventive co-creators. A recipe functions like an examination such as is described by Foucault in *Surveiller et punir*.[7] Written by the master for his students (identified as beginners or advanced cooks), the recipe is a unit combining a lesson and a test: it is both an attempt at transmitting knowledge, and an implicit request to do as well as the professional. The recipe is given (or sold or exchanged) as a valuable piece of information, but it is also the text of an examination for each housewife who intends to try it ; she will either pass or fail the test. If the meal is a failure, as in the case of the examination, no one will ever be able to determine if the recipe was 'bad' or if it was badly 'executed', if the knowledge passed on by the teacher was decontextualized, inappropriate, obsolete, useless, or if the housewife did not apply herself, if she lacked know-how, intelligence, flexibility, interpretive skills, etc.

Late twentieth-century recipes tend to play down their didactic aspect and refrain from overtly resorting to the rhetoric of examinations. Instead, they speak the language of desire, or invoke health. Recipes are illustrated with pages of glossy photographs representing appetizing meals. Our advertisement-ridden culture probably teaches us that it is more efficient to couch instructions in the language of temptation. But if we look at seventeenth-century cookbooks, written at a time when literature itself was not afraid to *instruire et plaire* [teach and entertain], we find that they tended to emphasize their roles as instructors. The word *enseigner* (teach) appears in most of the cookbooks titles or subtitles: *Le Cuisinier françois*, Varennes's famous treatise, one of the fetishized books which came to symbolize the standards of a certain French cuisine from 1651 to the beginning of the nineteenth century, bears a significant sub-title: 'enseignant la manière de bien apprester et assaisonner toutes sortes de viandes grasses et maigres, légumes, patisseries, et autres mets qui se servent tant sur les Tables des Grands que des particuliers'. [teaching the manner of properly preparing all kinds of meat, fat and lean, vegetables, pastries, and other dishes fit both for Lords' tables and the public]. The *Pastissier françois*, published anonymously in 1653, also presents itself as a book 'où est enseigné la manière de faire toute sorte de Pastisserie, très-utile à toutes personnes ...'. [in which is taught the manner of baking all kinds of pastries, very useful to everyone ...]. As for Bonnefons, author of *Délices de la campagne* (1654), he describes his work as the 'Suitte du *Jardinier françois* où est enseigné à préparer pour l'usage de la vie tout ce qui croist sur la Terre, & dans les Eaux ...' [in which one is taught how to prepare, for the purpose of life, everything that grows on the Earth and under Water ...].[8]

At the end of the twentieth century, the rhetoric has changed: the authors do not want to 'teach' us how to cook, they want us to 'be healthy', 'be fit' 'feel and look good', but the concepts of failure and success have not disappeared. Like students, cooks receive a grade at home: if the meal is a failure, even if the cook suggests that the recipe is to blame, she will be suspected of poor judgement. After all, she should have recognized that the recipe was 'bad' before carrying out its instructions. Unless individual cooks start comparing their experiences, unless a collective form of counter-discourse disrupts the lonely confrontation between the student and the test, the recipe-writer or teacher is not held responsible.

Once the meal is ready to serve, not only is the cook responsible for the guests' pleasure, but neither her own work nor her own pleasure is recognized. The labour involved in the preparation of the food tends to disappear from the scenario and even when the cook herself partakes of the meal, her status as a consumer remains ambiguous. In *Female Desires*, Rosalind Coward suggests that women displace oral satisfaction on to the pleasure of serving others. She agrees with Barthes and Lévi-Strauss that women's roles in the elaboration of meals symbolically reinforce the social and economic divisions between genders: men provide raw materials and, in return, they expect to enjoy services. The 'successful' dish becomes a sign of gratefulness and acquiescence to the system. Although she never enjoys the prestige of professional chefs, a good recipe reader is not primarily an educated consumer: she should be capable of following instructions but she is not really expected to enjoy the finished product. Although the recipe overtly claims to be 'teaching' her how to cook (for a generic eater including herself), it implicitly overemphasizes the guests' pleasure: the recipe teaches how to give and serve. While the professional chef usually receives a respectable salary, the woman who cooks for her family tends to present the meal as a gift: not only is her cake about to be devoured, but her work is minimized (it is unsightly, no one is interested in the preliminary stages). Before the first guest arrives, all traces of her labour are supposed to have been cleared away.[9]

Cooking food and presenting it beautifully is an act of servitude. It is a way of expressing affection through a gift. In fact, the preparation of a meal involves intensive domestic labour, the most devalued labour in this society. That we should aspire to produce perfectly finished and presented food is a symbol of a willing and enjoyable participation in servicing other people. (Coward 1985, 103)

Coward examines the photographs which often accompany recipes in a book or a magazine and argues that the photographer takes precedence over the cook. When a cook prepares a dish which will be used as example and illustration, the photographer will probably conclude that it is seriously flawed: it will not constitute a good photographer's subject. The *Focal Encyclopedia of Photography* (another compilation of recipes) states that 'the photographer learns by experience that certain foods do not photograph well'. When such is the case, 'he must be able to suggest reasonable substitutes'. Consequently, as Coward is prompt to notice, the photographer's intervention results in a paradoxical image:

Virtually all meals shown in these photos are actually inedible. If not actually made of plaster, most are sprayed or treated for photographing. How ironic to think of the perfect meal as destined for the dustbin. (Coward 1985, 104)

Images of inedible food photographed as representatives of ideal meals further contribute to erasing the cook's labour: like the recipe, the photograph suggests that only the ultimate stage of the cooking process is worth representing. The picture insists on perfection and suggests that all traces of previous labour are taboo.

A meal should really look like the pictures. And that's how the images produce complicity in our subordination. We aim at giving others pleasure by obliterating the traces of our labour. (Coward 1985, 104)

Reading recipes does not appear as a very rewarding activity. It occupies a strange, ambiguous slot among our cultural definitions of reading, it is neither exactly leisure nor intellectual work. I do not imagine the reader of recipes relaxing on the couch or intensely absorbed in a book among university students in the silence of a study room. Rather, I see a woman standing in front of the counter, glancing at the recipe from time to time while she performs the tasks described on the page, or leafing through a cookbook in an attempt to select a recipe for the next dinner party, or copying down a list of ingredients before going grocery shopping. Although I feel uncomfortable at the generalizing images generated by my imagination, I have trouble inventing other scenarios, other plausible versions. The reader of recipes is reduced to the role of eternal subordinate.

### Infiltrational practices: reading in bed and collecting recipes

On second thoughts, however, there is a very real possibility that the reader's role can be infiltrated and modified: after all, like all visual representations, the photographs occupy an ambiguous place which invites the infiltrator to alter the relationship between the powerful writer of recipes and their powerless user. It presents itself as the origin to be copied, but the reader is not supposed to reproduce it as a picture, and certainly not as an inedible meal to be photographed. These bright pictures of colourful salads or glazed poultry are reminiscent of the 'answers to exercises' one finds at the end of textbooks. The possibility of self-correction does modify the system of the examination even if its basic principles are not undermined. The presence of the photographs also changes the definition of authorship in the sense that we are reminded that the writer of recipes is also (or perhaps first and foremost) a cook himself. As such, he may also suffer from the potential erasure of the labour needed to manufacture the inedible meal. Even if the author of the book did not prepare the food himself, the trace of a certain amount of visible labour is preserved by the photograph, even if preliminary messy cutting, shredding and cooking are forgotten. Even if the picture per se tends to exclude the process of fabrication, it slightly modifies the distinction between written recipe and cooking as work.

Moreover, if these pictures impose a vision of what would be the successful dish, they are themselves representations and, as such, they do not systematically belong to the category of consultable texts: the photograph in the magazine is supposedly a translation, or an embodiment of the recipe, but because it is a graphic representation, its function as a model is complicated. Unlike the recipe, the image cannot be used directly, it needs interpreting, decoding, mediating. Images are narratives rather than a series of commands.

The paradox of the perfect dish destined for the trash-can because no one can eat it reminds me that I can no more represent a meal 'objectively' than any other so-called reality. The photographs of meals raise the same problem as other forms of representation: even the recipe, which presents itself as the origin, is finally displaced by a 'real' meal which both virtually precedes it and constitutes its consecration and transmission. The relationship between the meal and the recipe is as complex as that between the word and the letter, each claiming to be each other's memory, each claiming to be the real, the origin. It is easy to imagine a 'Plato's Pharmacy' of gastronomy (Derrida 1972, 71–197). The recipe is secondary compared to a certain gastronomic virtuality which came before but, on the other hand, it legitimizes itself as a set of instructions one must obey.

We have seen in previous chapters that the more rigidly defined categories are also the most desirable terrain from the infiltrator's point of view. The more visible the set of instructions, the more porous a terrain the cookbook becomes: the recipe so narrowly anticipates its docile reader's reaction that it is easy to thwart its implicit request for work and to indulge in subversive reading activities. Confronted with a text which gives her a series of simple orders, the female reader is almost invited to transgress. Coward herself suggests an interesting infiltrational reading practice for recipes: reading a cookbook in bed.

Few activities it seems rival relaxing in bed with a good recipe book. Some indulge in full colour pictures of gleaming bodies of Cold Mackerel Basquaise lying invitingly on a bed of peppers, or perfectly formed chocolate mousse topped with mounds of cream. (Coward 1985, 103)

Although Coward's formulation indicates that the visual part of the cookbook is the most easily infiltrated by the reader's gaze, she does propose a way of 'reading' recipes which has nothing to do with consulting texts. 'Indulging' in colour pictures cannot produce the kind of anguish experienced by individuals who eagerly search on their guests' faces, the transitive pleasure which takes the place of their own oral *jouissance*. Barthes states that:

Il rôde autour de la table une vague pulsion scopique: on regarde (on guette?) sur l'autre les effets de la nourriture, on saisit comment le corps travaille de l'intérieur; tels ces sadiques qui jouissent de la montée d'un émoi sur le visage de leur partenaire, on observe les changements du corps qui se nourrit bien. (Barthes 1975, 10)

[Around the table lurks a vaguely scopic function: one looks at (watches for?) the effects of food on others, one captures the signs of how the body works from the inside; like the sadists whose jouissance is caused by the rise of emotion on their partner's face, we observe the changes undergone by the well-nourished body.]

In the *Second Sex*, however, Simone de Beauvoir interprets the 'scopic' function in terms of alienation and servitude: Barthes's non-gendered subject becomes the female cook and the sadist's gaze is explained as a need for reassurance and the impossibility of enjoying food or nurturing herself:

C'est seulement dans la bouche de ses convives que le travail de la cuisinière trouve sa vérité; elle a besoin de leurs suffrages; elle exige qu'ils apprécient ses plats, qu'ils en reprennent; elle s'irrite s'ils n'ont plus faim: au point qu'on ne sait plus si les pommes de terre frites sont destinées au mari ou le mari aux pommes de terre frites. (Beauvoir 1949, 75)

[The validity of the cook's work is to be found only in the mouths of those at her table; she needs their approbation, demands that they appreciate her dishes and call for second helpings; she is upset if they are not hungry, to the point that one wonders whether the fried potatoes are for her husband or her husband for the fried potatoes. (Beauvoir 1952, 509)]

If the cook reads recipe books in bed, she alters the rapport between the recipe and its intended addressee, she interrupts the endless chain of pleasure displacement which sometimes borders on the grotesque (the husband being for the fried potatoes). It may seem silly at first to be reading ten pages of a recipe book every night before going to sleep, as silly as reading a telephone directory, or a timetable, or a table of algorithms. But it would let the cook reappropriate her own pleasure by allowing her to enjoy the spectacle of food prepared by others for others. She does not have to subordinate her pleasure to that of her guests, she short-circuits servitude, and redefines recipes: instead of a series of orders given by a gastronomic authority, the recipe becomes a fictional universe to be voyeuristically enjoyed.

Describing the kind of pleasure one is likely to experience in the face of 'l'énoncé gastronomique' [gastronomic statement] (1975, 24), Barthes notices that food always entails the presence of what he calls a 'perversion' ('l'exercice d'un désir qui ne sert à rien, tel celui du corps qui s'adonne à l'amour sans idée de procréation' [acting upon a useless desire, such as a body indulging in love-making outside the purpose of procreation][10]). Barthes would probably describe the contemplation of pictures in a cookbook as a form of perversion since, instead of producing a dish, the reader draws her pleasure from addressing a recipe as a text. The execution of the meal is replaced by the *jouissance* of reading. Coward even talks about 'Food pornography'.[11] But in *Female Desires*, this word 'pornography' is used to criticize a system which whets the female readers' appetite while systematically denying her the right to satisfy her desire (consumed by women, food will turn into aesthetically unpleasant fat cells, not to mention that she will be suspected of self-centredness if she caters to her own desires). Pictures are a form of 'pornography'. They both tempt and prohibit, offer and refuse.

But when a woman enjoys the recipe and the photographs for their own sake, the fetishization of food is not reinvested in the guests' satisfaction. The woman enjoying an imaginary feast infiltrates both the 'pornographic' and the 'scopic' functions described by Coward and Barthes. The potential cook replaces the guest with the mental image of her object of desire. A 'pornographic' or 'perverse' reading of the recipe allows the emergence of a form of feminine infiltrational gaze which takes advantage of the interdiction to satisfy her desire for forbidden food. This feminine gaze, that of the woman lying in bed devouring a cookbook, implicitly disempowers the recipe, because it temporarily obliterates other visions: a woman standing on her feet, peeling potatoes in front of a recipe book propped up on the counter; or a host, searching her family's face for the correct reaction of pleasure; or the housewife, disappointed by the inherent fragility of her work but determined to erase the traces of the preparations before the guests appear.

Another infiltrational use of cookbooks involves collecting and the slow collective or individual creation of a personal museum. The female cook then adopts the strategy of the historian, of the librarian.[12] Instead of treating the text like an expert one consults, or an order one executes, the collector distances herself from the recipe as individual text and indulges in another form of 'perversion': hoarding, preserving, collecting. The devoured cake is avenged by drawers full of disempowered recipes. Whether one casually throws recipes into an old shoe-box or meticulously copies them on alphabetically arranged index cards, the genre of the recipe is infiltrated and reinvented: a new canon emerges. When so many consultable texts are stored, each set of orders loses power. When recipes are accumulated, each recipe writer's authority is relativized: the unrealistic quantity of potential orders suggests that, statistically, very few recipes will indeed be executed. Although the collector does not overtly transgress the law of the genre, she is not a slave to utilitarian uses of her pleasure: when she clips recipes from magazines and newspapers, puts them away in some more or less secret box, when she dutifully writes down cooking tips offered by TV show hosts and relatives, the famous chef's recipes add to a body of fragmented and partial knowledge, the anonymous, collective body of an unrecognized written culinary tradition. The new canon is neither *grande cuisine* nor *cuisine populaire*, it is neither oral gossip nor published matter, it is an infiltrated space where gender and literary paradigms are reorganized. Closer to bricolage and collage than to culinary 'art', this practice grants the infiltrator the power and freedom of the critic: certain recipes will be annotated, or perhaps a date will be added, or a comment, a suggestion. A collection is not so easily claimed: its signature is relative and incomplete, at best provisional. It is difficult to ascertain what place such an infiltrated compilation occupies among other anthologies: how does one establish the relative importance of the different 'authors' turned infiltrators? When is such *bric-à-brac* publishable?

In other domains, the system resists the infiltrational tendency of disparate contents. For example, museums carefully reestablish hierarchies and differences between the collection and each visitor as potential collector. A whole array of symbolic barriers isolates the work of art, increases or creates the prestige of the displayed object by suitably belittling the visitor–consumer.

Personal museums of recipes do not confer the status of art on their collection. The knowledge stored in the private sphere of shoeboxes is usually of an ambiguous and heterogeneous nature: the box or drawer accommodates recipes but also a tip on how to remove stains, to take care of leather garments, to polish silver. If the collection has been alive for more than a few years, such tips may already sound quaint and naive. Although they present themselves as timeless practical wisdom, they are marked by the passage of time and their desire for eternity historicizes the collection. The consultable recipe becomes part of an infiltrated autobiography. In those drawers lies the tradition of a feminine audience, half-way between the private and the public sphere. A marginal history of women and their cuisine is thus preserved and can be read as the (Foucauldian) archives of infiltration rather than dismissed as a poor copy of successful and published cookbooks.

Of course, I do not think that the principles of collection and exchange are inherently infiltrational: in fact, when recipes are exchanged between family members, the system may reinforce the respective hierarchical status of each relative, and it functions as an effective way of perpetuating the status quo. And yet, the haphazard accumulation of recipes also questions the authority of the executable text over which the reader has such limited control. I suggest that a collection of recipes infiltrates both the genre of the recipe and the genre of the collection by turning both into interpretable archives, to be read, interpreted and historicized.

And when such a compilation is indeed read and interpreted, taken out of the realm of the private by an editor who wishes to publish the heterogeneous material, then, intriguing and complex cultural phenomena occur. Often, the collection attracts interest by proxy, because its owner was famous as a writer or an actor or a politician. Public recognition seeps into the humble private sphere and illuminates the contents of women's treasure boxes, ironically turning them into everlasting works of art.

Among the books recently published according to this method, two are particularly revealing of the relationship between women, food and writing. The first one, *La Table de George Sand*, is written by Christiane Sand, the last heiress to a feminine dynasty: she is the wife of Aurore Sand's adopted son. We are reminded that Aurore Sand is defined as George Sand's grand-daughter. The blurb on the cover states that Christiane Sand is the last survivor and guardian of the Sands' legacy: 'Depuis la mort de son mari en 1970, c'est sur elle que repose la lourde tâche de conserver le précieux héritage de George Sand' [Since her husband's death in 1970, the heavy burden of preserving George Sand's precious heritage rests on her shoulders].

In the foreword, Christiane Sand presents herself as the reader of an impressive quantity of loosely connected material, accumulated by the Nohant's female dynasty:

Aurore Sand avait pieusement conservé le moindre morceau de papier qui pouvait avoir un rapport avec sa grand-mère ou sa famille. Tous ces documents étaient entassés pêle-mêle dans des boites hétéroclites, dont certaines avaient abrité des chaussures de tous styles et de toutes les époques. … je découvris en les triant, que la publication des recettes de cuisine pourrait apporter une intéressante documentation sur la vie quotidienne de Nohant, d'Aurore de Saxe à Aurore Sand. (9)

[Aurore Sand had piously kept the smallest piece of paper having anything to do with her grandmother or her family. All these documents had been crammed into sundry boxes, some of which had contained shoes of all different styles and from different periods. … When I sorted them out, I discovered that the publication of recipes could provide interesting information about daily life at the castle of Nohant, from Aurore de Saxe to Aurore Sand.]

When Christiane Sand carries out her project, she does place the whole enterprise under the aegis of 'George Sand', a fetishized name whose literary fame is supposed to be both enhanced by revelations about her daily life and to guarantee the value of the collection. As a result, if the memory of a mythical George Sand benefits from the visibility of the book, her figure as a literary star is redefined and relativized by her re-insertion into a continuum of women. George Sand now belongs to a whole gallery of portraits of women which neither history nor literary canon is insisting on keeping alive. Ironically, it is because Aurore Sand so 'piously' and selflessly preserved her grand-mother's heritage that she now infiltrates the story as a (main) character. The details of this infiltration between the categories of the 'recipe' and 'literature', the famous woman and the humble cook, or even immortal (male) authors and dead and forgotten women result in a non-linear book which constantly asks the reader to reassess his or her own notion of what is important, what is meaningful, what is worth publishing and remembering (or quoting in this instance).

On the other hand, George Sand's exceptional fame is relativized when recontextualized within the dynasty of women bearing the same famous name. In fact, despite the commercial appeal provided by the reference to George Sand, the actual contribution of the author of *Indiana* to the corpus of recipes is remarkably slim: her name appears at the bottom of one single recipe for 'Gnocchis' (104). *Noblesse oblige*, the unremarkable text is described as a 'Manuscrit inédit de George Sand' (Unpublished manuscript by George Sand) although it is not clear how the signature of the author functions in this case: we do not know if George Sand created or invented the recipe (although this hypothesis is rather unlikely) we do not know whether she found it or copied it, etc. At this point, it is difficult to say whether literature is infiltrating recipes or if recipes are infiltrating literature: does Sand's fame unfairly spill over a rather boring text or does her presence serve to enhance the other women's creativity and work. One entire double page is devoted to George Sand's 'Gnocchis'. The left side is similar to all the other pages in the book (a printed reproduction of what appeared in the manuscripts or notebooks) but the right side introduces noise into the system by playing with repetition, reproduction, originality and authorship: 'A droite: recette manuscrite de George Sand' (On the right: handwritten recipe by George Sand). The attention to the author's handwriting confirms her literary status but also questions it as a type of slightly ridiculous cult. On the one hand, the double and redoubled presence of the 'Manuscrit inédit de George Sand' increases the prestige of the facsimile, on the other hand, some readers may start wondering if this so-called unpublished manuscript is worth the attention. Sand's contribution to the recipe part of the book appears so negligible that her name on the cover could be resented as a gross and deceptive advertising ploy. But, in the end, I realize that Sand's name is also the much-needed password into the other women's discursive universe of fiches and notebooks. George Sand's name becomes a master key, the unstable and meaningless yet all-powerful infiltrational element the effectiveness of which depends on its duplicity: it is both arbitrary and overdetermined.

In the same way, the presence of Litz, Flaubert, Alexandre Dumas, Balzac, Delacroix, Tourgeniev and Chopin is problematized by their status as guests in the book and at the castle of Nohant. They are summoned because they are canonized but not as canonical writers and musicians. The book isolates them from the recipes by placing them in a separate chapter intitled 'Hôtes et visiteurs', structured like a small-scale encyclopedia the undecidable title of which means either 'guests and visitors' or 'hosts and visitors'. As guests, the famous male creators are honoured, but they are also excluded and marked as outsiders. Only Dumas, faithful to his (ambiguous) reputation as a cookbook writer, contributes one recipe to the last part of *A la Table de George Sand*, and his 'Chou en Garbure' is presented as part of the 'Manuscrit d'Aurore Sand' (Sand 1987, 88).

Instead of focusing on great books and great men, *A la Table de George Sand* concentrates on the intricacies of a whole network of closely related women and in a sense, the book becomes part of the feminine tradition which it celebrates. What Christiane Sand does in this heterogeneous publication resembles what Aurore Sand, the guardian of little pieces of paper, did until her death.

Aurore de Saxe, Lina Sand, and Aurore Sand are all authors, scribes, keepers and interpreters: recipes, in the women's manuscript, are often attributed to others as if they insisted on giving credit to their friends instead of simply appropriating the information and knowledge necessary to use the recipe. The 'Mouton à la Turque' is from the 'Manuscrit d'Aurore' but is described as a 'Recette de Rose Renault' (142), the 'haricot de Mouton', appearing in the 'Manuscrit de Lina Sand', is a 'Recette de Marie Caillaud' (143), the 'Galantine ou Daube' ('Manuscrit d'Aurore Sand') is a 'Recette de Nounou'(148). The authorial privileges are both diluted and reaffirmed by means of short annotations: the titles of recipes are often followed by a critical comment such as 'Bon' 'Très Bon', 'Exquise' (re: 'Sauce Hollandais' 83), or information about the background or the context: the 'Confiture d'Orange' is described as a 'Recette excellente envoyée de Blidah' [Excellent Recipe from Blidah] (214), the 'Suprême au chocolat' is described as a 'Crème pouvant se conserver quelques jours au frais' [a cream that will keep several days in a cool place] (168). Sometimes the annotator and the author are two different persons, and this complicates the collaborative process: The 'Oeufs Farcis', a 'Recette d'Aurore Sand' are marked as 'Bon' by the author but the editor (Christiane Sand) also reports a second comment 'Recette inventée par Aurore' which she attributes to Lina ('La deuxième note est de Lina' 106). Similarly, the 'Recette pour le Curry' belongs to the 'Manuscrit d'Aurore Sand', but it is a 'Recette de M.H. Detouche' and a 'Note de Lina Sand' adds new information: 'Pour manger avec le riz' [Should be eaten with rice] (149). A phenomenon of what one might want to call 'reverse plagiarism' takes place: each woman in turn uses writing as a way of giving credit to other authors. Once used as an infiltrator into the world of publishing, the name of George Sand allows us to explore the world of other women, parents, relatives, friends or servants whose patience and collaborative art turn a collection of recipes into a sociological document. As Christiane Sand puts it, it is:

une intéressante documentation sur la vie quotidienne de Nohant, d'Aurore de Saxe à Aurore Sand. Tous les membres de la famille, en effet, figurent d'une manière ou d'une autre dans ce recueil, ainsi que tous les amis de toutes les générations. (9)

[an interesting documentation on daily life at Nohant, from Aurore de Saxe to Aurore Sand. One way or another, all the members of the family are present in this book, as well as all the friends of all the generations.]

George Sand is not redefined as an underrated author of recipes, but her writing skills do contribute to the interdisciplinary web: relegated to a secondary place, in the margins of the recipe, excerpts from her letters provide biographical details, adding a new layer to the collective authorship and annotation system, and counteracting the myth of the recipe as an anonymous, impersonal and authoritarian genre:

Marie Caillaud est adorable. Elle a une tête angélique et une diction qui prend le coeur d'un bout à l'autre.
G.S à Duvernet. 1958. (132)

[Marie Caillaud is adorable. Her face is angelic and her diction envelops your whole heart.]

Lina Sand. C'est une nature et un type: ça chante à ravir, c'est colère et tendre, ça fait des friandises succulentes pour nous surprendre, et chaque journée de notre phase de récréation est une petite fête qu'elle organise.
George Sand

[Lina Sand. A nature and a type: that little thing sings marvellously, can be angry or tender, makes delicious candy to surprise us, and everyday of our vacation is a little feast which she organizes.]

In the end, the strategic appeal of George Sand's mythical aura both uses and undermines the stereotypical definition of recipes as an authoritarian genre, and her recontextualized texts also enrich the cookbook with new ambiguities, by suggesting that it is amenable to quite varied appropriations. But George Sand is not actively infiltrating the genre itself, she remains in the margins, confined within the boundaries of literature. It would however be interesting to analyse the case of a woman writer who chooses not to separate cookbooks and literature, recipes and fictions, and I would now like to turn to a slightly different example of infiltration: Colette's recipes.

## Writing recipes in bed

In this particular instance, infiltration is achieved by a subtle adaptation of the voyeuristic and interpretive strategies deployed by the woman who reads (and writes) recipes in bed. As usual, this is made possible by the fact that recipes are such recognizable texts: their identity is so strong that it is possible to subvert them without abandoning the genre altogether. If the recipe, as consultable text, can be infiltrated by the reader, it can also be the object of reappropriative writing and infiltrational authoring strategies.

First of all, it is obvious that although the cookbook or the culinary treatise presents itself as an essentially masculine genre, this has never stopped individual women (or at least those who were already transgressing the rule according to which only men write) to publish recipes. Colette has signed a series of recipes in feminine magazines such as *Marie-Claire* and *Vogue* and, eventually, these recipes were reprinted in *Prisons et paradis*. As in the case of George Sand, a woman's literary status preserves the recipe from the fragility of orality and private shoe-boxes, or from the disposable quality of weekly magazines. Once republished in *Prisons et paradis*, Colette's recipes question the distinction between creative work and feminine labour, between labour and writing, between cuisine as art and the recipe as trace, between cuisine and literature and finally between a recipe and a short story.

When compared with other writings, recipes are perceived as inferior forms of literature, they are not even studied, or sold in that category. When the notion of 'recipe' is not contrasted with literature but used within its limits (when it refers to a writing strategy), it is systematically associated with negative connotations: in literature, resorting to 'recipes' is either a parodic stance or a failure. A writer suspected of following 'recipes', will unavoidably be suspected of borderline plagiarism or lack of taste and originality. Yet, the definition of 'styles' or literary genres functions like a reference to a set of implicit rules and I wonder how easy it would be to establish a clear theoretical difference between a literary genre and a culinary recipe.

Until the middle of the century, it was not uncommon for professors of French literature to assign 'pastiches' (which could be defined as following a so-called great writer's recipe).[13] But I don't think that the popularity of the exercise served to rehabilitate recipes:

rather, it underscored the link between fiction, writing, and the system of the examination embedded in the principle of the recipe. Pastiche and parodies often count on their pre-fabricated nature to provoke distance and satirical or burlesque effects. The famous Dadaist manifesto, claiming that a poem can be manufactured by following the specific advice given by a recipe, was precisely affirming, in a highly provocative and critical statement, that it disagreed with the traditional definition of poetry as a text emanating either from an inspired romantic hero, or a determined craftsman's 'perspiration'.

If one follows the Dadaists' 'recipe', the result is a poem whose composition rules are reduced to objective humour and chance. The resulting dadaist poem, however, has a non-creative aspect to it, because it relies on a very systematic method: creating such a poem supposes that one puts blind trust in the principle and the authority of the dadaist recipe and their series of verbs in the imperative only becomes ludic because it pretends to ascribe value to a recipe (a minor and/or feminized genre) at the expense of the mythically overvalued individual creation.

As for the real, literal recipe, it continues to be an object of implicit contempt in the spheres of high literature. Although 'gastronomy' remains associated with luxury and originally with aristocracy, food tends to infiltrate literature as a narrative rather than as a recipe, and only when processed and reinserted into more prestigious literary genres. Gastronomy is a literary theme rather than a literary genre. I am thinking of the long and accurate descriptions of meals in L'Assommoir or of Swann's knowledge of refined seasoning in La Recherche du temps perdu. But neither the recipe itself nor the culinary treatise is literary. In Un Festin en paroles, Jean-François Revel summarizes our prejudices:

Bien qu'en Occident, et particulièrement en France, il ne soit pas mal vu pour un auteur littéraire de montrer qu'il s'intéresse à la gastronomie, il ne serait pas pourtant considéré comme sérieux de sa part d'écrire des traités de cuisine proprement dits. Le Grand Cuisinier d'Alexandre Dumas fait exception, mais Alexandre Dumas n'est pas précisément considéré comme appartenant à la littérature dans ce qu'elle a de plus pur. (143)

[In the Western world, and particularly in France, it is not objectionable for a literary author to show interest in gastronomy, but it would not be considered serious for him to write actual cuisine treatises. Alexandre Dumas' Le Grand Cuisinier, is an exception to the rule, but Alexandre Dumas is not exactly considered as belonging to literature in its purest form.][14]

In other words, great writers (those who write 'pure' literature) will not make the mistake of fooling around in the kitchen, they will not write recipes, and if they do, then they are not great writers. Of course, such circular logic does not account either for Dumas' situation or for other recipe writers like Mallarmé, but the fact that the remark is argumentatively flawed does not make it any less convincing.

To this circular gesture of exclusion treating counter-evidence like further confirmation of the rule, I would like to oppose the texts of *Prisons et paradis* which infiltrate both the rule and the opposition between the exception and the rule. I see these short non-linear vignettes as doubly infiltrational because they both raise recipes to the supposedly superior status of literary genre and resist what, in the recipe, makes it an authoritarian construct: the consultable structure.

Because of their highly self-reflexive quality, certain passages from *Prisons et paradis* emphasize the work involved in the elaboration of a recipe as text by refusing to make the occasion of the writing transparent. Before becoming the sign of someone's culinary expertise, a recipe must be written, composed like a poem or a story. When recontextualized and historicized, the writing process of a recipe is reembodied and demystified: as a result, *Prisons and paradis* openly questions the implicit opposition between the labour involved in the concrete realization of the meal and in the production of the recipe. The supposedly masculine master text is exposed as a version of the supposedly secondary and uncreative reproduction of the recipe.

For instance, the text entitled 'Trente-huit cinq' (38.5, a reference to the temperature of a body suffering from the flu, for example) is a recipe which tells the story of a writer who finally comes to grips with the writing of a recipe after much hesitation and reluctant procrastination. Colette, or the I narrator, is bed-ridden and sick. On one level, 'Trente-huit cinq' is a micro-diary of the few days which she spends in her room, unable to get up. The disease causes a variety of painful symptoms, including a violent repulsion for food which seems to preclude the introduction of a recipe in the middle of the story:

Dîner? Qui a parlé de dîner! Pouah! ... Je viens de perdre, en deux heures de malaise, l'habitude, le dessein, l'envie et le besoin de manger. (362)

[Dinner? Who mentioned eating? Yuk! ... In a couple of hours of sickness, I have just lost the habit, the intention, the desire and the need to eat.]

Both stylistically and thematically, this is almost a non-recipe. The narrator offers us a tale of dis-appetite, of dis-taste and dis-gust.

Lundi. Mauvais, mauvais. Tout est mauvais. L'orange est amère. Amère la tisane sucrée. Amers les bonbons adoucissants. Qui m'a apporté ces bonbons des Borgia, vert poison dont chacun cache un piège glacial de menthol? Tout ce qui s'absorbe par la bouche est néfaste, et d'ailleurs désuet, révolu comme la coutume des repas. (363)

[Monday. Bad, bad. Everything tastes bad. The orange is bitter. Bitter too the cup of sweetened herb tea. Bitter are the throat lozenges. Who brought me these Borgia's poison green lozenges, each of which hides a frigid trap of menthol in its core? Whatever must be absorbed through the mouth is harmful and also obsolete, bygone like the tradition of meals.]

The narrator has lost all competence in the domain of taste. The sweet and the salty are confused with the bitter, food turns to poison and the ritual of meal is defamiliarized, seen as if from outside culture. The bed-ridden narrator has become a stranger in her own community.

Yet, at the very moment when the narrator proclaims her horror and distaste for all 'rite manducatoire' [manducatory rites],[15] a socialized voice, a voice from the outside, seeps into the sick narrator's text: from her bed, she overhears and reports a number of distinctly undesirable remarks. Filtered and mediated by the house-keeper who protects her from visitors, this voice represents the intrusion of labour, the call of professionalism, of the public sphere. It reminds the narrator that the flu has only temporarily removed her from the system of production and consumption of goods to which she belongs. In 'Trente-huit cinq', Colette is not a celebrated author who writes when inspiration or fancy strikes (or when her husband locks her up).[16] She is also a working woman, employed by a magazine as a free-lance writer.

The hated voice which intrudes upon the narrator's sickness and privacy is an order and a command: she must write. And, by a most ironic coincidence, the text that she is asked to write is nothing else but a recipe. The image of the famous chef whose Platonic recipes magically appear on a page as a result of a moment of culinary inspiration, or leisure, has to give way to another vision. The recipe is not only the commemoration of an abstract meal composed by one artist who then condescendingly shares his secrets. Here, the recipe writer is a sick, tired, and irritable woman who must produce a text for her employer, and who does not care to cultivate the image

of the inspired chef composing artistic master-pieces in a slick,
spotless and modern kitchen.

When the voice first reaches the narrator's ears, it is disembodied
and anonymous. At first, the reader does not know who is speaking.
'C'est aujourd'hui qu'elle devait envoyer à *Vogue* la recette de la
Poitrine de boeuf à la Languedocienne' [Today was the deadline: she
was supposed to send *Vogue* the recipe of Poitrine de boeuf à la
Languedocienne] (363). A little later, as the narrator overhears
fragments of a telephone conversation, the request for work reappears, insistent, monotonous, relentless:

Une voix au téléphone dans ma chambre: «Oh non, pas mieux au contraire.
Non, elle ne prend rien. Le docteur a dit ... Oh non, elle ne pourra pas
envoyer son article culinaire à *Vogue* ... Elle regrettera beaucoup ... Merci
Monsieur.» (363)

[A voice speaking on the telephone in my room: 'Oh no, not better, quite
the opposite. No, she is not eating. The doctor said ... Oh no, she will not
be able to send her culinary article to *Vogue* ... She will be very sorry ...
Thank you Sir.']

Two days later, the text reports yet another intrusion. Stubbornly,
the representatives of *Vogue* demand the production of the recipe,
unaware that the idea of a recipe is quite incompatible with the sick
narrator's lack of taste or desire for food:

Des sollicitudes à mon réveil s'égarent: 'Peut-être prendriez-vous une tasse
de bouillon de légumes?' Pourquoi pas une salade de hareng, aussi? Je
souris faiblement, mais c'est de mépris. On sonne: 'C'est rien, Madame,
c'est *Vogue* qui envoyait voir si ...'. (364)

[When I wake up, I am trapped in erring solicitudes. 'Do you think you
might like a cup of vegetable broth?' And why not a herring salad? My
smile is weak but contemptuous. Someone rings the door bell: 'It's nothing,
Madame, *Vogue* wanted to know if ...'.]

Let us assume for a minute that *Vogue* had obtained what they
wanted, that the sick narrator had made the effort of ignoring her
disgust and completed the assignment. Let us suppose that the recipe
in question had indeed been published in *Vogue*. The conditions of
work presiding at the elaboration of such a text would have been
completely erased. Instead, in lieu of a traditional recipe, the narrator
gives us a narrative describing the process of writing a recipe,
provides us with a context, and reveals the method of fabrication.

The story of the rude and untimely intrusion of *Vogue* into the sick room underscores the forgotten, yet obvious, fact that the relationship between the public and the writer is mediated by the professionals of writing. The conflict between the narrator's lack of appetite and her professional obligation as a writer ironically underlines the function of a recipe, which is supposed to whet the readers' appetite and excite their papillary buds. The bed-ridden writer does not give in to pressure altogether, and, finally, in the middle of this diary that has now become a linear narrative, the 'I' does insert a recipe, the recipe which should have been sent to *Vogue* after all. Of course, completely infiltrated as it is by the narrative, the recipe does not function properly anymore.

In fact, although a recipe does exist in this text, it is preceded and framed by the story of the recipe that was never written. *Vogue* did not exactly get what they asked: for after a third and last intervention, the exasperated narrator decides to punish the intruders. She no longer views the 'recipe' as a text addressed to the readers of the magazine, other women who might use or consult the recipe. Instead, the recipe is a sort of sacrificial meal she must offer to the magazine itself, the anonymous and symbolic magazine, writing manufacture, which starts resembling all the factories, mines, or workshops in nineteenth-century novels, mechanical ogres constantly chewing on human workers and spitting them out. Eating is now seen as the activity of the magazine. The recipe itself is to be eaten like a meal. The narrator thus announces her intention to satisfy 'l'appétit pantagruélique de *Vogue*' [Vogue's gargantuesque appetite] (364) rather than that of the readers. This craving for recipes is now presented as an intolerable form of cannibalism, and the original recipe requested by *Vogue*, the recipe of the 'Poitrine de boeuf à la Languedocienne', suddenly loses it prestigious gastronomic connotations to conjure up visions of Arcimboldesque raw and corrupt meat, disgusting in the materiality of displayed butcher's meat:

Ah! oui, *Vogue*, obsession, *Vogue* et sa poitrine de mouton, de boeuf, de mastodonte, ses gigots de plésiosaure, ses dinothériums farcis ... Mais ils ne pensent donc qu'à ça? ... (364).

[Oh yes! *Vogue*, obsession, *Vogue* and its breast of mutton, of beef, of mastodon, its legs of plesiosaurus, its stuffed dinotherium. Do they ever think about anything else? ...]

The angry comment inaugurates a switch in strategy: instead of refusing to do the job, the narrator consciously infiltrates the assignment. Her relationship with the magazine (she is the employee) is suddenly turned upside down as she decides that what *Vogue* really needs is not a recipe, but a good lesson. The moment when the persecuted recipe writer turns into an angry teacher is also the moment when the woman leaves the seclusion of her room to reoccupy her social role: she now communicates with her housekeeper, renounces the privacy of sarcastic smiles and introverted comments, and she dictates the text of a strange so-called recipe which fits snugly within her own fictionalized account.

As readers, we are ready to discover a somewhat eccentric recipe: prepared by the reframing tactic used by the narration, we know that we may expect a lesson and not a recipe. The allusions to 'dinothériums farcis' and other exotic inventions also warn us that, as amateur cooks, we are not supposed to take the rest seriously. At the very least, we are not invited to read the new recipe absent-mindedly, without paying attention to the context. The new recipe, the 'recette du lait d'amandes' announces itself as parodic, subversive: the reader is made an accomplice of a trick played on *Vogue*. The would-be 'recipe' starts as follows:

Dans toutes les familles qui se respectent, la poitrine de boeuf farcie est remplacée par le lait d'amandes fraîches. Pour deux litres de lait d'amandes, il faut plus d'un kilo d'amandes fraîches et saines, épluchées. Pilez dans un mortier de marbre etc... . (364)

[In every respectable family, the stuffed brisket of beef is replaced by the milk of fresh almonds. For two litres of almond milk, you will need a kilogram of fresh and healthy skinned almonds. Crush them in a marble mortar...]

The reference to 'respectability' becomes ironical, but also fulfils one of the narrator's goals: this is a lesson in good taste, in good manners, addressed to the people who have annoyed her. It is also a reappraisal of the very notion of taste insofar as the recommended substitution (one should stay away from 'poitrine de boeuf' and replace it with almond milk) is of course quite implausible unless one totally reconstructs our traditional meals or familiar nutritional customs. The tone of the 'lesson' is peremptory, the classic sequence of verbs in the imperative is present ('pilez..., ajoutez..., filtrez..., servez...', [crush..., add..., filter..., serve...]) but both the tone and the orders are undermined by the narrative frame of the whole passage which forces us to notice that the narrator's whim, when properly infiltrated into a legitimate cultural context (here, the publication of a 'respectable' and expensive magazine reserves one or several pages to 'articles' pompously designed as 'culinary'), immediately acquires the status of sociological models. Future culinary Messieurs Jourdain may then be tempted to adopt the new standard in the same way as they would hire a tailor to reproduce supposedly fashionable aristocratic outfits. Taste, this 'culture devenue nature' [culture turned into nature] (210), as Bourdieu puts it in *La Distinction* is both proposed and imposed in one discursive gesture: the respectability of almond milk is thus imagined at the same moment as it becomes a fact we should all take for granted. A taste for 'almond milk' is naturalized, presented as a piece of knowledge one should have acquired already unless one would rather be excluded from the circle of 'respectable' families. Colette humorously reproduces the pathologically tautological structures that Roland Barthes never ceased to denounce in *L'Empire des signes* or *Mythologies*.

The ludic distance between the authority of the recipe and the narrator's implicit disclaimer destabilizes the genre of the recipe. As waterlogged soil becomes slippery and treacherous if one insists on traversing it along old paths, the new 'text-recipe' disrupts the reader's comfortable habits. 'Trente-huit cinq' will not let us interpret the recipe as a set of instructions to be read by the reader and to be put into practice. The story presents us with the writer as a sick woman, and as a worker persecuted by her boss: we cannot fantasize the author of the recipe as a white-clad famous chef reigning over a kitchen, a professional culinary expert who reluctantly condescends to share his secrets with obscure housewives only because he knows that they will never rise to his artistic heights. Finally, what is questioned here is the distinction between the consultable text which wants to be obeyed, and the interpretable text which one is free to interpret in a different context from the one in which it was originally meant to be interpreted. As infiltration affects the reader, plurality of address becomes a reading practice rather than a function of a genre.

For if the method of infiltration in 'Trente-huit cinq' has to do with treating a genre with a degree of irony, displacing and rewriting, one can safely anticipate that this counter-recipe will not itself have the final word: it will be rewritten and reappropriated because it cannot be shielded from other infiltrational practices. Someone may, at any point, reframe the playful lesson into a 'real' recipe and reorganize Colette's 'vagabondages gourmands' [culinary meanderings].[17] Ironically, the recipe for almond milk would be taken at face value and considered as a respectable consultable text to be dutifully applied. This is exactly what happens in a recently published cookbook entitled Colette gourmande [Food-loving Colette]. This text is a complex hybrid, half biography, half cookbook, a non-linear collection of odd bits and pieces. Obviously written as an homage to Colette, this strange object subterraneously undermines the object of its own cult, infiltrating her texts with new agendas and new perspectives: for example, while 'Trente-huit cinq' was both making fun of the genre of the recipe and of the attempt to create some transparent mystique, here, excerpted and cut into little pieces, Colette's text is manipulated with frightening efficiency until the fake 'recipe' is reestablished in its consultable identity. But before examining what techniques are used by the authors to infiltrate Prisons et Paradis, let me briefly describe the system of address and the reading context implicitly adopted by Colette gourmande.

A beautiful and expensive hard cover, this book seems to believe that gastronomy is different from homecooking and that 'cuisine paysane' is only rehabilitated by Colette's famous character as a 'provinciale'. As in A la Table de George Sand, it soon becomes obvious that 'literature' and 'gastronomy' are considered incompatible or at least different disciplines. Colette's name is summoned here, not because her literary fame will lend credence to other women's work, but because she is herself a 'gourmande', a 'food-loving gourmet' who stuffed her literary texts with allusions to food, preparations, secret tips and know-how. Supposedly, Colette's literary creations are teeming with invisible recipes that the authors intend to extract. Thus carefully drained from supplemental material, the de-infiltrated recipes will be presented to the readers as if the non-recipe part of the work could be simply ignored. Colette gourmande presupposes an essential difference between the technical savoir-faire of a cook (who may or may not write cookbooks) and Colette's art as a writer (defined as an artist who writes for others). Between the two apparently watertight categories, this book has obviously chosen its camp: this is not literature, the authors seem to insist, this is a scientific enterprise. For example, Colette gourmande does not claim to belong to Colette's complete works (even though the text is mostly constituted by quotations drawn from the writer's work), it does not parade as a re-edition of some rarely available passages. And yet, it is seeking some of the recognition granted to canonical art: the authors carefully distinguish this book from traditional 'cookbooks' (probably suspected of being tainted with a certain degree of banality and vulgarity). The title Colette gourmande avoids any reference to recipes or cuisine; in fact, it echoes the title of Geneviève Dormann's Amoureuse Colette (translated as Colette: A Passion for Life), arguably the best known of Colette's biographies. Colette gourmande is an interesting mixture of the scholarly essay and art book sold in mainstream bookstores. The reference is not to some kind of new and improved recipe box, the value of which should be found in the authenticity of an old tradition. The 'Cahiers de recettes de Colette' [Colette's notebooks of recipes: the collection of recipes per se] are prefaced by two chapters entitled 'Gourmandes provinces' [Food-loving Provinces] and 'Un goût authentique' [An Authentic Taste]. The style of these two chapters oscillates between biographical narratives and critical articles: the authors focus on Colette's dwelling places, or write short articles laced with quotations from rarely published texts, and accompany their descriptions with philosophical or theoretical observations about taste in a given ideological context. The table of contents is that of a cookbook: it traditionally arranges recipes according to gastronomic categories and names of dishes but it also features a list of works cited which will probably look very respectable to any literary scholar. The authors carefully reference every cited text, the different editions used in the book, and the articles or manuals consulted during their research.

Since the revealed recipes are almost never signed by Colette herself (or are never couched in the language of recipes), the authors are very careful to protect themselves against potential accusation of fraud: the end-result of their research is legitimized by a detailed account of how much work went into the project. Both explorers and historians, the authors established the texts of recipes after a 'recherche [qui les] entraîna pendant plus de deux ans dans le tourbillon d'une véritable enquête' [a search which drew them into the maelstrom of a genuine investigation for more than two years] (93, my emphasis). The authenticity of the recipes is guaranteed by a strange mixture of references to literary texts treated like culinary archives and to an unwritten subtext of personal memories collected during interviews with Pauline, Colette's cook:

Quant au texte des recettes, il a été assemblé comme un puzzle et recomposé scrupuleusement en accord avec l'époque et le goût de l'écrivain. Là où Pauline ne pouvait se souvenir de tous les détails, notre large jeu de citations nous a permis en regroupant les termes, en les

analysant et en consultant les ouvrages de l'époque de retrouver exactement
ce qu'aimait Colette. (93).

[As for the text of recipes themselves, they have been put together like the
pieces of a jig-saw puzzle and scrupulously recomposed in agreement with
the period and the writer's taste. When Pauline could not remember all the
details, our large set of citations allowed us to group themes and, by
analysing them and consulting books written as the same time, to recapture
exactly what Colette liked.]

The 'recomposed' recipes are obviously yearning for legitimacy and
recognition. *Colette gourmande* is neither a gastronomic biography nor a
compilation of recipes written by Colette, who is neither quite the
author nor the object. And the book is also ambiguous as a
marketable commodity: it is an expensive decorative book complete
with photographs, sophisticated typesetting, first-rate quality paper,
and oversized format, one of these favourite gift books which
magazines like *Marie-Claire* and *Elle* recommend to their female readers
especially around the time of the 'fête des mères' (Mothers' Day).
Although it announces itself as a cookbook, I doubt that one would
use it in the kitchen for fear of ruining such a beautiful object. Before
rolling up her sleeves, a cook may be tempted to copy the recipes on
to a piece of scrap paper, as if this recipe book needed a mediator, a
less glamorous relay. *Colette gourmande* is a coffee-table book, and the
contrast between the luxurious publication and its overt purpose
mirrors the difference between Colette, lady of the house and
famous author, and Pauline, humble cook and servant. Once we
become aware that the authors of *Colette gourmande* used Pauline as
living archives, that she was approached as the guardian of a history
which a busy Colette did not have time to record, we may find it
rather distasteful that the relationship between the servant and her
famous employer should be described in the following terms:

Colette eut la chance de vivre à une époque où il était encore courant de se
faire servir ... Libérée de cette contrainte féminine, il est sûr que Colette ne
faisait plus souvent la cuisine et se consacrait à l'écriture. Devons-nous nous
en plaindre alors que sans l'aide de Pauline nous n'aurions peut-être pas à
lire toutes ces admirables pages de la littérature française? (88).

[Colette was lucky enough to live at a time when it was normal to have
servants ... Freed from this feminine chore, Colette surely did not cook very
often anymore and devoted her time to her writing. Should we regret it
when we think that, if it had not been for Pauline's help, all these admirable
pages of French literature would not have been available?]

Unlike the women of Nohant (some of which were servants), Pauline does not benefit from infiltrational practices. Once again, the problem of the relationship between the writer and other women is raised, even if the authors seem convinced that the imbalance of power and fame between Colette and Pauline is not an issue. Of course, as we rejoice in Colette's freedom from meaningless daily chores, we may regret that Pauline herself was never given the chance to choose between traditionally 'feminine' constraints and the possibility of contributing 'admirable pages to French literature'. Pauline and all the women who regularly use cookbooks in the privacy of their anonymous kitchens seem excluded. They are not worth 'investigating', their participation in the 'adventure' is at best secondary, even if the book is addressed to them.

It is perhaps no coincidence that the asymmetrical treatment of Pauline and her employer coexist with a refusal to respect Colette's resistance strategies to her own employers: in Colette gourmande, the text of 'Trente-huit cinq' undergoes a number of metamorphoses. On page 189, in the middle of a chapter entitled 'Boissons', one finds the following text:

---

Le lait d'amandes de Colette

---

RECETTE ORIGINALE DE COLETTE

«Pour deux litres de lait d'amandes, il faut plus d'un kilo d'amandes fraîches et saines, épluchées. Pilez dans un mortier de marbre, avec une petite quantité de sucre. Ajoutez, goutte à goutte, l'eau nécessaire à l'émulsion. Pendant la nuit suivante, le mortier et son contenu, voilés d'un linge, resteront au frais. Le lendemain, filtrez dans une poche de batiste, ou de mousseline à trame serrée. Ajoutez la quantité d'eau qui manque à vos deux litres. Si vous servez promptement vous pouvez remplacer l'eau par du lait fraîchement trait. Ne frappez jamais le lait d'amandes, mais laissez flotter sur son onde un peu bleue, crémeuse, une feuille de citronnelle verte, à peine immergée, effilée comme une jonque de Chine...Et n'oubliez pas non plus − tout est perdu sans elle! − la goutte d'essence de roses, une goutte, une seule...»

PRISONS ET PARADIS, 1932.

Rencontré au Maroc, ce lait d'amandes était devenu pour Colette la boisson favorite de ses moments de faiblesse. Quand quelque fièvre la fatiguait, il apparaissait, chauffé par les bons soins de Pauline et cet orgeat chaud, douceur laiteuse et parfumée, l'entraînait alors dans d'angéliques rêves peuplés de couleurs pastels...

The playful recipe, the 'lesson'-joke which the narrator of Prisons et paradis had concocted and sent to Vogue is utterly decontextualized. The passage is promoted to the prestigious status of 'original' recipe, the part of the story explaining how this so-called 'recipe' was manufactured, is amputated, as well as the very first sentence about 'respectable families', which, in Prisons et paradis, appeared between quotes: the irony of the 'respectable' substitution is thus lost and the oppositional gesture against Vogue is replaced by a column of comments. Separated from the text by a visible barrier, the marginal addition sounds as 'impersonal' and 'objective' as possible ('Rencontré au Maroc ...'). The note of exoticism however does not compensate for the disappearance of the first mischievous substitution.

At this point, I seem to be adopting the role of the better critic, the self-righteous oppositional voice blaming the authors of Colette gourmande for simplifying the narrator's humorous narrative. But this example is not representative of the whole book, and I would now like to turn to another passage that possibly redeems the unnecessary flattening out of 'Trente-huit cinq'. The system of collage in Colette gourmande (quotations, pictures, Pauline's unsigned revelations, comments, etc.) ironically undermines the authors' presuppositions about the primacy of one voice over another: in the end, whether they have been 'recomposed' or quoted from published texts, all the recipes collected in the last part of the book have the same status, none is more important, or more visible than others. We are now invited to treat every text (be it famous as a literary creation or not) like a recipe, a consultable text. We can try them, execute them.

Moreover, the technique used to reassemble the pieces of the puzzle is different for each recipe for the 'composers' of Colette gourmande have not been systematic in their infiltrational work. In the case of the 'almond milk', the authors' intervention consisted in manipulating quotations and reframing a narrative passage. But in the chapter entitled 'Volailles, viandes de boucherie et gibier', (Poultry, meat and venison) they draw from 'Trente-huit cinq' again and, this time, they transform it in a way which literary scholars might well find as scandalous as Vogue's editors when given the fake recipe. In the same way as Colette had infiltrated Vogue's demands, the authors of Colette gourmande infiltrate her manipulation and further complicate the distinction between recipes and narratives.

Colette had refused to divulge the recipe of 'Poitrine de boeuf à la

Languedocienne' as retaliation against *Vogue*. Consequently, her readers had been tempted and then denied the satisfaction of consuming the textual or material version of Colette's 'Poitrine de boeuf'. But Marie-Christine et Didier Clément have disregarded Colette's intentions and have taken it upon themselves to fill this vexing vacuum. They proudly present their readers with the (or a?) lost recipe of 'Poitrine de boeuf à la Languedocienne'.

---

Poitrine de boeuf à la Languedocienne

«Une voix dans ma chambre: 'C'est aujourd'hui qu'elle devait envoyer à Vogue la recette de la poitrine de boeuf à la Languedocienne...'.
[...] Ah! oui, Vogue, obsession, Vogue et sa poitrine de mouton, de boeuf, de mastodonte, ses gigots de plésiosaure, ses dinothériums farcis... Mais ils ne pensent donc qu'à ça?
Dans mes souvenirs, brumeux, tamisés et rythmés par la timbale de mes trente-huit cinq, il me semblait que Vogue s'occupait d'élégances...»

PRISONS ET PARADIS, 1932.

Colette écrivit périodiquement dans *Vogue* de 1925 à 1932. Ses chroniques gastronomiques – à partir de 1928 – furent toutes reprises dans *Prisons et Paradis*

*Dans une braisière, faites colorer 4 carottes taillées grossièrement, 4 oignons coupés en quartiers, une tête d'ail coupée en deux, 4 tomates bien mûres avec thym, laurier, une dizaine de grains de poivre, 2 clous de girofle et un bâton de cannelle.*

*Déposez dessus 2 kg de poitrine de boeuf coupée en deux morceaux. Faites colorer les pièces de viande puis mouillez avec une bouteille de vin blanc moelleux. Laissez réduire de moitié puis recouvrez d'un fond de viande. Laissez cuire pendant 3 heures en maintenant une cuisson douce et régulière.*

*Dans le plat creux, décantez la viande et arrosez de la sauce passée. Servez d'une garniture de cèpes escalopes, poêlés à l'huile d'olive et d'aubergines frites. Parsemez le plat de persil haché.*

The subversive quality of this insertion will only be noticed if one decides to compare Colette's complete works and the Cléments's book, but once this is done, it is difficult not to recognize that the non-telling of the recipe was crucial and constituted the textual foundation of 'Trente-huit cinq'. One may therefore wonder what effects are produced by the reinstating of this absence. My first reaction was to consider that Colette's remarkable infiltrational skills had been betrayed, but, on second thoughts, it occurs to me that Colette's silence was not innocent either. After all, even if the narrator's refusal to provide us with the information is amply justified by the context, some readers may resent the fact that they are being taken hostage as a result of a dispute between the professional writer and her boss. Perhaps some regretted that their desire for 'poitrine de boeuf' had been excited only to be frustrated by a vague allusion to a recipe which was never published. In *Colette gourmande*, the repressed recipe to which 'Trente-huit cinq' had denied us access miraculously reappears.

By demonstrating that any recipe can be turned into a narrative without losing the properties of the recipe, Colette had infiltrated the genre of the consultable text. The connections and distinctions between written recipe and oral tradition, feminine and masculine work, chef and 'humble' female cook, were consequently reconstructed as spaces to be infiltrated and possibly redefined. But the series of collages and the dilution undergone by her text also remind us that infiltration is not an ideological solution, at least never a permanent one, and that infiltrators are always susceptible to be infiltrated themselves.

Faced with the somewhat exasperating reappearance of the 'Poitrine de boeuf à la Languedocienne', I did not know what to do, how to rewrite, comment or annotate *Colette gourmande*. My first (critical, gastronomic or feminist?) impulse was to 'side' with Colette against the forces of institutionalized writing, professional duties and sickening deadlines. But I realize that I am not giving credit to the power of her infiltrational tactics by attempting to treat them as a frozen and solidified environment. My readers will probably wonder why I took the trouble of reproducing the entire recipes as they appear in *Colette gourmande* when I could have been content to quote one or two representative sentences. I certainly did not need to repeat the passage already quoted from *Prisons and Paradis*. At least, I did not need to reproduce the format.

But after all, I would be acting in bad faith if I did not realize that this chapter is itself threatened, or potentially enriched, by its readers' infiltrational strategies. The pattern described in Colette's *Prisons et paradis* or in Christiane Sand's *A la Table de George Sand* may also function here: when tired of my abstract and theoretical speculations about the distinction between genres, readers will not need my permission to forget about the argument and concentrate on the recipes. If they are seduced by Colette's almond milk 'original' recipe or even by the 'apocryphal' 'poitrine de boeuf' they may decide to try them or clip them and add them to their own collection. Perhaps, they will decide to appreciate them pornographically and read them in bed (thus paying homage to the anonymous team of typesetters). In which case, they might regret that I did not make the effort to include a reproduction of the photographs. Perhaps it is in this ultimate absence that I should have been looking for other infiltrations.[18]

## Notes

1 A literal translation misses the pun on 'ail' (garlic) and 'oeil' (eye). At first, the sentence seems to mean: 'We eat a lot of good food. I am putting on weight by the minute'. But in the set phrase 'à vue d'oeil' (before our eyes), the last word is replaced by the French word for garlic, 'ail,' which is pronounced almost like 'oeil'. A possibility would be to translate 'j'engraisse à vue d'ail' as 'I am on a see food diet' (as a way of respecting the written quality of the pun) but the reference is to a late twentieth-century joke which may obscure the fact that Colette's remark is the expression of a generalised and collective war-time obsession with food.

2 It would be interesting to analyse another cultural context which I will not cover in this text: the show and tell television cooking programmes where the oppositions between the male chef and the female follower almost entirely disappear.

3 About the different possible female communities imagined around recipes, see the important essay by Susan Leonardi: 'Recipes for Reading: Summer Pasta, Lobster à la Riseholme, and Key Lime Pie'.

4 See 'A Misunderstood Activity: reading' in the chapter entitled 'Reading as Poaching': 'In a society that is increasingly written, organized by the power of modifying things and of reforming structures on the basis of scriptural models (whether scientific, economic, or political), transformed little by little into combined 'texts' (be they administrative, urban, industrial, etc.), the binominal set production–consumption can often be replaced by its general equivalent and indicator, the binominal set writing–reading' (Certeau 1984, 167–8).

5 I have slighlty modified this translation.

6 Unlike *Elle* or *Marie-Claire*, coded as feminine magazine, *Le Nouvel Observateur* presents itself

as a serious weekly addressed to serious business men. That may be the reason why the categories 'Cuisine' or 'Gastronomy' have been discarded from the table of contents. Food and how we consume it have not disappeared however, but they are placed under more culturally eminent labels: the issue of December 8, 1990 features a story which has been placed under the 'Art de Vivre' rubric. The article is entitled: 'Trophée Coq Saint-Honoré: les cuisiniers sont des artistes'. [Coq Saint-Honoré Trophy: cooks are artists]. The paratactic association between the 'artist' and the 'trophy' seems natural, the writers of the article imply that artists and trophies belong in the same sentence, that artists are dependent on powerful patrons. The article describes the chef as an artist, only to have fleeting visions of Parisian Bohême reinserted into the world of contests, examinations, sports events or wars. Here, gastronomy owes its prestige to its artistic ambitions, but relies on 'trophies' rather than on galleries, exhibits (a more discreet form of examination): 'Après lecture des recettes qui nous sont envoyées, un comité sélectionne les huit finalistes qui prépareront leurs plats dans les cuisines de l'hôtel Nikko' [After reading the recipes sent to us, a committe selects the eight finalists who will prepare their dish in the kitchens of the hotel Nikko]: the chef must pass the written exam before being allowed to take the oral part.

7 See the second part of the chapter entitled 'Discipline' (186–96).

8 According to Jean-Louis Flandrin, Philip and Mary Hyman Montalba, the editors of a collection of three texts mentioned in this paragraph, the *Cuisinier françois* is 'un des grands succès de librairie de l'histoire du livre de cuisine [...] En outre, il est le premier ouvrage à avoir rompu avec l'ancienne cuisine médiévale et à s'être engagé dans les voies nouvelles qui sont encore à peu près celles de la cuisine actuelle. Enfin, c'est vers le moment où il est apparu que la cuisine française s'est imposée comme la première d'Europe, et c'est le *Cuisinier françois* qui en a été l'ambassadeur jusqu'au début du siècle' [a best seller in the history of cookbooks ... Also, it is one of the first books to break away from the old medieval cuisine and to move in new directions which are still mostly those of modern cuisine. Finally, it came out at a moment when French cuisine started dominating Europe, and the *Cuisinier françois* was its ambassador until the beginning of this century] (11).

9 This reminds me of a TV commercial for a brand of fast baking home-made cookies. The woman in the commercial is apparently leafing through a cookbook in the privacy of her kitchen, while a plate of cookies, obviously eagerly awaited by her family, sits in front of her on the counter. When the children ask, from the other room, if the cookies are ready yet, she pretends that she is still working on them. The idea is that she has to wait because it did not take her 'enough' time to bake the cookies. The commercial wants to sell the idea that little energy is needed to prepare this product but does seem to have internalized the contradictions of such a tempting proposition. The cook in the commercial has saved time for herself (she is alone, relaxing), but she is presented as stealing this time away from the others: she must be portrayed as a liar. In order to convince her children and husband that she did spend the mandatory amount of hard work on the dessert, she also covers her face with flour, apparently in an attempt to overcompensate for the guilt of not working enough. The exhausted-looking cook is somewhat incompetent and in bad taste, but it seems that nothing could be worse than the family finding out that the recipe did not demand much work. Interestingly enough, the children never set foot in the kitchen: for them, labour is invisible anyway. The commercial is reinforcing the invisibility of the woman's work by suggesting that even when a trace remains, it is probably a trick. It also teaches women that hard work is the only legitimate way of earning gratitude (not the successful dish, for example), that a decreased workload should remain a secret, and that guests, husbands or children

would not be able to appreciate her cooking if they did not assume that she spends her entire days in the kitchen. The commercial's logic further erases the woman's work by suggesting that what she does is never quite enough and that she must lie about it. Although it wants to sell simplicity and ease, it cannot bring itself to celebrate the absence of work without implying that it is accompanied by guilt and sneaky behaviour.

10 This quotation appears in the preface to Brillat-Savarin's *Physiologie du goût* (8). And Barthes adds: 'L'énoncé gastronomique, parce que le désir qu'il mobilise est apparemment simple, présente dans toute son ambiguïté le pouvoir du langage: le signe appelle les délices de son référent dans l'instant même où il en trace l'absence' [Because the gastronomic statement generates an apparently simple form of desire, it presents the power of language in its ambiguity: the sign calls for the delights of its referent at the very moment when it traces its absence] (24).

11 Most of the following quotations from *Female Desires* appear in a chapter entitled 'Naughty but Nice: Food Pornography'. Coward remarks that: 'This pleasure in looking at the supposedly forbidden is reminiscent of another form of guilty-but-indulgent looking, that of sexual pornography. Sexual pornography as a separate realm of imagery exists because our society defines some explicit pictures of sexual activitiy or sexual parts as 'naughty,' 'illicit'. These images are then made widely available through a massive and massively profitable industry' (99).

12 About the relationship between gender and collections, see Naomi Schor's article on the collecting of postcards, 'Cartes postales: Representing Paris 1990,' and especially her critique of Walter Benjamin, Susan Steward and Jean Baudrillard (199–203).

13 See the famous *A la Manière de* ... by Paul Reboux.

14 For an analysis of the specific place occupied by gastronomy in the French cultural imaginary, see Jean-Robert Pitte's *Gastronomie française*, especially the introduction ('De la passion gastronomique des Français') and the second chapter ('La gourmandise est-elle un péché en France?').

15 The phrase is used by Michel Tournier in the first story of *Le Médianoche amoureux*, 'Les amants taciturnes' [The Taciturn Lovers] which revolves around the connection between food and silence, meals and words.

16 Colette's biographers and critics have often commented on Willy's rather authoritarian influence on the beginning of Colette's career. It is more or less established that Willy used to lock up a reluctant Colette to make sure that she would produce her quota of pages. See for example Suzanne Relyea's 'The Symbolic in the Family Factory: My Apprenticeships'.

17 A book review of *Colette gourmande*, published in *Marie-Claire* Vol. 49 (November 1990), is entitled 'Les vagabondages gourmands de Colette'. I want to thank Denise Charvy who sent me the book from France. Her present gave me a chance to think about the possible uses of a recipe book that dare not speak its name.

18 Like the French version of this chapter, this text is dedicated to the late Lynn Salkin-Sbiroli. See the collection of articles edited by Monique Streiff-Moretti, Mireille Revol Cappelletti, Odile Martinez: *Il Senso del Nonsenso: Scritti in Memoria di Lynn Salkin Sbiroli*. (Editizione scientifiche italiane, 1995).

## 'Why should I swallow a toad?': self-defeating gender reversals

Le charme: s'entendre répondre oui à une question que l'on n'a pas clairement posée. (Camus)
[Charm is when someone replies 'yes' to a question I have not clearly asked]

In this last chapter, I have decided to mark the limits of infiltration as defined in this book. The notion of 'limits' may seem contradictory with the non-territorial conception of infiltration as a provisional fantasm of identity, embraced by those who do not want to choose between borderlands and mainland. It also seems futile, however, to claim that infiltration is a systematically prevalent activity which one could detect in any text, in any cultural production, provided they emanate from some minority or relatively powerless subject. If I want to treat infiltration as the attribute of specific fictional figures and as the tactic used by subjects or associations scripting their reality, I do recreate distinctions between infiltrators and their 'others'. In a sense, by proposing the translator, the interpreter, the spy, or even the cook as privileged objects of study likely to reinvent infiltrational cultural genres or to modify a subject's positioning, I do fall back on a differential pattern: the infiltrator depends, for his or her very existence, on his or her exceptional status as oppositional marginal. I would not want to give my reader the impression that infiltration, like Cartesian common sense, is 'la chose du monde la mieux partagée'. Infiltration does not do away with binary opposi- tions, nor does it try to undermine identities based on the belief in the extra-linguistic existence of binary oppositions. In fact, infiltra- tors will thrive in conservatively defined universes where paradigms are most strictly structured: it is easier to be an academic infiltrator when interdisciplinary research is not rewarded, one can only be a successful (textual or literal) spy if two powers insist on not sharing knowledge, one can only be a mole when the system creates insiders and outsiders.

But, as I hope to have demonstrated, the way in which the infiltrator redefines binary oppositions is not to expose their theoretical limitations. The infiltrator is not necessarily a demobilized individual who has given up on political organizations (the spy may report to a larger unit), but infiltration occurs when a direct confrontation with the ideological powers, which have created binary oppositions, seems useless and futile. Infiltrators do not claim that the distinction between inside and outside is not meaningful even if their ultimate goal is to modify the balance of power to the point where such systemic reappraisals may be possible. But theirs is a limited, provisional (and sometimes pathetically inefficient) tactic which will not necessarily be discovered.

To come back to my first geological metaphor, infiltration may, and will, be considered irrelevant, meaningless, inexistent, when it does not stop the farmer from ploughing the fields in such a way as he or she considers proper. In the same way, detective fiction or feast narratives will not necessarily call for a study of infiltration. And infiltration certainly does not exist as a hidden ingredient to be discovered by every critic in every object of study. Infiltration may be deemed desirable by the powerful as well as by the powerless, and I do not mean to imply that the less power one yields, the more infiltrational one should become.

I would like to analyse Renée Vivien's short stories as noninfiltrational discursive universes, not to demonstrate that these texts are less subtle or less politically aware than Colette's or Ega's reconstructions of binary pairs, but to suggest that they raise other problems for the reader: when infiltration is not an option, we are implicitly asked to use different interpretive strategies and different critical approaches. I am not saying that it would be impossible to discover infiltrators or infiltrational moments in Vivien's work, quite the contrary. I will instead argue in this chapter that, in Vivien's work, infiltration is a crucial element because it is repressed. If infiltration exists at all, it does not produce clearly identifiable or positive figures (like the interpreter in Maillet or the house-cleaner in Ega). Neither is infiltration a conscious writing strategy or a renegotiation of the relationship between the categories of cooking and writing (as in Colette's *Prisons et paradis*): in Vivien's work, there is no

obvious attempt to blur frontiers between territories, at least at the
level of the overt narration. In fact, her discursive universe is
founded on an all-pervasive division between two antagonistic
positions: the masculine and the feminine. These two extremely
hostile territories are defined in such a mutually exclusive way that
infiltration of one by the other seems absolutely impossible (let
alone desirable). When I suggest that in spite of the texts' thematic
efforts to impose their separatist vision, a reluctant infiltrational
element manages to survive, I refer to the impossibility of Vivien's
narratives to invent this conceptual non-porous essentialist gendered
terrain.

Before analysing the consequences of Vivien's non-infiltrational
premise in a few specific prose pieces, I would like to reflect upon
the relationship between the fundamental binarism of her texts and
the author's position within the canon. When an author's corpus
systematically grapples with the issues of separatism and gender
segregation, domination and oppression between genders, does it
influence the narrative produced by literary history about the work,
about the writer? Does the place of Vivien's literary production
within the canon mirror or contradict the imagined relationships
between men and women represented in her writings?

## Infiltration and canonicity

One of the current plausible discourses about Renée Vivien is that
she has recently been 'rediscovered' as a poet, and more specifically
as a woman and a lesbian. When Vivien was alive, her work was
received quite favourably by her male and female contemporaries,
and more recently, the works of a number of American and
European critics and publishers have made her texts available to a
relatively large public. Most of Vivien's writings had not been
reprinted since the beginning of the century, but in 1975, Arno
published Les Poèmes de Renée Vivien in a collection entitled 'Homosexuality: Lesbians and Gay Men in Society, History and Literature', and
her prose has been translated into English by Jeanette Foster, Yvonne
Klein and Karla Jay.[1]

I am, however, less interested in celebrating a 'rediscovery' or the
end of a collective amnesia as I am wondering about the modalities
which determine how a writer ('s work) is alternately pushed in and
out of the (academic) literary canon. More specifically, Vivien's

status as an outsider having to be reinserted into a corpus of texts
raises the question of whether or not to use infiltrating tactics. As
theoreticians have quite convincingly argued, it is difficult to fight
the exclusionary consequences of the literary canon other than on its
own theoretical ground. On the one hand, it is tempting to argue,
like Ross Chambers, that the canon is always differential, like power,
that no body of literature escapes the canon, that each selection
contains exclusion:

> When we accede to the idea that certain texts are in the canon while others
> are not, we are in fact acceding to the system of canonicity, of which the
> canon is a product. It is clear for example, that the supposedly canonical
> texts are so only by virtue of there being texts excluded from that category.
> ... What finally matters in the system of canonicity, then, is not so much
> which texts are included and which are excluded but what the criteria are
> that will count at a given time for exclusion or inclusion. (Chambers 1990, 18)

This position is not incompatible with that of Henri Louis Gates who
suggests that the time has come to invent and promote a canon of
Black literature without being paralysed by the fact that we do not
theoretically redefine the canon. Involved in the collection of texts
destined for the Norton Anthology of African-American Literature,
Gates writes:

> I am not unaware of the politics and ironies of canon formation. The canon
> that we define will be 'our' canon, one possible set of selections among
> several possible sets of selections ... those of us in feminist criticism or
> African-American criticism who are engaged in the necessary work of canon
> formation and reformation, confront the skepticism even of those who are
> allies on other fronts, over this matter of the death of the subject and our
> own discursive subjectivity. (Gates 1992, 111)

In a sense, Vivien's situation is a test case. When I ask the question of
her canonicity, my analysis resolutely accepts the categories of
inside–outside. I agree to recognize that no literature class in high
school or college ever introduced me to Renée Vivien's work, that I
knew about Baudelaire long before I discovered the existence of his
so-called female alter ego. Skirting the fascinating theoretical implications of my request, I ask that her name be put on reading lists,
that her books be translated, that her work be taught. And yet, I may
have been infiltrated by her thought long before I found out about
her existence: perhaps Vivien influenced Proust and Barthes and I
was indeed indirectly exposed to her work when I studied them. At
this juncture however, I would like to follow another path, a path

which will hopefully keep in mind both Chambers's healthy warning and Gates's passionate plea.

Critics' efforts to make Vivien's texts more accessible to the public are presented as a conscious political decision. In her preface to the second edition of Une Femme m'apparut (A Woman Appeared to Me), Gayle Rubin claims that the publication of such a text should be celebrated insofar as 'Lesbians, suffering from the dual disqualification of being gay and female, have been repeatedly dispossessed from their history' (Rubin 1979, iii). According to Karla Jay, whose book, The Amazon and the Page is entirely devoted to Renée Vivien and Natalie Barney, the two authors' work is:

long overdue for reconsideration. Their almost uncanny anticipation of the preoccupations of feminist writers whose work began almost sixty years after Vivien's death gives them a place as foremothers of feminist literatures. (Jay 1988, xv)

Late twentieth-century critics' interest in Renée Vivien is not restricted to her literary work: they are fascinated by her biography. The time has passed when Vivien's life among a community of women would have been considered irrelevant to the study of her poetry, for example. In fact, her life has been read as an early feminist manifesto and analysed in detail. Reading Vivien in the last decade of the twentieth century is often associated with a conscious gesture of resistance against the homophobic and misogynistic prejudices which, in a rhetorical and ideological coup de force, Vivien usually blamed on what she called the 'male principle'.

Vivien's life is not that of an infiltrator, rather that of a believer in separatism. She belonged to the famous community of women known as 'Women of the Left Bank' thanks to Shari Benstock's monumental study of the Parisian belle époque. At the time when a British court returns a guilty verdict against Oscar Wilde and sentences him to jail after a much publicized trial, Paris occupies a special symbolic and political place in Europe. The French capital is a relatively safe haven for gays and lesbians,[2] and it is not a coincidence that a group of women writers should have lived and worked there during that period. Colette and Pauline Tarn (Renée Vivien's real name), Radclyffe Hall, Gertrude Stein, Jean Rhys and others had not been born in Paris, and their encounter cannot be dismissed as a contingent accident. These women artists came from vastly different horizons, from French provinces (Colette's Burgundy), from England

(Radclyffe Hall), from the United States (Vivien), or from the Caribbean (Rhys), but they were united by their similar anti-patriarchal values and convictions. Their loosely bound community was explicitly involved in a fight against the male-dominated world within which their works are perforce inscribed. Although the 'Women of the Left bank' did not systematically work together, the group was coherent enough to constitute a distinct entity within the social and political tissue, and to generate specific narratives or descriptions. It is portrayed as an 'imagined community' in the texts written by the members of the group or by critics who appraised their literary productions. In Vivien's poetry and in her autobiographical novel, the same utopian desire recurs over and over again: the poet envisions the founding of a 'City of Women',[3] inspired by Mytilène and placed under the aegis of the mythic figure of Sappho. For Vivien, Sappho functions as a privileged female origin, she is the foremother, the absolute reference: it is believed that Vivien insisted on studying Greek (although her education as a woman would have been considered complete without her knowledge of the language) so that she could translate Sappho's fragments into French. She also made several trips to Lesbos with her lover, Natalie Barney, and the dream of an ideal female protected universe was imported back to Paris when the two women talked about creating the Academy of Women, meant as a space where women writers could find encouragement and an environment conducive to writing. As Natalie Barney had expected and hoped, all the authors who gravitated around the circle of the Academy of Women did influence and 'inspire each other' in a unique way.[4] These women appear as literary characters in each other's works, creating a dense network of fictional and biographical references. Renée Vivien, for example, became a literary character for both Colette and Natalie Barney, the former devoting a long passage to the poet in her *Le Pur et l'impur*, the latter offering us a detailed (if not flattering) portrait in her *Souvenirs indiscrets*. Symmetrically, Vivien's *Une Femme m'apparut*, Halls's *The Well of Loneliness*, and Colette's series of 'Claudine' books transform Natalie Barney into a fictional character. According to Shari Benstock 'Natalie Barney ... not only wrote a prolific record of her own lesbianism (as did Colette, Renée Vivien, and Radclyffe Hall) but also served as a fictional model of lesbianism in an astonishing number of works by other writers of the *belle époque*, appearing in works by Liane de Pougy, Renée Vivien, Ronald Firbank, Remy de Gourmont,

Colette, Djuna Barnes, Radclyffe Hall, and Lucie Delarue-Madrus (Benstock 1986, 59). Each fictionalization generates more texts in response, as the authors take issue with their representations and feel compelled to inscribe their own version. In *Souvenirs indiscrets*, Natalie Barney insists that both versions of Renée Vivien's *Une Femme m'apparut* are intolerably flawed: 'En relisant ces deux romans, j'ai la pénible impression d'avoir posé pour un mauvais portraitiste'. [When I reread these two novels, I get the painful feeling that I posed for a bad painter] (55).

Vivien's 'life' as written by others is not only an important textual layer, but it is becoming more and more difficult not to allow these texts to merge with what Vivien wrote as a poet and novelist. It seems that Vivien's biography and the kind of narrative it is likely to elicit has always exerted a more powerful attraction over literary critics than the works they were supposedly reading. Vivien's existence may be in the process of being rediscovered but her work is largely ignored. The French feminist movement of the 1970s, which has been taken to task by American critics for their tendency to look for models among male modernist poets, has not attempted to draw attention to Vivien's prose in spite of its sometimes uncannily prophetic tones. More recent studies tend to focus either on the history of Vivien's writing, concentrating on those who influenced the poet, or on why she was gradually forgotten after being so successfully received. In articles devoted to Vivien, it often strikes me that Baudelaire or Maurras's texts are more often quoted than her own poems for example.[5] Whenever a critic addresses Vivien's work, Baudelaire's unavoidable legacy looms large as the unavoidable reference and origin. His 'Fleurs du Mal' are supposed to account for the old-fashinoned symbolist techniques and for the lesbian thematics in Vivien' s poetics: she writes like another 'femme damnée'. As for Maurras's *Romantisme féminin*, which did offer Vivien a place among the pantheon of late nineteenth-century writers, it is often invoked as a justification or explanation for the current increasing attention given to her literary productions.

Vivien's life has now become a narrative, and, as such, it is likely to find its place among the imaginary museum that Bourdieu would call our cultural patrimony. Vivien's numerous partial and frag-mented biographies may be just as important as her work when they are used by some men and women as a positive history, a source of hope, intervention and involvement. By focusing on biographical elements, however, I do participate in a paradoxical venture: Vivien's work is not silenced, but it is not foregrounded either as the primary focus of the analysis. Silence around Vivien's poetry becomes relative and an oblique entrance into the canon is negotiated. Her literary production is neither silent nor powerful, or it is perhaps both silent and powerful, or neither powerless nor dominant.

The question of what happens in a text when silence and power are not mutually exclusive is far from irrelevant since women's silence is one of Vivien's thematic obsessions, especially in the prose pieces that constantly explore the issue. I suggest that the relative power of silence in the stories functions as a strange doubling of Vivien's alternate visibility and invisibility within the canon.[6]

## The male and female 'principles'

In *Une Femme m'apparut*, and in the short stories of *La Dame à la louve* (*The Woman of the Wolf*) silence is what female characters dread because it is imposed upon them, but it is also women's weapon against the male principle. Each text differs, however, in its strategic use of silence: in *Une Femme m'apparut*, the first person narrator proposes a radical reversal of gender roles. When not systematically excluded, the male principle is violently condemned: it has no redeeming qualities. At the same time, silence is presented as the feminine symbol of proud and heroic patience, the capacity to endure. The short stories are a particularly interesting elaboration on what I would call the right to silence, or more accurately, the right to remain silent when confronted with the enemy (the male protagonist), who is presented as an incessant talker. Men keep insisting on forcing the woman to talk to them, they harass them until they answer their questions and demands, while their resentful conversation partners remain silent as long as they can and only provide reluctant responses which are then systematically interpreted as arrogant, aggressive, hysterical, feminine. Silence, in itself, is not necessarily an anti-infiltrational principle, but here it is used to preserve and reinforce the apparently unbridgeable chasm separating two distinct entities. Even in the short stories, which are more complex than the poetry from a narratological point of view, silence is not infiltrational, it is a rebellious refusal to let language realize that its own constructions and paradigms of difference do not function without contradictions.

Originally, I had chosen to work on the short stories because they portray a form of rebellion against the male principle which seemed less manichean, perhaps a little more subtle, than the peremptory and polemic declarations of *Une Femme m'apparut*. Not that I consider 'subtlety' as inherently desirable in situations of struggle. After all, subtlety may well be the favourite weapon of the strong, of the educated, of the aristocrats, and perhaps it is self-defeating for the relatively powerless to indulge in it. But, it might be interesting to wonder what different effects are produced by the short fictional narratives that do not wage an open war against one gender. At first sight, the stories appear to be much less 'gynocentric' than the rest of the work.[7] Both Vivien's poetry and her prose are generally characterized by the proliferation of female characters, and an explicit celebration of lesbianism. Vivien resorts to strategies currently adopted among minority or feminist circles who have faith in the power of counter-histories: the poet rewrites narratives written by others, she systematically seeks to reinterpret or rediscover myths, and searches for foremothers in literature and philosophy like medieval knights in pursuit of a sacred grail. Sappho, or 'Psappha' (*A Woman Appeared to Me*, 7 and ff) is the ideal model, a heroine 'misunderstood and slandered' (8) by history, the ancient mother with whom Vivien can identify, as a poet, a woman, a lesbian, and a foreigner. Her poems sing the praise of the Kitharèdes, viewed as heroic figures of anti-patriarchal resistance. The point of view is exclusively feminine, and the poems are dominated from beginning to end by an autobiographical female 'I'. The few male characters endowed with a fictional existence never become narrators. Not only is their point of view contemptuously disregarded but they are presented as negative models, anti-heroes. Their portraits are caricatures, allegories of evil. They represent and embody ugliness, barbarism, evil. In *Une Femme m'apparut*, Petrus appears as a modern version of Molière's ridiculous Trissotin. Stupid, arrogant, fatuous, he is dubbed the 'Prostitué Mâle', and the text obviously shows no desire to question the violently negative stereotypes attached to prostitution. Sexuality is reconfigured according to strictly mapped territories. Vivien's divisions could be seen as a sometimes unconscious parody of the most extremist homophobic narratives in the sense that a simple reversal separates her text from such discourses: homosexuality is now the norm and heterosexuality is an abnormal and shocking disease. When asked if a 'woman ever loved a man'

(53), San Giovanni, the poet, replies: 'I can hardly conceive of such a deviation of the senses. Sadism and the rape of children seem more normal to me' (53). Every heterosexual act is 'lâche comme le pillage, brutal comme la rapine, sanglant comme le massacre, et digne seulement d'une soldatesque ivre et barbare' (*Une Femme*, 68) 'brutal as rape, bloody as massacre, and worthy only of a drunken and barbaric soldiery' (*A Woman Appeared to Me*, 62)

les actions des hommes ont toujours eu pour but l'unique asservissement de la femme à leur caprice stupide, à leur sensualité, à leur tyrannie injuste et féroce. (103)

There is no trace of infiltration between the two genders. The only strategic move away from the original dominant model is a recentering of the oppressed and marginalized feminine pole. This is accompanied by a radical gesture of exclusion and a reimagining of metaphorical and ideological frontiers between women and their other. For the female narrators, the presence of men signifies either a bitter, endless struggle or bottomless indifference, either no contact, or violent confrontation. Vivien's texts are only interested in borderlands insofar as they are battlefields. They thrive on reinforcing binary oppositions and paradigms rather than on deconstructing them, and they see no reason to invent strategies of interconnection:

Tout ce qui est laid, injuste et féroce, émane du Principe Mâle. Tout ce qui est douloureusement beau et désirable émane du Principe Femelle. Les deux Principes sont également puissants, et se haïssent d'une haine inextinguible. L'un finira par exterminer l'autre, mais lequel des deux emportera la victoire finale? Cette énigme est la perpétuelle angoisse des âmes. Nous *espérons en silence* le triomphe définitif du Bien et du Beau, sur le Principe Mâle, c'est-à-dire sur la Force Bestiale et la Cruauté. (37)

Everything that is ugly, unjust, fierce, base, emanates from the Male Principle. Everything unbearably lovely and desirable emanates from the Female Principle. The two principles are equally powerful, and hate one another incurably. In the end, one will exterminate the other, but which shall be the final victor? That riddle is the perpetual anguish of all souls. We hope *in silence* for the decisive triumph of the Female Principle, the Good and the Beautiful, over the Male, that is, over Bestial Force and Cruelty. (8, my emphasis)

The male principle, posited as essentially threatening and dangerous, would ideally disappear altogether. The text does not wonder what would happen to Good without Evil or Beauty without Ugliness. Instead, a survival tactic is adopted: the goal is to construct some sort of isolated enclave, populated by women who can exchange ideas and share their thoughts and opinions. The masculine is literally excluded from the narrative. As San Giovanni puts it: 'I never love or hate men ... What I hold against them is the great wrong they have done to women. They are political adversaries whom I want to injure for the good of the cause. Off the battlefield of ideas, I know them little and am indifferent to them' (11). Silence imposed by men is replaced by silence chosen by women and imposed upon men. There is no dialogue outside confrontation, no contact outside struggle. Infiltration has no part in this imaginary absence of dialogue.

*La Dame à la louve* presents a slightly different situation. Although role reversals are still very common, the so-called 'battlefield of ideas' is the focus of most of the stories. The male principle is not excluded altogether, rather portrayed and analysed in the way it relates to the feminine. Although the stories may appear as simple and didactic little fables, a close reading suggests that the text does not always succeed in presenting its female and male characters as essentially different and profoundly incompatible. In other words, the stories may be more difficult to read than the autobiographical novel: while it may be impossible to find any trace of infiltrational figures or writing strategies in *A Woman Appeared to Me*, the fictional universe of *La Dame à la louve* may be a case of denied or repressed infiltration.

The repression of infiltration is probably what makes the short stories more interesting than the novel: in these texts, conflicts are not solved and questions remain unanswered while the characters preserve absolute differences between genders or gender roles. Between the conclusion of the didactic fable and the fictional demonstration it proposes, a contradiction slips in. An ironic distance separates the point of the fable (the woman always wins), or rather the desire to function like a fable (there is evil and then again, there is good), and the self-contradictory infiltrational economy of the narrative as a whole (a woman who acts like a male always wins against a male acting like a woman, provided nobody realizes that a reversal has taken place).

In *La Dame à la louve*, male characters are not excluded, quite the opposite. In fact, these texts are obsessed by the theme of the encounter between men and women, rather than by a representation of a viable segregation between genders. Here, the elimination of the hated other camp recedes to the background. The resolution of 'espérer en silence' is abandoned and replaced by the production of scenarios from which neither the masculine nor the feminine is excluded. However, the perspective is still political and feminist, the narration focusing on issues of authority and domination, or more exactly on the ways in which authority and domination are expressed when the two genders are brought together.

In violent contrast with the tone of the poems, these stories are decidedly optimistic in their overt message: they claim that women are always the winners of a confrontation which they did not want and did not start, but that they could not prevent due to men's aggressive behaviour. Women do not want to fight and would be happy to be left alone, but a male character always initiates a hostile dialogue. The same pattern reappears in 'La dame à la louve' [The Woman of the Wolf], in 'La chasteté paradoxale' [A Paradoxal Chastity], in 'La soif ricane' [Snickering Thirst] and in 'Brune comme une noisette' [The Nut-Brown Maid]. Utopian constructions move away from the creation of an ideal lesbian world where love and friendships between women are celebrated, explored or invented, and unlike *A Woman Appeared to Me* or most of the poems. At first, *La Dame à la louve* did not seem very different from Edgar Allan Poe's 'Berenice' or 'The Fall of the House of Usher', or from some of Baudelaire's prose poems, or Barbey d'Aurevilly's short fictions. The short stories are not interested in telling the tale of a passionate relationship between two women, and whatever utopian element is to be found in the stories is about the unrealistic depiction of reversed power relationships between males and females.[8]

The confrontation is similarly constructed in almost all the stories: the conflict occurs because a male character insists on courting a female character and fails miserably in his seduction attempt. The same pattern is present in 'The Woman of the Wolf', in 'A Paradoxal Chastity', in 'Snickering Thirst' and in 'The Nut-Brown Maid': the 'I' narrator is a male narrator, who remembers a painful incident involving himself and a woman. While the rest of Vivien's work is dominated by an autobiographical 'I' celebrating its triple identity as woman, lesbian, and poet, the narrators of the stories are pathetic male losers, usually addressing a specifically male audience.

The same feminist, or even separatist, tenets are thus upheld, but they are couched in indirect formulations. As a male narrator speaks, some textual voice has to speak louder in order for his version to be exposed as untrustworthy and ridiculous. In fact, this louder voice is better defined as a loud textual silence: a seething irony implicitly accuses the narrators and a disapproving lack of authorial intervention greets their incessant babbling. Although the point of the narrator's story is to justify himself and accuse the woman of arrogance and malice, somehow, what gets emphasized is his failure to make his own case. The feminist programme consists of putting the male narrator on the stand and letting us be the jury recognizing his contradictions. The point of the text is to be silent while the 'enemy' makes his case worse.

The role of the silent female listener who brings about change without even pleading her case could be compared to the status of Vivien's text within the canon: I wonder if it is an infiltrational practice to describe hegemonic discourse as having a voice, while making sure that we perceive the clumsy narrators' use of their privilege as a way to discredit themselves. If access to story-telling leads to self-exposure because the male protagonist unwillingly reveals the extent of his pathetic errors, then, it is tempting to see the failed heroes as a prophetic incarnation of dominant literary criticism whose voices insist that Vivien's work is minor, second-grade. Perhaps the male narrators can be read as a parody of male readers: the narrators address 'men', while the text predicts its own condemnation at the hands of the mainly male literary establishment, and arrogantly refuses the value of the judgement by portraying its critics as fools and ignorant readers. The stories do make an effort to elaborate on the theme of 'reading' and 'interpreting': the male narrators are not indifferent to signs, simply, they consistently misread the woman's text. Although this silent trapping of the adversary's discourse does seem promising from the point of view of infiltrators, on second thoughts, I find the strategy very problematic on at least two counts. First of all, it is never very clear what agency wants to claim silence as a signature. Moreover, it could be said that the stories are not infiltrational because they constitute a simple reversal of what stereotypically happens in the 'real' world or in realistic narratives: predicting the reaction of the male audience and equating it with a male narrator does not allow for the possibility of non-essential and critical gender (masculine) reconstructions. On the other hand, it is quite an interesting infiltrational strategy to tell the story of a women's strength using the channel of a conservative male voice. This possibility suggests that feminist critics may not be limited to collecting women's stories when they seek to give them a voice. It also suggests that each silenced individual may identify powerfully with the woman in this text.

Since each text tells the story of one confrontation, one limited encounter, I am tempted to compare them to the 'récits de partie', analysed in the *Practice of Everyday Life*:

A mémoriser autant que mémorables [les récits de parties] sont des répertoires de schémas d'action entre partenaires. Avec la séduction qu'y introduit l'élément de la surprise, ces mémentos enseignent les tactiques possibles dans un système (social) donné. (Certeau 1980, 66)

To be memorized as well as memorizable, they are *repertories of schemas of action* between partners. With the attraction that the element of surprise introduces, these mementos teach the tactics possible within a given (social) system (Certeau 1984, 23).

The reference is not innocent since it appears in a chapter entitled 'Popular cultures'. When Michel de Certeau describes 'récits de parties', he has in mind 'la belote d'hier soir ou le petit chelem de l'autre jour', he imagines card games played in popular cafés, usually among men. Perhaps, the parallel with Vivien's characters can only be ironic: far from being working class characters, her heroes evolve in highly stylized pastoral settings and do not seem concerned with practical problems or economic considerations.

The point is, however, that when players explain how a game developed, why someone won or lost, a repertory of tactics is constituted: a story is a case-study and a set of stories may amount to a sort of jurisprudence, setting precedents, establishing the effectiveness of certain strategies. If a collection of short stories presents upper class women as powerful hunters and travellers, rather than blaming the text for its unrealistic portrayal and simple reversals, the reader could choose to read it as jurisprudence. For Gayle Rubin,

Vivien scoured her sources for themes of female independence. Amazons, androgynes, and archaic female deities abound in her writing. Many of her prose pieces are tales of women as magnificent rebels. There are noble virgins, independent prostitutes, queens who choose poverty and freedom to the slavery of an unloved royal bed. (Rubin 1979, ix)

The magnificent rebels' narratives are thus endowed with a performative value. Like Bretécher's children, Vivien's heroines may be said to reappropriate the feminine and use their minority performance to rewrite their gender role. But the question of who is the heroine, who is the winner of a textual confrontation, does not exhaust the problem of power and identity: having tried to problematize the 'consultable' text and its intended uses, I obviously cannot hope to treat these short stories as recipes and turn to them as though they did not require interpretation and mediation. The confrontation between a male and a female character does not reassure me that women are generically protected by their silence. Besides, the stories insist on maintaining essentialist distinctions between male and female principles while reversing the power structure, which means that women's superiority is viewed as a consequence of men's weakness and ignorance. In other words, the male principle is always defeated, not because of the superiority of his adversary's strategy but because it never represented a threat to begin with.

## 'The Woman of the Wolf': the infiltration of silence

A more intriguing aspect of the stories is their insistence that there is a direct link between power and the use of a certain type of language: Vivien's text presupposes that men and women do not speak the same language, even if they think they do. In fact, the characters' way of using language is determined by their biological sex: another way of putting it is that men and women, in these stories, are allegories of discourse. Each sex speaks in a different tongue.

Naturally, the invisible discrepancy results in impossible dialogues, especially as the language issue is doubled by an incompatibility between man and woman's respective desire. Vivien's text thus offers a two-fold explanation of the characters' failure to engage in meaningful conversation: the nature of desire is different for each biological sex, and language, which might mediate this difference, cannot help solve the problem because man fails to interpret woman's discourse. Dialogue is replaced by silences and misunderstandings.

When a conflict occurs, it is almost always for the same reason: a man and a woman are brought together by textual fate (a voyage, a hunting trip, a visit to a brothel). A man meets a woman, and can relate to her only as an object of generic sexual desire. He courts her, and tries to win her over using every possible rhetorical tool. The woman's reaction is invariable: she does not feel attracted to the protagonist, or to anyone else. The male character talks about desire, and when he meets with a characteristically sobering response, he then keeps talking as a way of interpreting the woman's disappointing gestures or the few words she deigns to utter. Most of the time, however, the female character remains silent as long as she can, deferring the moment when she absolutely has to pay attention to her companion's ceaseless babble, usually to stop the narrator from acting on what he thinks is a clear agreement to further sexual games. His discourse is intended as a kind of foreplay, while she only uses language to mark the limit of their encounter.

In each dialogue, men make desperate efforts to interpret the woman's sparse sentences and gestures, only to meet with resounding failure. As a result, a tense situation finally degenerates into open conflict. When a male character insists on interpreting, on understanding, he only produces more hostility, more resentment, more violence: if man reads the woman's text, he usually starts a war and the initial situation of separation and misunderstanding escalates into a moment of physical violence. One of the two characters then becomes the victim of the male character's failed attempt to interpret the woman's words.

For example, in 'The Woman of the Wolf', the heroine is the only female passenger on a ship and the narrator decides to court her. Humiliated by this 'péronnelle' [little pretentious madam] who rejects him without a second thought, he apparently takes a sadistic pleasure in watching her drown when the ship sinks into the ocean. The reason given by the narrative for the woman's death is that, in spite of the captain's order, she refuses to part with her pet-wolf, and is therefore denied access to the life-boats. Because she refuses to abandon her own definition of important affections, because she clings to the she-wolf as the only object of her love and desire, the woman must be sacrificed. The captain and the narrator obviously consider that her priorities are at best childish, at worst, perversely abnormal. How can a woman prefer an animal to humankind, how can she suggest that a human being be sacrificed so that her wolf can take her place in the life-boats?

But the implicit questions about the definition of the human versus the animal would not necessarily find their answers in the kind of theoretical works produced by Donna Haraway, for the text suggests that the woman is not so much guilty of not respecting hierarchies between human and animal as of rejecting her male suitor. The narrator presents her death as the direct result of her refusal to talk to him. He suggests that, had she not humiliated him, he would have been willing to help her out of her predicament. According to the narrator, women's safety depend on men's willingness to save them (from themselves), and ultimately women have to agree to it in advance by allowing the narrator's interpretation of desire to prevail. According to the short story, the woman is killed by men's incapacity to accept her chaste silence:

Quant à moi, je ne pouvais véritablement pas m'embarrasser d'une semblable péronnelle. Et puis, elle avait été si insolente à mon égard! Vous comprenez cela, n'est-ce pas messieurs? Vous n'auriez pas agi autrement que moi. (20)

[For myself, I honestly could not burden myself with this pretentious little madam. And furthermore, she had been so insolent to me. You understand that, gentlemen, don't you? You would not have acted any differently from me. ('Woman of the Wolf', 13, slightly modified translation)]

In 'A Paradoxal Chastity', the situation is similar except that the narrator himself, rather than the woman, is the victim of the violence caused by his insistence on being desired. The heroine of the short story is a brothelkeeper, who, as the title indicates (perhaps ironically), is paradoxically 'chaste'. The narrator apparently believes that the fact that she employs a whole crew of prostitutes necessarily means that she is willing to sleep with their customers. Like the narrator of 'The Woman of the Wolf', the narrator proves incapable of questioning his own premises and of understanding what the woman says when he expects a different response from her.

When the heroine refuses to let him kiss her, he cannot interpret her refusal other than as the typical coquette's manoeuvre:

'Vous vous trompez, signor', répondit-elle, très calme. 'Je suis la marchande, je ne suis pas la marchandise'.
Je rencontrai son regard altier.
'Vous êtes une coquette de premier ordre', ricanai-je. 'Mais vous me plaisez. Tout l'or que vous me demanderez, je le verserai dans le creux de vos mains.
– Je vends les autres, mais je ne me vends point'.
Fou de désir, je l'attirai contre moi:
'Aime-moi car je t'aime'.
Et j'imposai à ces lèvres froides mon baiser fébrile. ('La Chasteté' 109)

['You have made a mistake, sir', she replied very calmly. 'I am the merchant, not the merchandise'.
I met her haughty look.

'You are a first-rate coquette', I laughed nervously. 'But you please me. I will pour all the gold you ask for into the palms of your hands'.
'I sell the others, not myself'.
Mad with desire, I pulled her against me. 'Love me, for I love you'.
And I imposed my feverish kiss on her cold lips. (61)]

As usual, the male narrator insists both verbally and physically, but, this time, the woman does not try to commit suicide: she stabs him with a 'stiletto – a filigreed and jeweled marvel which hung decoratively from her belt' (61). Only then does he finally realize that he had misconstrued the woman's discourse.

The point of both stories is apparently crystal-clear: whenever the narrator fails to interpret the woman's message, extra-textual violence ensues. If she means 'I have no desire (for you)', and if he understands instead 'you have desire for me', then a verbal duel develops and finally escalates into a life-threatening situation: one of the protagonists ends up dead, or maimed, or wounded.

As readers of Vivien's short stories, we may choose to hear a distinct warning in such endings: after all, should we not suppose that the woman writer identifies with her heroine and considers that her writings are likely to be misconstrued, interpreted as the equivalent of the coquette's speech? Are we implicitly warned that the text considers its point as obvious, and that we are not expected to look for supposedly ulterior motives or hidden meaning?

If, as readers, we try to engage in a dialogue with the stories, are we guilty of the same mistaken assumption as the narrators who approach the 'Woman of the Wolf' or the chaste brothelkeeper? When I try to interpret the stories, I am also confronted with what appears to be a relatively mysterious set of signs, which I hope to decipher thanks to my experience as a literary critic. The denouement of Vivien's parables lets us know that when a male character is guilty of arrogant misinterpretation, he will either perish or kill her. When I read *La Dame à la louve*, will I also misunderstand a woman's text? And should I fail to interpret, am I in danger of being violently aggressed by the text (perhaps I will be bored, or shocked, or distressed by what I imagine to be a pessimistic separatist and essentialist ideology). On the other hand, I could symbolically eliminate it like the narrator who does not want to take responsibility for the woman of the wolf (I could insist, for example, that I will not teach Vivien's short stories because they are 'poorly written', or 'weird', because they did not try to seduce me: 'You understand that, gentlemen, don't you? You would not have acted any differently from me'.) One may then wonder if the text provides solutions for the dilemma, but we are mostly confronted with anti-models of readers: the series of rather foolish male narrators. We are implicitly asked to do the opposite of what they do.

The vexing parameter of the narrators' failure is that it does not result from an absent-minded, hasty, or casual reading. They read the woman's text earnestly. When they narrate the encounter, after whatever disaster has befallen them, they sound a little like literary critics: not only do they tell us what conclusions they had reached, what meaning they ascribed to the woman's text, but they also elaborate on the process of decoding. They comment on their own interpretive skills, on their experience as readers of women, they tell us what reading method was used. The fact that they are neither negligent nor ignorant is troubling: it means that our good intention as readers of a text will not guarantee that we can avoid repeating the narrator's mistake. Obviously, we cannot hope that our (honest) desire to understand and our critical interest will save us from dangerous misunderstandings. Strangely enough, by refusing the thematic possibility of infiltration between the female character (always interpreted and incomprehensible) and the male character (incessant and failed interpreter), Vivien's stories infiltrate gender issues into the reading position and de-essentialize our own relationship to masculinity: in a sense, whatever our extra-textual biological sex, when we read *La Dame à la louve*, the text puts us in the position of the male narrator.

## Portrait of the critic as male reader

In the stories, women are case-studies, difficult texts. Their words, gestures, postures, and facial expressions must be minutely analysed according to a certain code. The male characters believe that they have acquired mastery of this code, and usually, they condescendingly refer to it as a 'platitude'. In the 'Woman of the Wolf', for example, the narrator brags that he can decipher, with accuracy, the meaning of the heroine's discourse because he 'had long studied the psychology of the feminine face' (6) [étudié depuis longtemps la psychologie sur le visage féminin (8)]. When the woman says, 'Allez-vous en [...]' (Go away), he does notice that the words have been uttered 'with almost savage decisiveness' (6) [avec une décision presque sauvage (8)], but he chooses not to interpret this 'allez-vous en' as an order or an injunction. As was the case with Colette, the problem revolves around the definition of different types of discourse and enunciation: the narrator's naivety lies in his refusal to admit that some texts are not interpretable at the level of daily practices. He constantly fails to identify orders, and he does perceive the difference between rhetorical tactics. Ironically, he carefully comments on his decision, he presents himself as an informed interpreter who is privy to specialized knowledge about women:

Voyez jusqu'où allait la fourbe de cette femme! Elle affectait, en m'écoutant, une distraction lunaire. On eût juré qu'elle s'intéressait uniquement au sillage d'écume, pareil à de la neige en fumée. (Les femmes ne sont point insensibles aux comparaisons poétiques.) Mais moi qui étudie depuis longtemps la psychologie sur visage féminin, je compris que ses lourdes paupières baissées cachaient de vacillantes lueurs d'amour.

Un jour je payai d'audace, et voulus joindre le geste flatteur à la parole délicate, lorsqu'elle se tourna vers moi, d'un bond de louve. 'Allez-vous en', ordonna-t-elle avec une décision presque sauvage. Ses dents de fauve brillaient étrangement sous les lèvres au menaçant retroussis. Je souris sans inquiétude. Il faut avoir beaucoup de patience avec les femmes, n'est-ce pas? Et ne jamais croire un seul mot de ce qu'elles vous disent. Quand elles ordonnent de partir, il faut demeurer. (8–9)

[Observe to what length this woman carried her deceitfulness! Listening to me, she adopted an air of moonstruck distraction. One would have sworn she was interested only in the foaming wake which looked like steaming snow. (Women are by no means indifferent to poetic comparisons.) But I, who had for so long studied the psychology of the feminine face, understood that her heavy, lowered eyelids concealed the vacillating glimmers of love.

One day, when I was particularly bold, uniting flattering gestures with delicate words, she turned toward me with a she-wolf's bound. 'Go away', she commanded with almost savage decisiveness. Her wolf-like teeth glittered strangely beneath lips drawn back in menace. Without anxiety, I smiled. You must have patience with women, must you not? And you must not believe a single word they say. When they command you to depart, then you must remain. Really, gentlemen, I am rather ashamed to serve you up such warmed-over and mediocre banalities. (7, translation slightly altered)]

I find it intriguing that the narrator's interpretation of the woman's words completely ignores the semantic content and concentrates exclusively on the rhetorical structure, on the type of discourse. The decision 'not to believe' what is said implies a knowledge of the

difference between declarative and performative statements, the
similarity between a coquetterie and an invitation: 'You must', 'you
must not'. Incapable of understanding the order as an order, the
narrator turns the interpretation of an order into a recipe.

The same pattern recurs in 'The Nut-Brown Maid', 'Snickering
Thirst' and 'A Paradoxal Chastity'. The male narrators cite the
woman, then propose a signification and a commentary that explain
their reading method. They refer to a code which they (we?) must
respect scrupulously. They thus legitimize the supposedly obvious
interpretation of their female protagonist, implying that each woman's text is generically encoded and that their knowledge makes the
encoding transparent. But their expertise as a critic and reader has
only one application: their goal is to understand so as to better
succeed in winning the woman over. A successful translation reveals
the woman's mandatory desire for man and its just as mandatory
coquettish expression.

Like experienced critics, male characters resort to a whole array of
interpretive strategies: a complex set of formulaic rules constitute the
canon of their interpretive skills. As we already know, 'Woman are
by no means indifferent to poetic comparisons' (6) [Les femmes ne
sont pas insensibles aux comparaisons poétiques (8)]. Besides, 'You
don't have to be crafty with women. They always notice it, but since
they are cleverer than you, they pretend not to notice it' (81) [Il ne
faut pas être roublard avec les femmes. Elles s'en aperçoivent
toujours, mais, comme elles sont plus fortes que vous, elles font
semblant de ne rien voir] (149).

Interpretive skills involve a mastery of a proverb-like knowledge
that is presented as the most obvious and banal truth. The recurrent
use of 'must you not?' [n'est-ce pas?] at the end of sentences recruits
us as sympathetic (male) readers that share the same canonical
wisdom and the same condescending attitude towards women. Such
knowledge is unquestionable, shared by the community at large. If
we argue that we are not conversant with those mating rituals, then,
we are either ignorant or we do not belong. The male narrator's
discourse is invaded with endless series of 'You must', 'you must
not' which they paradoxically present as useless reminders. Men are
thus portrayed as predictable readers who constantly use the same
strategy.

The text also insists that interpretive skills are used for a single
end. All narrators use dialogue as a prelude to more overtly sexual

exchanges, and they all define seduction in the same way: for them courting a woman means forcing her to reveal the genuine meaning hidden behind hostile rejoinders. Woman's desire is always veiled by rhetorical games, and man's role is to make sure that he sees through her ruses. Seduction is thus defined as a specific form of interpretation. One must read and respect the deciphering code in order to trick the other into expressing her desire.

Male desire is thus described as a generic interest for whoever is female and resists. It exhausts itself in the determination to force women to reveal their hidden desire, it is closer to a sophist's game than a post-Freudian concept. In 'The Woman of the Wolf', the narrator explains:

Elle n'était ni belle, ni jolie, ni charmante. Mais enfin, c'était la seule femme qui fût à bord. Je lui fis donc la cour. J'observai les règles les plus solidement étayées sur une expérience déjà longue. (6)

[She was neither beautiful, nor pretty, nor charming. But she was the only woman on board the ship. Therefore I courted her. I observed those rules which I had firmly established through long experience. (5)]

The amusing consequence of the narrators' firm belief that they master the rules is that the more self-confidence they express, the more ridiculous they sound to the reader, since the plot exposes their interpretation as ludicrous nonsense. Whenever a male character insists on forcing the woman to talk and to reveal what her silence hides, a superior narrative agency mercilessly denounces them as incompetent and stupid. In each story, the text makes it absolutely obvious that women remain silent out of disdain and contempt, not out of coquetterie. Two forms of silence combine to drive the same point home: an implicit and unformulated feminist perspective is at work behind the blabbering fools, and confirms the validity of the female character's reserve. The four stories discussed in this chapter are built on the same pattern: a silent woman does not deign to engage in a dialogue with the narrator, but his point of view is dismissed by textual irony.

In spite of their constant bragging and verbose explanation, the male narrators are portrayed as pathetic failures. Their much-publicized knowledge of deciphering rules only serves to highlight their blunders as bad translators and incompetent readers. The more insistently they refer to the woman's supposedly obvious coquetterie, and to the code of seduction that we all supposedly recognize and admire, the more irony the story mobilizes against them. Their would-be knowledge is exposed as crass ignorance and their would-be insights are marred with arrogance and self-congratulation. According to the narration, the male characters' error is two-fold: not only are they wrong to imagine that they know how to seduce women (their tactics are totally ineffective) but they are also wrong to believe that seducing any woman is a matter of skill, of strategy. Women, the irony of the text claims, simply will not be seduced because they cannot feel any sexual desire for men (or, one suspects, for anyone else). And each story insists on describing the heroine as a lofty and supposedly superior asexual being.

## 'Negative' ironies

But like all the forms of ironies that pretend to be superior to (outside of) the system they denounce, this form of critique is a very problematic *coup de force*. In 'Irony and the Canon', Chambers proposes a distinction between 'negative' and 'appropriative ironies':

Where negative irony is simultaneously adversative (with respect to its butt) and amnesiac (with respect to its own systemicity), appropriative irony is both anaclitic and anamnestic with respect to the system in which it is being inscribed ... Negative irony, in other terms, wants to have the last word; appropriative irony signals that it is not, and cannot be, the last word, that it is part of an open-ended historical process. (Chambers 1990, 23)

The silent woman does appear as a fictional alter-ego of the silent and ironic omniscient narrator that rejoices in the male narrators' discomfiture. But a 'system', to which the text is oblivious, supersedes the irony directed against the male characters: in fact, the text and the male character are not so different. The story interprets its characters in exactly the same way as the male character treats the female characters. In the same way as men think that every discourse produced by the woman can be analysed in terms of coquetterie and veiled desire, the stories, from their ironic vantage point, also impose a unique interpretation. The statement: 'Every woman is a coquette' is systematically replaced with another proposition: 'Any suspicion of coquetterie is arrogantly male and stupid because women do not desire'. The male character becomes ridiculous only if we are convinced by the implicit assumption, if we let the text 'have the last word'. To demonstrate that the male narrators are fools, 'The Woman of the Wolf' must presuppose that women are immune from seduction: no discourse can move them, or influence their position. Any attempt to elicit desire from them is always doomed.

The assumption raises two questions for me: first of all, is it possible (let alone desirable) to create a character that would be totally insensitive to seduction? A desireless character which no one's discourse could ever hope to move or touch? Are Vivien's characters not already influenced by other (male) representations when they try to embody some worn-out Parnassian cliché? Why do we need to portray women as a 'rêve de pierre' to prove that they will not be taken in by men's discourse? And secondly, from a literary point of view, how does the story as a whole know better than the narrator what women want (or rather do not want)? What superior reading principle allows the text to criticize the male narrator and make him the butt of the irony?

The story replaces the narrator's ideology (presented as a stereotype) with another ideology (to which we are invited to adhere unconditionally). Vivien's position reminds me of what I would call a Swiftian paradox: when Jonathan Swift, in his famous 'modest proposition', suggests that one should consider eating Irish children as a way out of economic crises, the ironic point of the story is made because it never occurs to us that cannibalism could be acceptable. The impossibility of accepting the solution literally leads to a search for an ironic interpretation. But it strikes me that our decision to look for irony also marks our belonging to a certain historical or social context which absolutely refuses to question certain assumptions. Swift's story is amusing because we do not think twice before associating 'cannibalism' with generic enemies (barbaric people, those we colonize and civilize), and because our political or literary unconscious idealizes children as innocent victims. It is already problematic that, in order to mend social injustices, Swift must appeal to some supposedly universal morality, which was part of the system that created them in the first place. But what would happen if we replaced 'cannibalism' with a given ideological position that does not function as an obvious, or hegemonic truth (the legalization of drugs for example)? What if the position chosen to fill the spot of 'cannibalism' does not strike us as either obviously 'right' or obviously 'wrong', or if we are convinced that it is 'good'? In Vivien's case, the problem is further complicated by the fact that her philosophical basis is utopian: in these stories, women always win, women are always powerful enough to impose their point of view, they never need to negotiate since the text marks them as 'right' from the beginning. By refusing to let male and female characters stage a dialogue for the reader, the text presupposes that we will instinctively share its ideological position. We should simply agree that the male narrators are wrong and that their interpretation is erroneous. But should we find ourselves in the position of a male narrator (having to interpret a woman's text and its silence), what guarantee do we have that we would not repeat their mistake? What do the stories propose as a superior interpretive strategy?

It seems to me that the text requires that we believe in a pre-conceived truth that is just as powerful and authoritarian as the patriarchal constructs it purports to undermine: it is almost as if we had to have read the rest of Vivien's work to appreciate the irony. The text's superior reading principle is intertextually guaranteed by the ideological infrastructure laid out in *Une Femme m'apparut* and the poems. The short story implicitly assumes that we know about the eternal struggle between the feminine and the masculine, and that we agree that the elimination of one of the principles is the desired goal. Vivien's feminist utopia functions as a reference, as an uncon-tested hegemonic discourse.

*La Dame à la louve* wishes to replace the narrator's vision by a system of its own in which the discourses of men and women are just as predictable and generically determined. The arrogant and ignorant narrator fails to seduce the woman, and he is exposed by a morally superior textual agency. An implicit judgement condemns the narra-tor, accuses him of being a poor reader, and provides no positive model other than a systematic reversal of roles. As Karla Jay correctly points out in *The Amazon and the Page*:

[the] conviction that men were fully replaceable by women in all areas of human existence was potentially a revolutionary one, but it led them [Barney and Vivien] merely to alter the gender of participants in traditional literary scenarios, without subjecting the resultant relationships to any sort of feminist analysis. (Kay 1988, 121)

## The disinfiltrated toad

I would now like to turn to one final story, 'The Nut-Brown Maid', in an attempt to explore the problems raised by the lack of what Jay calls 'feminist analysis'. I propose the text as an example of disinfiltration in which the woman's so-called victory over the male principle is seriously limited by the assumption that gender categories function like symmetrical territories. In 'The Nut-Brown Maid', the issue of correct (or at least efficient) reading becomes crucial because the text unwillingly admits that its own theories are not without ambiguities: it could be argued that the point of the 'Woman of the Wolf' is to insist that (all) male narrators are (always) poor readers. But this hypothesis is undermined by one of the pieces of the puzzle, 'Brune comme une noisette', in which a female character ends up suffering unnecessarily from her own interpretive error and serious misreading. From a more general point of view, the short story is sobering in its perhaps reluctant warning that reading errors cannot be used to define the 'other'.

On first reading, the story is quite similar to the others: a male narrator is in love with (or generically attracted to) his female companion, while her feelings for him are affectionate and chaste. As usual, the narrator's vain effort and frustration will eventually lead to a climactic (or anticlimactic) violent scene, the episode of the toad. Here is how the narrator describes the episode: one day, after exhausting his rhetorical resources in vain, he had tried to kiss Nell, and had been rewarded the following response:

'J'aimerais mieux avaler un crapaud que de me laisser embrasser par toi', dit-elle en montrant du doigt la minuscule bête brune qui lui avait suggéré cette comparaison peu flatteuse pour ma personne. (152)

['I would prefer to swallow a toad than to let you kiss me', she said, pointing her finger at the minuscule brown beast which had suggested to her this hardly flattering comparison. (83)]

Like the narrator of 'The Woman of the Wolf', the man immediately distances himself from the intensity of the refusal and he starts analysing the text: he concentrates on the rhetoric of the woman's text. Unlike his male counterparts, he does not jump to the conclusion that the 'coquetterie' structure provides an overarching explanation. In fact his first analysis is correct, he correctly understands that Nell's discourse constitutes a comparison, that she is, in effect, calling him a toad. I am interested in his reaction to the comparison because it is both similar to the other male narrators and quite different at the same time: like the others, he does not give up, he does not interpret the woman's text as an order. But, unlike the

others, he resorts to a very efficient and devious tactic. Instead of
suggesting that Nell means the opposite of what she says, he
pretends that she means exactly what she says:

Une idée assez lâche, je l'avoue, mais ingénieuse, traversa ma cervelle. Tout
endolori, je me livrai à une chasse effrénée, qui eut pour résultat la capture
du petit crapaud.
'Avale-le tout de suite', ordonnai-je, 'ou je t'embrasse de force'.
Elle me regarda bien en face. Grave, elle comprit que je ne plaisantais point.
Un mépris inexprimable serpenta sur ses lèvres minces, lèvres d'ascète,
lèvres d'hermite. Elle prit l'affreuse bestiole, et l'avala, un peu plus pâle
seulement. (152–3)

[An idea, a cowardly one, I admit, but ingenious nevertheless, crossed my
mind. Totally in pain, I abandoned myself to a frantic chase, which resulted
in the capture of a little toad.
'Swallow it right away', I ordered, 'or I'll kiss you by force'.
She looked at me right in the face. Looking solemn, she understood that I
was not joking in the least. An expression of unutterable scorn crept onto
her thin lips, the lips of an ascetic and a hermit. She took the horrid little
beast and swallowed it, turning only a little paler. (83–4)]

Apparently, once again, the woman has won. And, once again, her
victory reinforces the dichotomy between the demonized masculine
and the idealized feminine, once again, the female heroine is
perceived as perfectly capable of resisting man's impure desire but
we know nothing about her own desires. And at this point, I wonder
if feminist readers would not share (rather than mock) the male
narrator's discouragement. On the one hand, one may celebrate the
fact that the female character is not a passive stereotype. A possible
summary of the episode is that the narrator is utterly ridiculed for
refusing to understand that 'no means no' (if I may anachronistically
borrow the slogan) and, after all, for a modern reader familiar with
the slogan, the conclusion of the incident may have therapeutic or
deterrent value.

But I still wonder what kind of victory is celebrated in this text. Is
it not disappointing to realize that the only way in which a woman
can convince a narrator is to transform her metaphor into literal
absorption of a toad? If she chooses to express her disgust through a
metaphor, an admittedly ferocious comparison between her suitor
and a small ungraceful animal, why must she be forced to literalize
it, why must she use her body to make her point when the
effectiveness of her strategy came precisely from her power to
imagine a comparison? It seems to me that the woman loses out

when she gives up her privilege to metaphorize her feelings. I would argue that, in the end, the male narrator's 'cowardly and ingenious tactic' is indeed successful, since the woman is seduced into internalizing the very symbol of her repulsion. After all, she swallows her words at the same time as the toad and one may wonder just how deadly and self-destructive it is to swallow one's words instead of food.[9]

From a narratological point of view, the reader may also legitimately ask yet another question: does the text really justify Nell's self-sacrificial gesture? What narrative logic is invoked at the moment when the female character accepts to do violence to herself by swallowing a 'hideous' beast. Suicide and self-sacrifice are leitmotivs in the entire book, but Nell's position is particularly ambiguous compared to the 'Woman of the Wolf', for instance. Although that character remains calm among the terrified crowd, she does not want to die. If she finally drowns, it is because she was forced to make a tragic choice: either she abandons the wolf and saves herself, or she remains faithful to her companion and dies with her. The text makes it clear that the two alternatives are imposed upon the woman. Symbolically, she must choose between the narrator's crude overtures and her exclusive love for her animal alter ego, she must recant or commit suicide. Thematically, the fact that she chooses death is a proof of her loyalty to her beliefs, but more importantly it proves that the male narrator is a bad reader: the woman's suicide confirms that the 'allez-vous en' was indeed an order and not a 'coquetterie'.

I argue that Nell's gesture is much more ambiguous because it contradicts and invalidates, rather than confirms, the meaning of her declaration. From a literary point of view, her gesture is still spectacular, it is more original than the ophelic disposition of the woman of the wolf, and it is a symbolically rich gesture of ambivalent internalization. But from a strategic point of view, Nell's feast marks the limits of an imaginary universe which seeks to exclude the problems of seduction altogether. Seduction is, in itself, a form of infiltration in the sense that it implies that someone's desire does not necessarily preexist discourse or that someone's desire can be changed by discourse. If the text, in order to make its point, must claim that the woman can never partake in a seduction enterprise, then Nell's gesture becomes contradictory and impossible to understand.

Let me cite the passage immediately preceding the spectacular denouement of the toad episode in an attempt to explain what troubles me about Nell's strategic logic or lack thereof. The narrator remembers:

Nous étions en pleine forêt, par un soir très vert, lorsque je tentai de l'embrasser sur la bouche. Elle me planta entre les deux yeux un coup de poing si formidable que j'en fus défiguré pendant plus de deux semaines ... Deux semaines pendant lesquelles mes camarades de chasse me raillèrent impitoyablement. (152)

[One green evening we were in the middle of the forest when I tried to kiss her on the mouth. She punched me between the eyes with such a tremendous blow that I was disfigured by it for more than two weeks ... two weeks during which my hunting companions teased me mercilessly. (83)]

After such a demonstration of physical strength, I really wonder what Nell fears from Jerry. It seems to me that this episode demonstrates that the woman is far from powerless, and that she is in a position to make sure that her words are taken seriously. When the narrator demands ('commande'), 'Avale-le tout de suite ou je t'embrasse de force', it seems to me that he has just demonstrated that he is in no position to indulge in this kind of ultimatum. He is bluffing, his show of authority is not guaranteed by any real power and he cannot act upon his threat since Nell is so obviously stronger than he is. Then why does she not laugh at him instead of swallowing the toad? Why is she taken in by his bluff? Is the narrative contradicting itself, suddenly adopting a different logic of realism?

Nell's incomprehensible surrender is all the more vexing as the relationship between physical strength and gender is treated in a most ambiguous manner in almost all of the stories. Vivien plays with the stereotype according to which men are naturally stronger than women. Faithful to her favourite tactic, she reverses gender roles. All her female characters are strong, resilient, all her male characters are 'nervous', weak and impressionable. But, in spite of the systematic reassignment of traditional gender attributes, Vivien's texts are apparently not interested in celebrating strength as a feminine feature: strength remains a male characteristic, as if the text could not bring itself to admire and celebrate it once it has been reappropriated by the feminine principle. Strong female characters remain exceptions to the rule, even after the rule has become a statistical exception. Individual characters and gender roles are still perceived as separate and incapable of influencing each other.

For instance, in 'Snickering Thirst', Jim readily admits that he is a 'feverish weakling' (18) [un fiévreux débile].[10] Polly, on the other hand, is 'disgustingly healthy' (18) [vigoureusement saine (29)]. During a bitter quarrel, the narrator makes the point that he only refrains from violence because he knows that he will not have the upper-hand:

> Je l'aurais volontiers fait taire d'un coup de pied ou de poing mais des expériences réitérées et douloureuses m'avaient persuadé que la vigueur physique de Polly surpassait de beaucoup la mienne. Je n'avais sur elle qu'une vague supériorité mentale. Et encore! Le bon sens de ma compagne m'a souvent tiré d'un mauvais pas, ce que n'auraient pas pu faire mes divagations de songe-creux. (27)

> [I would happily have slapped her or kicked her, but too many unhappy former experiences had convinced me that Polly was far stronger than I. All I had over her was a vague mental superiority. And yet, my companion's good sense had often gotten me out of a bad spot, something which my visionary meanderings could never have done. (16)]

Recognizing Polly's physical strength does not modify the system which paralyses the two protagonists: an unshakable prejudice pervades Jim's conclusions. Neither he nor apparently the omniscient narrator can interpret Polly's strength and his own powerlessness as anything but a freak occurrence, what I called a 'weak performance' in the first chapter. Gender roles are not altered at all: 'She is tougher and more solid than a man. She could send me rolling six feet with the flick of her wrist' (18) [Elle est plus hardie et plus solide qu'un mâle. Elle m'enverrait rouler à dix mètres d'une chiquenaude (29)].

Strangely enough (or perhaps precisely because of this lack of infiltration), the narrators have a very realistic idea of their limited strength, and yet they never lose confidence in their own superiority. They remain arrogantly confident although they lack the power to enforce any decision. They are endowed with this 'vague mental superiority' (16) [vague supériorité mentale (27)] that they can neither describe nor transform into authority or domination. If the principle of lingering 'vague' power is problematic from a political and strategic point of view, I have to admit that I am interested in Vivien's description as an explanation of contemporary debates: power, even in its most diffuse and differential Foucauldian manifestation, does not simply change hands when new epistemic para-

*digms of knowledge (feminism, ethnic studies) gradually emerge as relatively dominant.

Even if they are not stronger, male characters are always tempted to resort to force as a guarantee of the performative value of their statements. The 'Avale-le tout de suite ou je ...' is almost a case of generative syntax: a formula that could serve as the basis of a male narrative grammar. The narrators stick to their ultimatum even if, as in the case in this story, they are quite incapable of establishing their physical superiority.

In the 'Woman of the Wolf', the narrator must 'beat [his] retreat, mildly humiliated' (4) [battre en retraite, légèrement humilié (5)] as soon as the woman turns against him. In 'A Paradoxical Chastity', the man is executed in a split second as soon as he tries to kiss the heroine, and, in 'Snickering Thirst', Jim must be content to bitterly rehash impossible dreams of revenge:

Je la hais férocement parce qu'elle est plus forte et plus vaillante que moi ... Je la hais comme une femme exècre l'homme qui la domine. Je finirai certes par la tuer un jour pour le plaisir de la vaincre, tout simplement. (34)

[I hate her ferociously because she is stronger and more valiant than I. I hate her the way a woman detests a man who masters her. One of these days I will wind up killing her, for the pure pleasure of conquering her ... (21, translation slightly modified)]

In most cases, the narrators need the category of 'feminine weakness' to interpret women's texts, but they are themselves better representatives of this supposedly feminine attribute. They are caught in the most visible of contradictions and the narration does not spare them any humiliation. Yet, the pattern makes me wonder what logic is invoked when the story suggests that Nell takes Jerry's threat seriously. After all, the ultimatum emanates from a rather pathetic adversary. Why does she swallow a toad if he is so weak? He could not have kissed her by force.

The question troubles me because one of the possible answers is that Nell makes exactly the same mistake as the male narrator of the 'Woman of the Wolf': she is confused about the genre of discourse being used by her interlocutor. The man took an order for a coquetterie, interpreted 'go away' as a sign that he should stay, while Nell here reads a rhetorical bluff as an order. The former thought he could use a power that he really did not have, Nell thinks that she does not have a power which she really has. She is as bad a reader as he is because she allows a powerless character to trap her into an alternative without questioning the fact that the system which has produced the alternative cannot enforce it. Instead of pointing out to Jerry that he is in no position to force her to choose between being kissed by him or swallowing the toad, she does swallow the toad.

The fact that the woman does not avail herself of a very real possibility to refuse to play the game, to refuse to choose between two insufferable options, is in contradiction with the insistent message in the stories which seems to be, precisely, that she must be given the option not to choose (to choose between men or between men and women). The text claims the right to say neither yes nor no, it claims the right to silence and indifference, but when a woman has enough power to choose silence, then, she has become enough of a man to have turned into a poor reader who reproduces the narrator's mistake.

I would therefore argue that it is somewhat self-contradictory to present the toad episode as a victory for Nell. Isn't she indeed taken in by Jerry's 'cowardly ... but ingenious' tactic? After all, this clumsy narrator, who, unlike others, does not claim to comprehend female psychology, is capable of seduction in the sense that he manages to lure Nell into willingly doing something that is contrary to her own interests.[11] Nell is deceived by a character who feigns to believe that he can overpower her and finally does so when she swallows his bait. Jerry pretends that Nell's grandiloquent declaration about the toad is literal, even though he knows very well that it is a 'comparison' and she does not stop to consider that she certainly has the right or, at any rate, the power to identify her metaphor as a rhetorical trope.

I call this 'seduction' because when the text portrays a female character who thus chooses to hear Jerry's challenge (or bluff) as an order, I wonder if the implication is not that Nell is in fact attracted to a stereotypical image of the male hero. She jumps at the opportunity to show off her contemptuous courage and iron deter-mination. By insisting on demonstrating that she is fearless and capable of extreme self-control, she ends up valorizing her enemy's values and reinforcing stereotypical definitions of powerfulness. Instead of celebrating the effectiveness of her metaphors, she gives in to literalization. After all, the kind of strength she displays for Jerry is more Spartan than Sapphic. Like the crow who takes it upon itself to put its voice to the test when it could have been content to bask in the fox's flattery of its beauty, Nell is seduced into demonstrating how heroic she is and how weak her opponent is. Since her own discursive universe places courage and strength on the side of masculinity, I suppose that it is not too far-fetched to suggest that she is tricked into trying to pass for a male. Jerry's victory is to turn her into a reluctant infiltrator who uses infiltration against herself.

Like Polly, Nell is undoubtedly 'plus hardie qu'un mâle'. Yet, she still answers to the authority of an abstract construction which opposes masculine strength and feminine weakness and tries to make a point which her adversary has already conceded. In order to overpower Jerry, she has to buy into the ideology that glorifies physical strength and despises whoever does not live up to such stoic values. Like Jerry, like all the other male characters, Nell would rather dominate the 'weaker' protagonist than try to understand their different use of language. Seduced into showing her contempt for this weakling of a male, Nell does not realize that the price she pays for her victory is higher than the price she would have had to pay for a so-called defeat: I would argue that her impulsive response to Jerry's fake challenge leads to self-victimization. By accepting to go through the unnecessary ordeal set up by Jerry, Nell does not prove anything new: Jerry would not have kissed her by force anyway since he does not have that kind of strength. In a sense, Jerry's seduction attempt is a success thanks to this clever use of an ideology which continues to make him the representative of power (as a male expected to be brave and strong). I wonder if this contradiction is the ultimate irony of the short stories. The overt message is the male narrators' efforts at interpreting will forever be defeated: the woman's text is always crystal clear, its only meaning is that she is immune to seduction. But this is never convincingly demonstrated. The narrators, it is true, consistently make the same dangerous mistake (they believe that woman is *always* about to be captivated by their discourse), but the text cannot impose, as a counter-proposition, that it necessarily follows that woman will *never* be seduced by language. I wonder if that irony is not the only infiltrational twist in a text which ultimately recognizes that all discourse will be mediated by different readers, that each text is interpretable, and that desire cannot be so easily controlled, even in the name of resistance to undesirable power structures.[12]

# Notes

1  *A Woman Appeared to Me*, translated from the French by Jeanette H. Foster came out in 1976 (Naiad Press) and was reprinted in 1979. *The Woman of the Wolf* was published by the Gay Presses of New York in 1983, translated by Karla Jay and Yvonne Klein.

2  See Shari Benstock's discussion of the relative tolerance to lesbian cross-dressers in Paris and of the strategies used by women to oppose the *préfet de police*'s prohibition (Benstock 1986, 177 ff).

3  I borrow Elyse Blankley's phrase: her article on Renée Vivien is entitled: 'Return to Mytilène: Renée Vivien and the City of Women'.

4  In her *Souvenirs indiscrets*, Barney claims that she was at the origin of the foundation of the Academy: 'Pourquoi dis-je à Renée, ne rassemblerions-nous pas autour de nous un groupe de poétesses comme celles qui entouraient Sapho à Mytilène et qui s'inspireraient mutuellement'. [I said to Renée: 'Why not gather around us a group of women poets like the ones who lived with Sappho at Mytilène and inspired each other,' my translation (51)]

5  See for example Elaine Marks' important article on Renée Vivien. Marks suggests that the reasons why Renée Vivien's work has been excluded from the canon, are paradoxically the same as those invoked to justify its inclusion into literary anthologies. Comparing Charles Maurras's text on Vivien in *Le Romantisme féminin* and Gayle Rublin's introduction to *A Woman Appeared to Me*, Marks criticizes both Maurras's 'nationalist, monarchist and antisemitic' (178) reading and Rubin's feminist approach on the ground that they participate in the same ideological construction. She concludes that 'If it is unpardonable to proscribe her because she and her texts are dangerous to humanity, it is equally unpardonable to prescribe or proscribe her because she either is or is not part of an imaginary lesbian-feminist family' (189).

6  I do not necessarily equate silence with powerlessness or invisibility but the question belongs to the larger issue of who is speaking for whom. For an interesting discussion of the fact that 'It is almost impossible to write about writing without using metaphors of speech' (247), see Christopher Miller's chapter on 'Senegalese Women Writers, Silence, and Letters: Before the Canon Roars' (Miller 1990, 246–53). See also the introduction to *Out of the Kumbla* for a discussion of the concept of 'voicelessness' (Davies and Fido 1990)

7  In her introduction to the English translation, Karla Jay adopts a different point of view. According to her, 'Though some of Vivien's other works, including *A Woman Appeared to Me* ... are gynocentric – that is, place women at the core of human experience – it is in *The Woman of the Wolf* that her stance is most explicit' (ii). Jay, however, is especially referring to the short story entitled 'The Veil of Vashti,' which rewrites the biblical figure of Vashti into a positive rebellious heroine. 'The Veil of Vashti' takes two well-known Biblical tales – the stories of Lilith and of Vashti – and recreates them so that these women are no longer peripheral figures but become central ones. In the Bible the rebellious Lilith is merely a preface to obedient Eve as the disobedient Vashti precedes the faithful Esther' (ii).

8  The themes of the stories are not explicitly lesbian, except for one fairy-tale in which Vivien ironically and humorously rewrites the classic 'bed-trick' from a feminist perspective. In 'Prince Charming' [Le Prince Charmant], the hero of the story will of

course turn out to be a charming princess (*La Dame à la louve* 39–45, *The Woman of the Wolf* 23–8).

9 The choice of the toad as an expression of disgust is probably not innocent either: should we wonder if the interiorization of disgusting non-food has something to do with anorexic behaviours? One of the prevalent biographical myths about Renée Vivien is that she starved herself to death. Is the woman with the toad reminiscent of the eccentric character depicted by Colette in *Le Pur et l'impur*? Colette remembers a woman drinking glasses of 'trouble elixir' [cloudy elixir] which she thought tasted like acid [some sort of vitriol] (67). She also alludes to a letter written by Vivien in which she complained that she had inadvertently gained ten pounds and was leaving for ten days on a starving retreat (71–2). Or, should we see the episode as a humorous rewriting of the ways in which fairy tales use toads and other supposedly disgusting animals? Little girls or princesses often start spitting out toads or serpents when they do not say what they are expected to say. Should we also notice that, in Vivien's text, the toad never turns into Prince Charming, and that Nell refuses to believe that the symbol of her disgust could magically be turned into an object of desire as the result of a story?

10 Jim matches the typical description of *femmes fiévreuses* as portrayed in late nineteenth-century decadent literature. See especially Rachilde's *Madame de Sade* or *L'Animale*.

11 Contrary to the narrator of 'The Woman of the Wolf,' Jerry perceives himself as a rather incompetent reader: he has 'never had the time to study women' (80) [jamais eu le temps d'étudier les femmes (147)] and the only conclusion he can draw is that 'with women, everything is possible and nothing is certain' (81) [avec les femmes tout est possible et […] rien n'est certain (148)]. Yet, like other male narrators, he expresses his self-declared ignorance through proverb-like generalizations and formulas. Jerry claims: 'women get on my nerves. I understand nothing of their ways, I prefer wild animals' (81, translation slightly modified) [les femmes m'agacent, je ne comprends rien à leurs façons, je préfère les fauves (147)].

12 An earlier version of this chapter appeared in French in *Atlantis* : see 'Renée Vivien: résistance et velléité,'*Atlantis* 17.2 (spring–summer 1992): 32–43.

# Conclusion

# James Bond as civil servant: the limits of infiltration

> Although the political discourses that mobilize identity categories tend to cultivate identifications in the service of a political goal, it may be that the persistence of disidentifications is equally crucial to the rearticulation of democratic contestation. (Butler 1990, 4)

> A kind of fragile community can be composed of people who disagree with one another. (Gilroy 1993, 253)

Infiltration, as described in this book, is not an event: I have started from the premise that I usually imagine the infiltrator as an outsider who suddenly or gradually seeps into a more coherent structure. This has allowed me to focus on relatively powerless infiltrators that the system calls foreigners, women, lesbians, housecleaners, people of colour. What I hope to have demonstrated is that I need this definition of the infiltrator as someone who penetrates a closed territory, only to expose it as power's fantasy. What the infiltrator and the infiltrational texts know, is that, from the very beginning, what parades as the core is always already a juxtaposition of disparate elements that needs to represent itself as a series of binary and unequal oppositions: the insider versus the outsider, the whites versus the blacks, the rich versus the poor, the straight versus the queer. Infiltration is not a critique of binary oppositions *per se*, rather, it is a desire to know when exactly and for how long it may be necessary to adopt the discourse of binary oppositions in order to survive, when one places oneself in a position from which one can undermine the system.

There are obviously limitations to such an enterprise. In conclusion, I would like to stress the ambivalence of the infiltrator as a

cultural, social, moral agent, but also as a textual figure. Once I
accept the hypothesis that the core is always the very site of
infiltration, it becomes evident that fluids and solids are a convenient
but paradoxical opposition. As a result, even if I start from the
assumption that the infiltrator is closer to water because of the
historical layers of metaphors which construct our discourse, I also
know that it will not be tenable to insist that there is an essential
distinction between the infiltrator and the infiltrated. The process is
always reversible because, from the beginning, it was both a
dynamic phenomenon (a constant exchange or displacement of
elements) and the structure of the territory itself (at any given time,
what appears as the coherent part of the core is, in reality, a
juxtaposition of fluid and solid parts). The infiltrating element itself,
especially if it is a subject with agency, is part of the process and
becomes an infiltrated element too. Infiltration, as soon as it is
recognized as a form of relationship, as the definition of communities, works both ways. The infiltrator is infiltrated by the juxtaposition of old and new, dissimulation and exposure, secret and
revelation; he or she is at times the insider, at times the outsider,
accepted as a foreign element or as one of 'ours', always in danger of
(or saved by the possibility of) being mistaken for a fluid or a solid
element. Like the 'post-colonial' as described by Ella Shohat, infiltration does not, ultimately authorises a meaningful distinction between the passive and the active voice:

While one can posit the duality between colonizer/colonized and even neo-
colonizer/neo-colonized, it does not make much sense to speak of post-
colonizers and post-colonized. (Shohat 107)

Even the conscious infiltrator who works at undermining a given
system (as opposed to the immigrant who thinks that survival is at
the price of assimilation for example) could be ironically deprived of
his or her oppositional position by time and circumstances: let us
imagine that a spy is assigned a mission. Let us call this spy John
Dunbar or Kevin Costner. In order to establish a temporary safe
house within the foreign country, he must become one of 'them'.
He must speak like them, act like them, break all ties with the
organization to which he officially belongs, and, like Bretécher's
little girl, he must learn the cultural acceptable performances. Even if
he carefully preserves his identity as an infiltrator for himself, no
narrative should be able to distinguish him at this point. (The fiction

of) his original self is only preserved by the knowledge, shared by a few individuals, that, when the time comes, he will secretly or openly perform the series of destructive acts described in his assignments. Time, in this scenario, is the metaphor for the infiltrator's ambivalence: there is indeed a moment during which nothing distinguishes the spy from the others. His differed difference is similar to that of each subject in the group. Let us now imagine that a contact, sent by the 'outside' (the infiltrator's supposedly real 'inside') is supposed to signal the end of invisibility. Let us also imagine that, as the result of a stupid espionage book accident, the contact in question dies or disappears before he has had a chance to meet with the isolated spy. Not knowing that this identity as an infiltrator is now a figment of his own imagination (or that he is the last repository of such a story), the spy continues to 'pass' successfully, waiting for a message that will never come. He now lives what would be called an infiltrated life, both as an infiltrator and as an infiltrated subject: if we agree that a culture does not exist outside the discontinuous practices and discourses reinvented by each subject's acts of enunciation, then, our spy is both part and creator of, this culture which he is supposedly imitating. When the spy dies, of natural causes, without having had a chance to complete his mission, was he a model citizen fantasizing himself as a spy? A failed spy? A failed citizen? Or was he the very image of our own mixture of loyalty and treason towards whatever power both protects and oppresses us?

When I say that 'time' is of essence in this case, or that time is the metaphor for the infiltrator's ambivalence, I might as well reformulate and suggest that the identity of the infiltrator depends on what narrative is produced about him or her: in my example, I can isolate an ambiguous period, during which the spy waits for the moment when he can reveal his 'real' allegiance, but I know that this 'period' is arbitrary, that, rather than being a period of latency and anticipation, it could also be viewed as the infiltrator's positioning. When I imagine that the contact never reaches him, I am choosing a particular form of scenario, I am writing one of the possible infiltration stories. I suggest that there are, basically, two ways of telling such a story: either I emphasize the temporary and supposedly artificial quality of the period during which the spy is indistinguishable from the infiltrated culture (I insist on the difference, I recruit my reader as an accomplice of the power that sent the infiltrator), or, on the contrary, I stress the ambivalence and ironies of the spy as infiltrated agent. Whether I concentrate on the period of time which precedes the actual enactment of the mission, or on the mission itself, a very different picture of the infiltrator obtains. In the former case, I focus on the ambivalence of the spy as infiltrated, or contaminated by, the culture he or she supposedly wanted to endanger (typical scenarios include the story of the spy who falls in love with the enemy, who makes friends with the natives, etc.). In the latter case, my narrative will make sure that I preserve the difference between the spy and the infiltrated structure by maintaining (technological) contact for example.

The first kind of story, carried to an extreme, suggests an oppositional use of infiltration narratives: what I would call the 'imagined infiltrator' syndrome. If I start from the premise that millions of infiltrators have eventually lost touch with their original goal, I suspect each and every member of my community of being an outsider who wants to deprive me of my power. But, in my powerless moments, I can also hope that everyone is a potential ally. The fear, hope and mistrust bred by such a realization, is, I suspect, as creative as it is destabilizing: it deprives me of a form of power (the belief in my identity, in my own legitimacy) which I sometimes use to exclude and oppress others without knowing it. It forces me to remain a step ahead of my own prejudices, to question my previously accepted definitions of superior and inferior, powerful and powerless. Concretely speaking, it prevents me from using my own power in a non self-conscious way. We have seen an example of this in the chapter on *Lettres à une noire*. Reading my (a) housecleaner's diary makes me become aware that I may be the object of study rather than (or at the same time as) a powerful employer. If I start looking at each of the members of my 'community', and if I start looking at myself as always already infiltrated and infiltrating, a new metaphorical and discursive universe is created: I *imagine* infiltration as the always possible explanation for identities. This, admittedly, requires a leap of faith, it requires the belief that untold stories of infiltration circulate outside of myself, that infiltrators are not necessarily the visible heroes of detective fiction. If I imagine the other as an infiltrator, disorder, contamination, impurity all become part of a chaotic system to which I belong and I can potentially provide an oppositional narrative even of my own powerlessness: for example, Lorna Goodison, in an interview with

Wolfgang Binder, suggests that Afro-American or Caribbean slaves could be imagined as infiltrators and that such utopian constructions could foster hope and encourage the struggle for dignity.

> I could not believe that everybody was left back in Africa, in places were slaves were taken from. Not everybody was taken, and they were seeing their fathers and mothers, and relatives taken off to what obviously could not have been a pleasant experience. And I could not believe they did not do anything at all, that they were absolutely powerless. So it came to me that maybe, just maybe, Nanny could have been deliberately trained and sold into slavery to fight this resistance war. (Goodison, 53)

Nanny, one of the most famous female leaders of Jamaican maroons, has achieved the status of 'national hero' (sic) since the independence of Jamaica in 1972. It may thus be said that her story has been slightly flattened and that her struggle is now difficult to distinguish from the other heroic deeds of national figures from other times, other countries, other traditions. As desirable as it is to have her 'recognized' as a liberator, her story is now trapped by the paradoxical structure examined in the chapter on Michèle Maillet. Goodison's invention of Nanny as infiltrator is even more satisfying and rich in opposition potential even if it must remain a 'maybe, just maybe' narrative. Goodison's vision preserves the infiltrator's invisibility, the ambiguity of his or her positioning, and refuses to stabilize Nanny's identity. Her ambivalence becomes the potentially eruptive power of each slave, who, maybe, just maybe, was trained alongside with Nanny of the Maroons. I can also imagine pedagogical implications of Goodison's vision: I wonder for example what it would mean to become an underground feminist, or to prepare infiltrated reading lists for MA courses. The series of texts presented here could have functioned as the promotion of an invisible canon (had I not given away the story of how the book was composed in the introduction). For the delicate balance between silence and voicelessness is also a matter of determining when and how revealed infiltration is most useful and more desirable. The 'just maybe' of Nanny's untold and unofficial story is both the greatest danger and the most powerful ingredient of imagined infiltration. It is dangerous because the infiltrator runs the risk of dying without achieving any archivable change, of leaving surviving infiltrators isolated and utterly deprived of the support provided by the fiction of a community; it is however powerful because the story does not need to be told, nor to be heard, to function as a reservoir of oppositional hope. Not to mention that, if I perceive myself as a member of the country that is being infiltrated by 'others', if I forget that I am an agent of contamination and infiltration myself, I may be tempted to violently resist the hypothesis that I am surrounded (indeed traversed by) constant, shapeless, yet ultimately efficient, processes of infiltration.

Surely, the knowledge that each infiltrator can be infiltrated too is politically disturbing both when one is aware of 'fighting this resistance war' and when one perceives oneself as opposed by illegitimate outsiders. Which is why the second narrative, that I will now try to outline, is probably much more frequent and easily recognized as a plausible scenario: for the sake of convenience, I will call the second such type of narratives the 'James Bond stories'.

James Bond is the opposite of Nanny of the Maroons because his career has nothing to do with silence, powerlessness, and tentative identities. James Bond is infiltration as recuperated by a system that needs to avoid invisibility and ambivalence while recognizing its inability to totally eradicate them. Telling a tale which forgets that the infiltrator's story could be a powerful form of silence entails manipulating time: I must indicate, very specifically, when the process of infiltration begins and when it ends. If I want to control the infiltrator, I must pretend that infiltration accepts closure, I must ignore the fact that each process of infiltration is always already infiltrated, I must control the opposition between inside and outside when the theme of my story has already undermined it. In a sense, whenever I tell the overt story of an infiltrator, it is always the story of a failed infiltrator. In order to retain control over the spy sent behind the enemy lines, I must constantly reidentify him or her as one of ours, I must reveal the secret over and over again, force him or her to 'come out'.

We all know, before the film or the book begins, that James Bond is a hero, and that he is a spy. Even his adversaries usually know him and address him as Mr Bond in the first and predictable encounter scene. Mirrored by the character's popularity, James Bond's visibility within the story fixes his identity as an infiltrator (something which most of our less powerless characters resolutely try to avoid). The system is safe as long as we all agree that the infiltrator is an exception and that our cultural competence allows us to recognize him. Naturally, this is a paradoxical move which severely restricts the fictional infiltrator's freedom and that other writers have not hesitated to criticize.[1]

Not only do James Bond stories refuse to consider the spy as an invisible mole, but they usually lead to a paradoxical conclusion. I have suggested that infiltration is the art of the 'in the meantime': it is impossible to say whether distinctions between genders, races and classes will ever be obsolete, and it is equally impossible not to hope (in the current state of our cultural reflection) that they will indeed be replaced by more egalitarian constructions of inclusion. Because the infiltrator bases his or her strategies on the very system he or she would like to undermine, his or her imagined story lacks closure. As an infiltrator, I place myself in the paradoxical situation of hoping for change while being unable to theorize change without resorting at least partly to old narratives of progress. Infiltration does not let me envisage an end to the process but forces me to concentrate on the here and now. Even if I actively construct myself as a newcomer to infiltration, if I become a spy with a specific goal in mind, this specific goal, which I imagine as the reason for the choice of infiltrational tactics, may never be realized. First of all, because infiltration takes an amount of time over which I have no control. And during the time it takes me to infiltrate the system, I know that the system will infiltrate me as well. Interdependence will result in the creation of a chaotic space of imagined isolations. Often, as an individual, the mole also has to trust that a larger organization (of which he or she may gradually forget that he or she is part) knows which ultimate purpose is better served by which specific strategy. If my assignment is to sneak into someone's office at night to Xerox secret documents, I may be quite ignorant of the contents of the document or of their relative meaningfulness. If any 'change' is indeed effected by my actions, it may be invisible to me, I may never see any results. Not that change does not occur, but it may be more accurately conceptualized as the chaotic fluctuations in a turbulent flow. Changes cannot exist independently from the profound changes that I am experiencing as an infiltrated infiltrator. From my point of view, it may be unpredictable and even undesirable. The differing of difference also affects what I see as the results of my infiltrational position. The infiltrator does not necessarily have to wonder whether it is possible to destroy the master's house with the master's tools. He or she is more like a termite the slow and imperceptible work of destruction of which may remain invisible for years, may be stopped, or may result in the total destruction of a system and of the population of termites. Like Serres's parasite, the infiltrator is this bête petite qui, en se multipliant pour changer d'échelle, produit des épidémies mettant à mort des ensembles géants de gros animaux, mais qui, du coup, s'expose à disparaître. (Serres 1990, 80)

[small animal which, by multiplying to reach a different scale, causes epidemics fatal to giant groups of large animals, but which, at the same time, exposes itself to extinction.]

In order not to risk extinction, the spy as star needs to reinvent closure as a spectacle. At the end of almost every single James Bond film, the viewer is treated to a visual and cathartic apocalypse. The enemy's microcosm (usually symbolized by a desert island, or an underground bunker) is pulverized by a gigantic explosion, usually caused by the destruction of its own evil technology. Workers of the micro-order are killed by the dozens, but they are rationalized as the accomplices of evil forces. The final explosion is not very different from a commemorative celebration involving fireworks and marching bands. The infiltrated system collapses like the House of Usher, engulfed in flames and eventually swallowed by the earth, the ocean or space from which it should never have emerged as distinct.[2] On the one hand, this spectacular change is meant to represent success for the spy. If the infiltration is efficient, then, the infiltrated territory (its evil philosophy, evil leaders, evil subordinates and evil technology) will indeed crumble and collapse upon itself, offering the rather pleasing spectacle of an aestheticized conflagration. Such endings seem to be nostalgic of the kind of head-on confrontations in which the infiltrator simply cannot indulge. I suggest that the system which tells the story needs to reassure itself that such endings are possible and become an intertextual reference for real infiltrational operations (recent wars may be a case in point). When the war becomes a spectacle thanks to the combined effects of intertextual references to James Bond stories and the technological advance of media techniques which bring physically harmless images back from the other side of the world, then it becomes obvious that the aesthetic or spectacular side of violence is precisely what permits media coverage. Imagining that the infiltrator is separable from the terrain allows what Christopher Miller calls the 'remote control' effect.[3]

On the other hand, the fact that some [remote] control remains possible explains why the infiltrator is never part of a new order. The infiltrated terrain is treated as a self-contained territory which had usurped the right to exist in the first place and which must now be identified as what had infiltrated the larger world order to begin with. The infiltrator, therefore, had better not be part and parcel of that infiltrated micro-culture when change occurs in the form of a violent yet innocent revolution: when the destruction of the other's other is a satisfying form of closure, the infiltrator, narratively speaking, has but one solution: pull out as fast as he can. Part of the (rather limited) suspense in James Bond stories is indeed the final escape, the last minute but always successful attempt to abandon what is by now a sinking ship. As if some dominant narrative discourse was toying with the idea that it might indeed be impossible for the infiltrator to dissociate him or herself from the havoc his or her intervention has wreaked, as if the possibility was entertained, and immediately rejected, that the infiltrator and the infiltrated territory are indeed, one and the same entity. In other words, when infiltration does succeed, when change is effected, it is also at its most reactionary because it is content with destroying one micro-system in order to fall back on an older, better, more organized purveyor of identities, which, needless to say, prefers to think of itself as a non-infiltrated system. If some infiltrators such as Maméga, Bretécher's children or Maillet's Sidonie, may understandably lament the fact that their infiltrational tactics are barely effective enough to let them survive, let alone to change the system that oppresses them, maybe there is hope in the realization that when the infiltrator is portrayed as a successful hero, he has, in fact, long ceased to be an infiltrator, he has become a civil servant. At the end of each movie, James Bond is usually granted a moment of capitalist paradise. Like the faithful employee rewarded for 355 days of labour, he is allowed by the script to take off to a (safe and colonized) tropical island, the image of the kind of order he has helped restore or maintain. Still linked to the authority by some electronic umbilical chord, he usually makes the point of ignoring troublesome orders to return, wrapped as he is in a rather unclad and suntanned heterosexual embrace. The mixture of annoyance and acceptance then displayed by his employer puts the finishing touch to the portrait of the spy as a naughty little boy whose moments of freedom are still perfectly contained and predicted by some totalizing Secret Intelligence Services.

By concentrating on the implausible moment of closure, such narratives pretend to forget the ambivalent moment when the infiltrator is also perfectly infiltrated, and to avoid to recognize that the infiltrator is also, like the infiltrated terrain, always already contaminated. Perhaps, it is unavoidable that the most popular infiltrator should remain a failed infiltrator since the first type of narrative would either result in an untold story or in a series of paradoxical statements that would hardly add up to a coherent whole.

The infiltrator is at his or her most successful as long as he or she has not succeeded yet, when nothing happens, when no hero can be isolated. The infiltrator as an individual cannot take credit for what might or might not happen since the amount and quality of change brought about by his or her intervention is not quantifiable. The infiltrator may be most efficient when he or she is the accomplice of the system to be undermined rather than of the outsider to which he or she wants to be loyal. Finally when a 'real' event occurs (when the Berlin Wall collapses, when the women of Brewster Place destroy theirs, when a Schoelcher announces that slavery is abolished), the infiltrator may consider this as the final apocalypse from which he or she wants to dissociate him or herself by either bailing out or by taking a safe vacation.

Infiltration is always tainted by ironic distance if I understand irony as the archetypal self-reflexive trope: like the infiltrator, the ironist is always aware of the irony of being one step ahead of one statement and one step behind the statement that is about to appropriate it. The danger of course is to celebrate the infiltrator as an agent of ambivalence, of ambiguity and to imagine that his or her ambiguity can be valued as such. Julia Epstein and Kristina Straub's warning against 'the temptation ... to reify ambiguity and to celebrate the disruption of binary oppositions without asking concrete questions about how power is distributed through that disruption and ambiguity' (Epstein and Straub 1991, 5) is worth keeping in mind. Infiltration is not nihilistic (it entails a will to survive, a will to change, a will to challenge the status quo) but it cannot be content to idealize even successful resistance to hegemony. The ironic and imagined infiltrator probably remembers (and this is a source of pleasure and pain) that for each emergent field of study, there is an infiltrator which both questions the new frontier and makes it exist by positioning his or herself or by being positioned as the new other.

When the story is not recast as a James Bond scenario, no cataclysm ever signals a happy ending. The site of infiltration remains mobile, unstable and ambiguous. I suggested earlier that infiltration is not a theory and I will even go as far as saying that it cannot even be called a tactic unless one is absolutely aware that results cannot be controlled. Which is why I would not want to celebrate the infiltrator as a new and improved solution to the problems of complicity raised by oppositional tactics. Like hybridity, infiltration cannot be analysed out of context even if infiltration makes the notion of self-contained context just as problematic as the illusion of a self-contained system of power.[4]

One cannot build a theory on a future landslide. Thinking like an infiltrator is the opposite of 'building' when the metaphor implies accumulation, linear progression, historical progress. The infiltrator exposes the fact that each structure is built on sand and infested by termites. The infiltrator, especially when he or she does not have a story to tell (like Suzanne in L'Etoile noire) does not disappear in the midst of a cloud of smoke, but he or she leaves a subtle trail of slow disintegration, fissures, slippages, movements in a turbulent flow. As Serres puts it:

Nous ne savons ni ne pouvons habiter sur cette faille, cet axe ou dans ce tourbillon: qui bâtirait sa maison au milieu du courant? Aucune institution, aucun système, nulle langue, pas un geste, ni une pensée ne se fonde sur ce lieu mobile. (Serres 1990, 54)

[We cannot, we do not know how to inhabit this crack, this axis, this vortex: who would want to build one's house in the middle of the current? No institution, no system, no language, no gesture, no thought can be founded on this unstable site.]

Who indeed? Except perhaps all the already marginalized subjects who are not given a chance to build a house anywhere, those for whom identity is a painful confinement on some outside of the imagined community, those who know that their own hybridity is all the more violently rejected as they ironically redouble the molecular infiltration of the core. Who would ironically build in the middle of a maelstrom except a poetic and megalomaniac infiltrator who would suddenly have a vision of him or herself as Power: for after all, this agent that traverses, infiltrates, seeps through, 'passes' and pretends, is not only what resists power, it is Power as it resists itself. Infiltration is the embodiment of power because power is infiltration. Power, as Foucault has taught us, is what 'pervades the very conceptual apparatus that seeks to negotiate its terms, including the subject position of the critic' (Butler 'Contingent Foundations', 6).

In the same way as Butler claims that gender is drag (Butler 1991) power is infiltration and infiltration is power. My hope is that it is indeed up to every one of us to know when to mourn this ambivalence as a vicious circle and when to use it as the precondition of critical thought.

## Notes

1 John Le Carré's anti-heroes are usually analysed as a mirror-image of the implausible secret agent as star. Gadget-ridden James Bond, who benefits from the ideological, financial and technological support of a recognizable superpower is the glamorous alter ego of a Leamas, who remains a dull and ordinary middle-class character. James Bond's Hollywood glitz, however, does not make him less of a civil servant as I will try to demonstrate. See for instance John Le Carré's *The Spy Who Came In From the Cold* and *Tinker, Tailor, Soldier, Spy*.

2 For example, Lewis Gilbert's 1979 film *Moonraker* ends on the 'finale of whiz-bang gadgetry and firepower' (as the cover of the video puts it) when the evil microcosm, a station in space, is finally destroyed. This self-contained replica of Noah's Ark is Hugo Drax's dream or, as 007 points out, nightmare of a 'super-race' born of his megalomaniac imagination in the 'untainted cradle of the heavens'. Interestingly, James Bond (Roger Moore) and his American counterpart (Corine Clery) find an unexpected ally in the person of one of their worst enemies, 7'2" giant 'Jaws' (Richard Kiel). While Jaws' monstrous size and supposedly animal power has, until now, been appropriated by Hugo Drax, who has used him as a faithful henchman, he finally turns against his master, and, almost single-handedly, causes his demise when James Bond makes it clear to him that neither he nor his bespectacled and goofy-looking fiancée belong to the 'super-race' due to their non-standard physiques. Although, as usual, the picture of the aspiring fascist is painfully self-righteous, the presence of this last minute revelation of Jaws as infiltrator is not a bad trick in the sense that it shows that the fiction of a pure system was already 'tainted' from the beginning. Jaws and James Bond can never form a community but their alliance is based on the mutual knowledge that no system is safe from infiltrators.

3 'The "remote control" that has always characterized colonialism is now perfectly updated and literalized by the technology of "smart" bombs, cruise missiles, and panoptical video recordings that allow us to "be there" with the pilots, to ride bombs down to their targets, to participate in the war as if it were a video game' (Miller 1989, 63). See also Judith Butler's 'Contingent Foundations: Feminism and the Question of "Postmodernism"': the author makes the point that when one 'newcaster remarked that the US weapons were instruments of "terrible beauty"' (10), such a discourse 'celebrates prematurely and phantasmatically its own capacity to act instrumentally in the world to obliterate its opposition and to control the consequence of that obliteration. But the consequentiality of this act cannot be foreseen by the instrumental actor who currently celebrates the effectivity of its own intentions' (Butler 'Contingent', 10).

4 For a critique of hybridity as a fundamentally liberatory trope, see Ella Shohat's (1992) 'Notes on the "Post-Colonial"'. See also *Outside in the Teaching Machine*, where Spivak warns us against the danger of teaching strategies 'as though they were theories, good for all cases' (Spivak 1993, 4).

# Bibliography

Alibar, F. and P. Lembeye-Boy (1982), *Le Couteau seul...*, *la condition féminine aux Antilles* (Vol. 2, Vies de Femmes), Paris, Editions Caribéennes.

Altman, J. (1982), *Epistolarity, Approaches to a Form*, Columbus, Ohio State University Press.

Anderson, B. (1991), *Imagined Communities, Reflections on the Origin and Spread of Nationalism*, (2nd edition), London, Verso.

Anzaldúa, G. (1987), *Borderlands, La Frontera, the New Mestiza*, San Francisco, Spinsters, Aunt Lute.

Bâ, M. (1981), *So Long a Letter*, trans. Modupe Bode-Thomas, London and Nairobi, Heinemann. Originally published as *Une si longue lettre*, Dakar, Les Nouvelles Editions Africaines.

Badinter, E. (1980), *L'Amour en plus, Histoire de l'amour maternel (XVIIe–XXe siècle)*, Paris, Flammarion.

Baker, H. (1993), 'Beyond the Culture Wars, Identities in Dialogue', *Profession 93*, 6–11.

Barney, N. (1960), *Souvenirs indiscrets*, Paris, Flammarion.

Barthes, R. (1957), *Mythologies*, Paris, Seuil, collection Pierres vives.

Barthes, R. (1970), *L'Empire des signes*, Genève, Editions Albert Skira.

Barthes, R. (1975), 'Introduction', *Physiologie du goût*, Anthelme Brillat-Savarin, Paris, Hermann, 7–32.

Bataille, G. (1957), *L'Erotisme*, Paris, Minuit.

Baudelaire, C. (1961), *Les Fleurs du mal*, Paris, Garnier, [1857].

Beauvoir, S. de (1949), *Le Deuxième Sexe*, Vol. II, Paris, Gallimard.

Beauvoir, S. de (1952), *The Second Sex*, trans. H.M. Parshley, New York, Alfred A. Knopf.

Benaïssa, A. (1990), *Née en France, l'histoire d'une jeune beur*, Paris, Payot.

Benstock, S. (1986), *Women of the Left Bank*, Austin, University of Texas Press.

Berg, E. (1982), 'The Third Woman', *Diacritics 2*: 2, 11–21.

Bernabé, J., R. Confiant and P. Chamoiseau (1989), *Eloge de la créolité*, Paris, Gallimard.

Bhabha, H. (1986), 'Signs Taken for Wonders', *'Race', Writing and Difference*, H. L. Gates, ed. Chicago, Chicago University Press, 163–84.

Bhabha, H. (1990), 'DissemiNation, Time, Narrative and the Margins of the Modern Nation', in *Nation and Narration*, H. Bhabha, ed. London and New York, Routledge, 291–321.

Blankey, E. (1984), 'Return to Mytilène, Renée Vivien and the City of Women', *Women Writers and the City, Essays in Feminist Literary Criticism*, Susan Squier, ed. Knoxville, The University of Tennessee Press, 45–67.

Bonnefons, N. de (1654), *Les Délices de la campagne*, Paris, Pierre Des-Haynes.

Boulaga, F. E. (1968), 'Le Bantou problématique', *Présence Africaine* 66, 3–40.
Bourdieu, P. and J. C. Passeron (1970), *La Reproduction*, Paris, Minuit.
Bourdieu, P. and J. C. Passeron (1979), *La Distinction*, Paris, Minuit.
Bourdieu, P. and J. C. Passeron (1985), *Les Héritiers*, Paris, Minuit.
Bretécher, Claire (1975, 1977), *Les Frustrés*,Vol. I, Paris, Presses Pocket.
Bretécher, Claire (1978), *Les Frustrés*, Vol. II, Paris, Presses Pocket.
Bretécher, Claire (1987), *Frustration*, trans. A. Mason and P. Fogarty, New York, Grove Press.
Brillat-Savarin, A. (1975), *Physiologie du goût*, Paris, Hermann.
Butler, J. (1990), *Gender Trouble*, New York and London, Routledge.
Butler, J. (1991), 'Imitation and Gender Insubordination', *Inside/Out*, D. Fuss, ed. New York and London, Routledge, 13–31.
Butler, J. (1992), 'Contingent Foundations of Feminism and the Questions of "Post Modernism"', *Feminists Theorize the Political*, New York and London, Routledge, 2–21.
Butler, J. (1992), 'Sexual inversions', *Discourses of Sexuality, From Aristotle to AIDS*, D. Stanton, ed. Ann Arbor, University of Michigan Press, 344–61.
Certeau, M. de (1980), *L'Invention du quotidien*. Paris, UGE.
Certeau, M. de (1984), *The Practice of Everyday Life*, trans. S. Randall, Berkeley, Los Angeles, London, University of California Press.
Certeau, M. de (1994), L. Giard, P. Mayol, *L'Invention du quotidien. 2. habiter, cuisiner* (2nd edition), Paris, Gallimard.
Césaire, A. (1989), *Discours sur le colonialisme*, Paris, Présence Africaine.
Césaire, A. (1995), *Notebook of a Return to my Native Land/Cahier d'un retour au pays natal*. trans. M. Rosello with A. Pritchard, Glasgow, Bloodaxe Books.
Césaire, A. (1970), *La Tragédie du Roi Christophe*, Paris, Présence Africaine.
Chabram-Dernersesian, A. (1992), 'I throw Punches for my Race but I don't Want to Be a Man', *Cultural Studies*, C. Nelson, L. Grossberg and L. Treichler, eds. New York and London, Routledge, 81–95.
Chambers, R. (1990), 'Irony and the Canon', *Profession*, 90, 18–24.
Chambers, R. (1991), *Room for Maneuver, Reading (the) Oppositional (in) Narrative*, Chicago, The University of Chicago Press.
Chaney, E. and M. Garcia Castro (eds.) (1989), *Muchachas No More, Household Workers in Latin America and the Caribbean*, Philadelphia, Temple University Press.
Chodorov, N. (1978), *The Reproduction of Mothering*, Berkeley, University of California Press.
Cixous, H. (1977), 'La venue à l'écriture', *La Venue à l'écriture*, M. Gagnon, H. Cixous and A. Leclerc, Paris, UGE.
Clément, M.-C. and D. (1990), *Colette gourmande*, Paris, Albin Michel.
Clifford, J. (1988), *The Predicament of Culture, Twentieth-Century Ethnography, Literature, and Art*, Cambridge, MA and London, Harvard University Press.
Clifford, J. (1992), 'Traveling Cultures', *Cultural Studies*, Larry Grossberg, Cary Nelson and Paula Treichler, eds. New York and London, Routledge, 96–116.
Colette (1949), *Prisons et paradis* in *Oeuvres Complètes*, Vol. VIII, Paris, Le Fleuron.

Colette (1986), 'Bâ-Tou', La Maison de Claudine, Oeuvres, Vol. II, Paris, Gallimard, Pléiade, 1061–4.

Condé, M. (1986), Moi, Tituba sorcière noire de Salem, Paris, Mercure de France.

Confiant, R. (1988), Le Nègre et l'amiral, Paris, Grasset.

Coward, R. (1985), Female Desires, New York, Grove Weindenfeld.

Daudet, A. (1994), 'Les trois messes basses', Lettres de mon moulin, Paris, Ramsay.

Davies, C. B. and E. S. Fido (1990), 'Introduction, Women and Literature in the Caribbean, An Overview', Out of the Kumbla, C. B. Davis and E. S. Fido, eds. Trenton, NJ, Africa World Press, 1–19.

Davis, C. (1994), Elie Wiesel's Secretive Texts, University Press of Florida.

Deleuze, G. and F. Guattari (1980), Mille Plateaux, Paris, Minuit.

Derrida, J. (1967), De la Grammatologie, Paris, Minuit.

Derrida, J. (1972), La Dissémination, Paris, Seuil.

Dery, M. (1992), 'Cyberculture', The South Atlantic Quarterly 91:3, 501–23.

Détienne, M. and J.-P. Vernant (1970), Les Ruses de l'intelligence: la mètis des Grecs, Paris, Flammarion.

Dormann, G. (1985), Colette amoureuse, Paris, Albin Michel, 1985.

Duras, C. de (1979), Ourika, Paris, Des Femmes, [1823].

Ega, F. (1978), Lettres à une noire, Paris, L'Harmattan.

Ega, F. (1989), Le Temps des madras, Paris, L'Harmattan.

Epstein, J. and K. Straub (eds.) (1991), Body Guards, The Cultural Politics of Gender Ambiguity, New York and London, Routledge.

Esch, D. (1992), 'Deconstruction', Redrawing the Boundaries, S. Greenblatt and G. Bunn, eds. New York, MLA, 374–91.

Farb, P. and G. Armagelos (1980), Consuming Passions, The Anthropology of Eating, Boston, Houghton Mifflin Company.

Felman, S. and D. Laub (1992), Testimony, Crises of Witnessing in Literature, Psychoanalysis, Freud, Lacan, and Derrida, New York, Routledge.

Fisher, P. (1992), 'American Literary and Cultural Studies since the Civil War' in Redrawing the Boundaries, S. Greenblatt and G. Gunn, eds. New York, MLA.

Flandrin, J.-L., P. and M. Hyman Montalba (eds.) (1983), Le Cuisinier françois, Paris, Montalba.

Flannigan-Saint-Aubin, A. (1988), 'Reading Below the Belt, Sex and Sexuality in Maryse Condé et Françoise Ega', The French Review 62, 219–29.

Flannigan-Saint-Aubin, A., (1992), 'Reading and Writing the Body of the Négresse in Françoise Ega's Lettres à une noire', Callaloo 15:1, 49–65.

Fontenay, E. de (1976), 'Pour Emile et par Emile, Sophie ou l'invention du ménage', Les Temps Modernes 358 (Petites filles en éducation) (Mai), 1774–95.

Foucault, M. (1969), L'Archéologie du savoir, Paris, Gallimard.

Foucault, M. (1972), The Archeology of Knowledge, trans. A. M. Sheridan Smith. London, Tavistock.

Foucault, M. (1972), Histoire de la folie à l'âge classique, Paris, Gallimard.

Foucault, M. (1975), Surveiller et punir, Paris, Gallimard.

Fuss, D. (1989), Essentially Speaking. Feminism, Nature and Difference, New York and London, Routledge.

Gates, H. L. (1992), 'The Master's Pieces, On Canon Formation and the African-American Tradition', The Politics of Liberal Education, D. J. Gless and B. Herrnstein Smith, eds. Durham and London, Duke University Press, 95–117.

Gilroy, P. (1993), The Black Atlantic, London, Verso.

Gless, D. and B. Herrnstein Smith (1992), The Politics of Liberal Education, Durham and London, Duke University Press.

Glissant, E. (1990), Poétique de la relation, Paris, Seuil.

Godard, L. (1985), 'Pour une nouvelle lecture de la question de la "femme", Essai à partir de la pensée de Jacques Derrida', Philosophiques 12, 161–4.

Goodison, L. (1991), 'Interview with Wolfgang Binder (October 1st 1988)', Commonwealth Essays and Studies 13:2, 42–8.

Graff, G. (1992), 'Teach the Conflicts', The Politics of Liberal Education, D. J. Gless and B. Herrnstein Smith, eds. Durham NC and London, Duke University Press, 57–73.

Grafigny, F. de (1990), Lettres d'une Péruvienne, (Preface by Colette Piau-Gillot), Paris, Côté-femmes [1747].

Greenblatt, S. and G. Gunn (1992), Redrawing the Boundaries, New York, MLA.

Griaule, M. (1938), Masques Dogon, Paris, Institut d'ethnologie.

Haraway, D. (1991), Simians, Cyborgs and Women, London and New York, Routledge.

Holmund, C. (1990), 'The Lesbian, the Mother, the Heterosexual Lover, Irigaray's Recodings of Difference', Feminist Studies 17:2, 283–308.

Hountondji, P. (1977), Sur la Philosophie africaine, Paris, Maspero.

Hugo, V. (1967), 'Les Mages' (XXIII) in Les Contemplations, Oeuvres poétiques, Vol. II. Paris, Gallimard, Pléiade, 780–99.

Hugo, V. (1985), Les Misérables in Oeuvres complètes, Vol. II, Paris, Laffont.

Irigaray, L. (1977), Ce Sexe qui n'en est pas un, Paris, Minuit.

Irigaray, L. (1981), Le Corps à corps avec la mère, Paris, La Pleine lune.

Irigaray, L. (1985), Parler n'est jamais neutre, Paris, Minuit.

JanMohammed, A. R. and D. Lloyd (1990), 'Toward a Theory of Minority Discourse, What is to be Done?' The Nature and Context of Minority Discourse A. R. JanMohammed and D. Lloyd, eds. New York and Oxford, Oxford University Press.

Jay, K. (1988), The Amazon and the Page, Bloomington and Indianapolis, Indiana University Press.

Johnson, B. (1980), The Critical Difference, Baltimore, Johns Hopkins University Press.

Kessas, F. (1990), Beur's Story, Paris, l'Harmattan.

Kristeva, J. (1988), Etrangers à nous-mêmes, Paris, Fayard.

Kritzman, L. (1995), Auschwitz and After, Race, Culture and the Jewish Question in France, London and New York, Routledge.

La Fontaine, J. de (1929), *Fables*, Paris, Hachette.

Le Brun, A. (1990), *Vagit-Prop, Lâchez tout et autres textes*, Paris, Ramsay.

Leonardi, S. (1990), 'Recipes for Reading, Summer Pasta, Lobster à la Riseholme, and Key Lime Pie', *PMLA* 104:3, 340–7.

Levy, B.-H. (1990), 'A propos du Carmel d'Auschwitz', *Questions de Principe Trois*, Paris, Libraire Générale Française, 84–7.

Lionnet, F. (1989), *Autobiographical Voices, Race, Gender, Self-Portraiture*, Ithaca, Cornell University Press.

Lyotard, J.-F. (1978), 'On the Strength of the Weak', *Sémiotexte* 3:2, 204–12.

Lyotard, J.-F. (1983), *Le Différend*, Paris, Minuit.

Maillet, A. (1986), *La Sagouine*, Montreal, Leméac.

Maillet, M. (1990), *L'Etoile noire*, Paris, François Bourin.

Marks, H. (1988), 'Sappho 1900: Imaginary Renée Viviens and the Rear of the Belle epoque', *Yale French Studies* 75, 175–89.

Maximin, D. (1981), *L'Isolé Soleil*, Paris, Seuil.

Miller, C. (1990), *Theories of Africans, Francophone Literature and Anthropology in Africa*, Chicago, Chicago University Press.

Miller, C. (1993), 'Nationalism as Resistance and Resistance to Nationalism in the Literature of Francophone Africa', *Yale French Studies* 82:1, 62–100.

Miller, M. C. (1989), *Boxed In: The Culture of TV*, Evanston, Northwestern University Press.

Miller, N. K. (1991), *Getting Personal, Feminist Occasions and Other Autobiographical Acts*, New York and London, Routledge.

Minh Ha, T. (1989), *Woman, Native, Other, Writing Postcoloniality and Feminism*, Bloomington, Indiana University Press.

Mizla, O. (1988), *Les Francais devant l'immigration*, Paris, Editions complexe.

Montferrand, H. de (1990), *Les Amies d'Héloise*, Paris, Fallois.

Montferrand, H. de (1991), *Journal de Suzanne*, Paris, Fallois.

Montreynaud, F. (in collaboration with F. Audi, C. Helfter, L. Klejman and M. Perrot-Lannaud) (1989), *Le Vingtième Siècle des femmes*, Paris, Nathan.

Moraga, C. and G. Anzaldúa (eds.) (1981), *This Bridge Called My Back, Writings by Radical Women of Color*, Wattertown, MA, Persephone Press.

Morrison, T. (1970), *The Bluest Eye*, New York, Washington Square Press.

Mudimbe, V. Y. (1982), *L'Odeur du père. Essai sur les limites de la science et de la vie en Afrique noire*, Paris, Présence Africaine.

Mudimbe, V. Y. (1988), *The Invention of Africa, Gnosis, Philosophy and the Order of Knowledge*, Bloomington and Indianapolis, Indiana University Press.

Offen, K., R. Pierson and J. Rendall (eds.) (1991), *Writing Women's History*, Bloomington and Indianapolis, Indiana University Press.

Paulson, W. (1988), *The Noise of Culture, Literary Texts in a World of Information*, New York and London, Cornell University Press.

Philip, M. (1990), 'The Absence of Writing or How I Almost Became A Spy', *Out of the Kumbla*, C. B. Davies and E. S. Fido, eds. Africa World Press, 271–8.

Pitte, J.-R. (1991), *Gastronomie française*, Paris, Fayard.

Pratt, M. L. (1991), 'Arts of the Contact Zone', *Profession* 91, 33–40.

Rabasa, J. (1990), 'Dialogue as Conquest, Mapping Spaces for Counter-Discourse', *The Nature and Context of Minority Discourse*, A. JanMohamed and D. Lloyd, eds. Oxford, Oxford University Press, 187–215.

Reboux, P. (1925), *A la Manière de* ..., Paris, Grasset.

Relyea, S. (1981), 'The Symbolic in the Family Factory, My Apprenticeships', *Women Studies* 8:3, 273–99.

Revel, J.-F. (1979), *Un Festin en paroles*, Paris, Jean-Jacques Pauvert.

Riccoboni, M.-J. (1979), *Lettres de Mistriss Fanni Butlerd* (with introduction and notes by J. Hinde Steward), Genève, Droz, [1757].

Rosello, M. (1987), *L'Humour noir selon André Breton*, Paris, Corti.

Rosello, M. (1991), 'Franquin et Reiser: Vers une éthique de l'humour noir comme surenchère', MLN 106:4, 880–93.

Ross, A. (1989), *No Respect, Intellectuals and Popular Culture*, New York and London, Routledge.

Rousseau, J.-J. (1964), *L'Emile* , Paris, Garnier, [1762].

Roy, O. (1991), Ethnicité, bandes et communautarisme, *Esprit*, 169, 37–47.

Rubin, G. (1975), 'The Traffic in Women, Notes on the "Political Economy" of Sex', *Toward an Anthropology of Women*, R. R. Reiter, ed. New York, Monthly Review Press.

Rubin, G. (1979), 'Introduction', *A Woman Appeared to Me*, R. Vivien, trans. J. Foster, Tallahassee, The Naiad Press, iii–xxii.

Russo, M. (1984), 'Female Grotesques, Carnival and Theory', *Feminist Studies/Critical Studies*, T. de Lauretis, ed. Bloomington, Indiana University Press.

Sand, C. (1987), *A la Table de George Sand*, Paris, Flammarion.

Sartre, J.-P. (1943), *L'Etre et le néant*, Paris, Gallimard.

Schipper, M. (1985), '"Who Am I?" Fact and Fiction in African First-Person Narrative', *Research in African Literatures* 16:1, 53–79.

Schor, N. (1992), 'Cartes postales, Representing Paris 1900', *Critical Inquiry*, 8:2, 188–244.

Schwarz-Bart, A. (1967), *La Mulâtresse Solitude*, Paris, Seuil.

Schwarz-Bart, S. (1972), *Pluie et vent sur Télumée Miracle*, Paris, Seuil.

Schwarz-Bart, S. (1979), 'Interview with Simone et André Schwarz-Bart, Sur les pas de Fanotte', *Textes-Etudes-Documents* 2, 13–23.

Sebbar-Pignon, L. (1976), 'Mlle Lili ou l'ordre des poupées', *Les temps modernes* 358, Petites filles en éducation, 1796–1828.

Segalen, V. (1978), *Essai sur l'exotisme*, Montpellier, Fata Morgana, [1904].

Sembène Ousmane (1962), 'La Noire de...', *Voltaïques*, Paris, Présence Africaine, 149–74.

Serres, M. (1980), *Le Parasite*, Paris, Grasset.

Serres, M. (1990), *Le Tiers instruit*, Paris, Bourin.

Serres, M. (1992), *Eclaircissements* (entretiens avec Bruno Latour), Paris, Bourin.

Shohat, E. (1992), 'Notes on the "Post Colonial"', *Social Text* 31–32, 99–113.

Silverman, M. (1990), 'The Racialization of Immigration, Aspects of Discourse from 1968–1981', French Cultural Studies, 1:2, 111–28.

Spivak, G. (1988), 'Subaltern Studies, Deconstructing Historiography', In Other Worlds, Essays in Cultural Politics, New York and London, Routledge, 197–221.

Spivak, G. (1988), In Other Worlds, Essays in Cultural Politics, New York and London, Routledge.

Spivak, G. (1990), The Post-Colonial Critic, S. Harasym, ed. New York and London, Routledge.

Spivak, G. (1992), 'Teaching for the Times', The Journal of the Midwest Modern Language Association, 25:1, 3–22.

Spivak, G. (1993), Outside in the Teaching Machine, London and New York, Routledge.

Stanton, D. (1986), 'Difference on Trial, A Critique of the Maternal Metaphor in Cixous, Irigaray and Kristeva', The Poetics of Gender, N. K. Miller, ed. New York, Columbia University Press, 157–82.

Stavans, I. (1992), 'Moctezuma's Revenge', Transition 56, 112–22.

Taguieff, P.-A. (1990), La Force du préjugé, essai sur le racisme et ses doubles (2nd edition), Paris, Gallimard, Tel, [1987].

Tempels, P. (1959), Bantu Philosophy, trans. C. King, Paris, Présence Africaine.

Terzian, D., L. Irigaray (1985), 'Discours de l'homme ou de la femme?' Constructions, 119–25.

Tobin, R. (1990), Tarte à la crème, Comedy and Gastronomy in Molière's Theater, Columbus, Ohio State University Press.

Todorov, T. (1989), Nous et les autres, la réflexion française sur la diversité humaine, Paris, Seuil.

Tournier, M. (1989), Le Médianoche amoureux, Paris, Gallimard.

Veeser, A. (1991), 'Re-Membering a Deformed Past, (New) New Historicism', The Journal of the Midwest Modern Language Association, 24:1, 3–13.

Vivien, R. (1977), La Dame à la louve, Paris, Régine Desforges.

Vivien, R. (1977), Une Femme m'apparut, Paris, Régine Desforges.

Vivien, R. (1979), A Woman Appeared to Me, trans. J. Foster, Tallahassee, The Naiad Press.

Vivien, R. (1983), The Woman of The Wolf and other stories, trans. K. Jay and Y. M. Klein. New York, Gay Presses of New York.

Warhol, A. (1975), The Philosophy of Andy Warhol (From A to B and Back Again), New York, Harcourt Brace Jovanovitch.

Warner-Vieyra, M. (1982), Juletane, Paris, Présence Africaine.

Williams, P. (1991), The Alchemy of Race and Rights, Cambridge, MA and London, Harvard University Press.

Yaeger, P. (1988), Honey-Mad Women, Emancipatory Strategies in Women's Writing, New York, Columbia University Press.

Yaguello, M. (1984), Alice au pays du langage, Paris, Seuil.

Zwinger, L. (1992), 'Blood Relations, Feminist Theory Meets the Uncanny Alien Bug Mother', Hypatia 7:2, 74–90.

# Index